SILICON VISIONS

SILICON VISIONS

The Future of Microcomputer Technology

The Waite Group
Dan Shafer

A Brady Book
Published by Prentice Hall Press
New York, NY 10023

A Brady Book
Published by Prentice Hall Press
A Division of Simon & Schuster, Inc.
Gulf + Western Building
One Gulf + Western Plaza
New York, New York 10023

PRENTICE HALL PRESS is a trademark of Simon & Schuster, Inc.

Designed by Geraldine Ivins
Manufactured in the United States of America

1 2 3 4 5 6 7 8 9 10

Library of Congress Cataloging-in-Publication Data

Shafer, Dan.
    Silicon Visions

    Includes index.
    1. Microcomputers.   I. Waite Group.   II. Title.
QA76.5.S443   1986   004   86–12339
ISBN 0–89303–845–8

DEDICATION

This book is lovingly dedicated to my children: Sheila, Mary, Christy, and Heather. It is to them and their generation that the future only hinted at here truly belongs. I pray they will have better wisdom than this generation in using it.

REGISTERED
TRADEMARKS

Apple, Apple II, ImageWriter, LaserWriter, MacDraw, MacWrite, and MacPaint are registered trademarks of Apple Computer, Inc.

Amiga is a registered trademark of Commodore-Amiga Corporation.

CP/M-86 is a registered trademark of Digital Research Inc.

Filevision is a trademark of Telos Software Products.

DG/One is a trademark of Data General.

CompuServe is a trademark of CompuServe, Inc.

Ashton-Tate, dBase I, and Framework are trademarks of Ashton-Tate.

IBM, PC-DOS, and IBM PC are trademarks of International Business Machines Corporation.

Jacuzzi is a registered trademark of Jacuzzi Brothers, division of Kitte.

Lotus, 1-2-3, and Symphony are trademarks of Lotus Development Corporation.

KAMAS is a trademark of KAMSOFT.

MicroVAX, VAX, and DEC are trademarks of Digital Equipment Corporation.

PC-TALK is a trademark of FREEWARE.

XENIX, MS-DOS, and MSX are trademarks of Microsoft Corporation.

Radio Shack and TRS-80 are registered trademarks of Tandy Corporation.

VisiCalc is a trademark of VisiCorp, Inc.

The Source is a trademark of Source Telecomputing Corporation, a subsidiary of The Reader's Digest Association.

Turbo Pascal, Sidekick, and Superkey are trademarks of Borland International.

Zenith is a trademark of Zenith Radio Corporation.

WordStar and WordStar 2000 are trademarks of MicroPro International Corporation.

Softcasting is a trademark of Softcast Corporation.

UNIX is a trademark of AT&T, Bell Laboratories.

ZAPMail is a trademark of Federal Express Corporation.

TinkerToy is a registered trademark of Questor Corporation.

LaserJet is a trademark of Hewlett Packard.

CONTENTS

Index   305

PREFACE

Predicting is difficult, particularly when it concerns the future.—Anonymous

The prophesying business is like writing fugues; it is fatal to everyone save the man of absolute genius.—H. L. Mencken, Prejudices

---

I have, in the course of writing this book, talked to more than 200 people. Some I've met personally. Others I've talked with only by telephone. Still others are telecommunications friends whose voices I would not recognize. I know, though, that I could have talked to 2,000 such people and still not made a significant dent in the cadre of thinkers and visionaries, producers and movers and shakers, who are "out there" somewhere.

No one book could hope to be comprehensive in its review of all the possible scenarios, products, technologies, people, and ideas that will shape the electronics revolution in the last half of the 1980's. This book does not claim to do so. If I omitted something you strongly feel should have been included, please write to me about it. I'm still in a learning mode, and I do publish a monthly newsletter designed to provide people with continuing updates of the information in this book. Feel free to drop me a line at 1220 Edgewood Rd., Redwood City, CA 94062, or on CompuServe at ID 71246,402. Leave me an address and a phone and I promise I'll contact you.

Yet, despite all of the people I've met and interviewed, read and argued with, laughed and agreed with, the final responsibility for what is in this book is mine and cannot justly be shared with anyone else. Mistakes, and there are always some, are attributable to me and not to any other person. So, too, with oversights.

I hope you enjoy this book. May you find here a future in which to participate in some exciting way. The future does indeed belong to those who are prepared for its promise and its pitfalls.

ACKNOWLEDGMENTS

The primary thanks for the reality of this book goes to two groups of people. The first group includes Mitchell Waite, Barry Richmond, and Robert Lafore, all of the Waite Group and all of whom believed enough in this project to give me the freedom to research and write, and guess and be wrong. There is more creativity in that group than I have had the pleasure to encounter in many other places in my life.

The second group includes hundreds of people whose ideas, thoughts, opinions, writings, projections, and conversations have somehow influenced the contents of this book. Many of them are mentioned by name, but the vast majority are not. This is not because they are not worthy to be included; they are. It is simply because, for various reasons ranging from space and time limitations to their own need for anonymity, they have not been included specifically.

As with my other books, Don Huntington has been an invaluable and very human resource throughout this project. He has worked late nights, deprived himself of sleep, and his family of himself, researched, written, and edited. The quality of the technical tutorials in this book can largely be attributed to his willingness to research, revise, discuss, revise, and revise some more. Thanks, Don.

My family and many of my friends also deserve thanks for not making me feel guilty for the many, many hours I spent in dialogue with subjects, on the telephone, locked in my den writing, or otherwise being inaccessible.

If this book enjoys any success, I would like to publicly share it with all of these people. They deserve it at least as much as I.

ABOUT THIS BOOK

This is a book about the future of microcomputer technology. It does not deal with computers in the distant future, but focuses on things you should know about the technology, and what is likely to happen to it in the next five years or so. Furthermore, this book concentrates exclusively on the *small* end of high technology: microcomputers and systems built around or using them. The small systems will have the most immediate and fundamental impact on the daily lives of Americans in the next five years.

Silicon Visions: The Future of Microcomputer Technology will demonstrate that the most important and fundamental changes in the microcomputer industry in the next few years will focus on making computers at once more *human* and more *humane*. By "human," we mean more usable and understandable by and accessible to humans. In other words, a great leap beyond "user-friendly."

The next five years will move us close to the place where we won't have to think about computers; they will simply be tools and appliances for dealing with our world.

By "humane," we mean that computers in the next few years will be brought to bear on solving problems and addressing needs that transcend the world of business, the searches of science, and the demands of education. The emphasis will be on creativity at a personal level, extending our minds, enabling us to develop more interpersonal relationships and become key players in adding to the culture around us.

This will happen in large part because of the kinds of people who are involved in shaping the revolution. You will have the chance to meet a few of them in the pages of this book. You will be struck, as we were, by the fact that most of them are not engineers and hobbyists designing gadgets for the admiration of their fellow engineers and hobbyists. They are multifaceted, multi-talented people with strange amalgams of backgrounds. Deep interests in philosophy, religion, music, and art permeate their lives. Technology is not their *raison d'etre* but rather one of several focal points in their filled and fulfilled lives.

For Whom It Was Written

Silicon Visions: The Future of Microcomputer Technology is aimed, in a general sense, at intelligent readers who have little or no background in high technology but are curious about microcomputers and how they are going to affect their lives.

More specifically, we have tried to provide direct advice, guidance, and interpretation of these events for three types of people:

- those making *career decisions*, either about what to study in college or how to shift a stagnating career in midlife;
- those making *investment decisions* who want to be sure they have taken into account the major, visible near-term trends in high technology;
- those making *management decisions* about how their companies are going to assimilate, respond to, and capitalize on these advances.

(To the career-minded, incidentally, we have a word of caution: The era of the multicareered life has arrived. Most people in the next decade will not go through their lives in one profession or occupation; as things change, so will their jobs. The emphasis is thus on being prepared for change more than on acquiring specific job skills.)

In each case, the ground-floor opportunities, challenges, and prospects for the rest of the 1980's are presented, discussed, and analyzed briefly to enable the reader to answer the question: "What does all of this mean to me?"

How the Book is Organized

The book is divided into two major sections, each of which is further divided into chapters. Each chapter includes a main essay and a collection of "profiles." The profiles are optional reading. Some describe in detail specific people and products, enabling the interested reader to get a more in-depth appreciation for the people who are forging the next phase of the electronics revolution and the products they are using to do so. Some profiles are tutorial in nature. If you encounter a new idea or concept in the main essay, you will often find a reference to a profile that will clarify its meaning for you.

The world of the electronics revolution does not lend itself easily to convenient compartmentalization; an intimate relationship binds the pieces together. We will, for example, discuss AI and expert systems separate from hardware and memory advances, but the two are inextricably linked to one another. How we organize our thinking about them is inevitably artificial. Nonetheless, some organizational scheme must be imposed. The one chosen interferes little with the process of reading and assimilating the information in the pages of the book.

The Proof

Our belief that the next few years will see advances destined to make microcomputers at once more human and more humane is borne out by evidence presented in the pages that follow.

It is supported by the emergence of products like Mind Reader, a word processor that tries to anticipate what we are going to type before we've even thought about it, making typing on a computer possible even for people who thought they'd never use a keyboard.

It is sustained by the development of expert system development tools that will ultimately put at everyone's disposal massive amounts of reliable data, organized, and accessible in such a way that we will all benefit from the brains and experience of a few.

It is encompassed by the emergence of on-line psychological counseling services available by computers using telephones, the creation of whole new towns built around the need for information in our society, and by the introduction of electronic universities that permit us to enjoy a degree of freedom in education we never before thought possible.

It is perceptible in the stirrings of computer-generated music and art, including poetry.

It is found in the beginnings of a new sub-industry of speech and voice processing that will ultimately enable us to speak in plain English (or whatever our native tongue is!) to our computers and have them respond as if they were friends and collaborators.

And it is evidenced in the development and publication of computer programs that don't make demands and place expectations on us, but rather place those demands and expectations where they belong: on the computer.

The pages of this book will introduce you to products that exactly fit these descriptions—and to dozens of others that will intrigue, excite, provoke, and disquiet you.

The Revolutionaries

In its final assessment, *Silicon Visions: The Future of Microcomputer Technology* is ultimately about people. For it is people who make revolutions. Some of the products in this book will die premature deaths before the ink is dry on its pages. Others will undergo radical transformations and look entirely different from what we have predicted. But the people shaping them, whether or not the specific personalities will be the same, will continue to be the bold, aggressive, interesting, confident, and thought-provoking people you'll meet in these pages.

The other people this book is about are people like you, who read it, assimilate it, and make things happen for themselves and for others. To that end, let us begin to see if we can share a Silicon Vision together.

1

FOREGROUND

The Content of the Coming Changes

Introduction

Silicon Visions: The Future of Microcomputer Technology is divided into two major parts. The first part, Foreground, deals with emerging applications of microcomputer technology in specific products and ideas. The second part, Background, discusses features of the technology itself.

This Foreground section will discuss the changes that will take place in the microcomputer industry during the next five years or so. It will focus especially upon the *content* of these changes. In other words, the section will assess the immediate impact of those changes on our lives rather than examining their technical details. The changes in the near future will be concentrated in three main areas.

Extending Our Minds Through application of the principles of Artificial Intelligence, the microcomputer has the potential to become a true appliance of the mind. Tools like levers, gears, wheels, and hoes have extended the power of our muscles and made it possible for us to perform physical labor that would otherwise be beyond our capability. In a similar way, the microcomputer can, if managed correctly, extend our minds to do things easily that might otherwise be difficult.

We must remember, however, that the computer cannot be more than a tool. It is not capable of turning the tables on us and running our lives, any more than a lever or a wheel can take over the world. Like the implements of sinew extension, however, the microcomputer is capable of doing damage if we let it. Our job is to prevent that while harnessing its power.

This chapter will present ideas and introduce people and products who will have a great deal to say about how well those tasks are carried out in the remainder of this decade.

Broadening Our Community We think nothing of sending pictures and sounds through thousands, even millions, of miles of space to one another. We pick up the telephone and call a friend in Bangkok and hardly give it a second thought.

Before this decade is over, we will adopt the same casual "of course I can" posture with regard to using our computers to tap into vast data bases all over the world. The expansion that will take place in the telecommunications industry between now and 1990 will be staggering in its implications for our lives. We can already bank, send mail, and locate data using our computers and a telephone line. The range of services available "on-line" will explode in the remainder of this decade. We will find ourselves bridging space and time with such regularity that we will wonder why we ever wondered at the prospect.

Enhancing Our Life Style   There are many ways that the microcomputer will make the quality of life better for all of us. This section will review some of those ways. We'll take a look at how the arts—musical, visual, and written—will be affected by the emerging technology. We will glimpse the impact of the movement on education and review how the availability of books, magazines, newsletters, and newspapers on demand, delivered electronically with incredible immediacy and speed will alter our sense of the world.

How will the computer affect how and where we work and what we do while we are there?

Will robots be an important part of the high-technology scene before the end of the 1980's?

These and dozens of other important questions will be answered in this discussion.

Come. Let us wonder together.

1
Extending Our Minds

> Much learning does not teach a man to have intelligence.—
> Heraclitus
>
> The test of a first-rate intelligence is the ability to hold two
> opposed ideas in the mind at the same time, and still retain the
> ability to function.—F. Scott Fitzgerald
>
> . . . the strange flavor of AI work is that people try to put
> together long sets of rules in strict formalisms that tell inflexible
> machines how to be flexible.—Douglas R. Hofstadter

We will be crystal clear at the outset: No single field of endeavor
connected with the electronic revolution has more potential for
shaping and influencing the world in the future than the work
being done by a group of zealots collectively referred to as the "AI
community."

Artificial intelligence (AI) defies definition. The members of the
AI Community themselves don't even agree what artificial intelligence is (see What is Artificial Intelligence? Don't Ask the
Experts!). But whether or not it can be precisely defined, AI will
certainly be the *chef d'oeuvre*, the centerpiece, of the electronic
revolution's next phase.

"Expert systems" comprise one of the most important types of
AI products. Expert systems are those ingenious computer programs that embody the expertise of a specialist in some area and
then apply that knowledge in helping their human users make
decisions or giving them advice. Expert systems have been applied
to many knowledge areas—from BELLE, which knows appropriate responses to brilliant gambits in master-level chess play—
to MYCIN, which provides remarkably accurate diagnoses of
patients' ailments on the basis of their complaints.

Contrary to the expectations of many, AI will produce commonly available and useful microcomputer-based products during the next five years. Most industry observers *do* agree that AI *concepts* will be integrated into and brought to bear upon dozens, perhaps hundreds, of products before 1990. They argue, however, that "true AI products" won't be available on microcomputers for at least 10 years.

The truth is, however, that such systems are already beginning to emerge in the microcomputer industry. People who ignore them or treat them as "mere toys" rob themselves and their companies of a chance to deal in real-world applications of artificial intelligence.

Artificial Obstacles

Members of the AI community who maintain that "expert systems" will not be commercially available for microcomputers before 1990 point to two factors in support of their skepticism: inherent hardware limitations and lack of available micro-based development tools.

The two misgivings are unwarranted.

When talking about hardware limitations, skeptics of the feasibility of micro-based AI programs typically focus on limited storage capacity and processing speed. They argue that no microcomputer—even one with as much as a million characters (a "megabyte") worth of memory capacity—can store enough knowledge in its core memory to be able to carry on real artificially intelligent activities. A megabyte of memory is considered insufficient to deal efficiently with even a small sub-set of the knowledge base required for genuine expertise in a particular area.

Even if ways are found to overcome the problem of limited internal memory in microcomputers, it is thought that the disks on which microcomputers store their main data or knowledge bases are too small to accommodate the *hundreds* of megabytes of information that comprise any real area of expertise.

Finally, conventional wisdom maintains that microprocessors are not nearly fast enough. AI is thought to require larger computers that take advantage of specialized processors with inherently faster execution speeds and huge amounts of memory for rapid processing of information.

These objections are not without *some* merit. Certainly a computer with more memory, greater disk capacity, and a faster central processing unit (CPU) will perform any task, AI-based expert systems included, more effectively than a smaller machine. It is also true that the traditional design and implementation of expert systems that have been developed for larger computers require huge amounts of memory.

But the fact goes unrecognized that such systems grow so large in part because they *can* grow large. In other words, their size may be more a function of nature's (and programmers') abhorrence of vacuums than of an intrinsic necessity for large scale. The position that microcomputer hardware is incapable of supporting a "real" or "useful" expert system fails to account for the ingenuity of people who design software for micros. After all, a few years ago few observers saw the possibility of an integrated software package with the capability of Framework or Symphony.

New AI products like Expert-Ease (see Expert-Ease: Expert Systems for Everyman?), and others overcome memory limitations by two basic techniques: knowledge base compilation and virtual memory emulation. Those two phrases are shorthand ways of expressing two interesting ideas that have been used on the larger mainframe computer systems to a degree. If the knowledge base—the facts and rules making up the expert system—were stored in the same ways text and spreadsheets are stored and used inside microcomputers, they would quickly occupy all of the system's available memory before they were of a usefully large size. However, compilation uses techniques that condense the amount of memory such information requires. Compilation streamlines the way in which such information is accessed, and thus goes a long way toward overcoming the problem of memory shortage. Compiled knowledge bases maximize available memory.

Besides compiling the knowledge base, expert system development tools for microcomputers also take advantage of a long-standing mainframe computer technique—virtual memory. This technique makes the micro act as if it has more memory than it really does. The mass storage medium—almost always a diskette these days—is treated as if it were merely an extension of the computer's main memory. Thus, the real limitation on the size of a knowledge base for these new programs is not the amount of memory the computer has or even the capacity of a single disk. Multiple disks become memory extensions. The technique permits expert systems of theoretically unlimited size on micros. We say "theoretically" because issues of practicality intervene at some point where the user of the expert system is unlikely to tolerate the inconvenience of adapting to the computer's limits if those limits impose a too-cumbersome burden on the user's patience or time.

Definition, Please

The disagreement that clearly exists within the AI community over the feasibility of developing "true" expert systems on microcomputers centers on a clear understanding of what an expert system really does or should do for its user.

An expert system recommends decisions or produces specific advice about a course of action in a particular set of circumstances. Viewed from that limited definition, there would be little dispute among various groups that a microcomputer-based expert system is feasible despite the limitations of today's technology. When we begin to examine *how* an expert system reaches its conclusions, we approach the area of disagreement between those who believe that micros are incapable of supporting "true" expert systems and those, like this author, who disagree.

An expert system is ultimately a collection of rules and factual statements (axioms) that make up a knowledge base—the information on which a decision is based. We will deal later with the question of how these rules are arrived at and "taught" to the computer. But the rules themselves tend to look something like this:

```
IF circumstance 1 is true
    THEN apply rule 14
        ELSE apply rule 11
```

Of course the complete set of rules that makes up any given knowledge base is far more complex than this, with hundreds or even thousands of interconnected IF-THEN-ELSE sets of rule groups. But the fundamental principle remains the same. An expert system is given a set of circumstances—most often as a series of answers to questions it poses to its human user—from which it is asked to make a recommendation. It then applies its rules to the set of circumstances and reaches a conclusion.

The disagreement between those who believe that micros can be hosts to expert systems and those who believe that current microcomputer technology makes that impossible centers generally on three issues: (1) the ability of the system to use probabilistic or "weighted" outcome methods; (2) the system's ability to "explain" how it reached a particular conclusion; and (3) how automatically the system gets the additional knowledge needed to add to its understanding of the class of problems it is being asked to solve. We will examine each of these issues in order.

Many large expert systems on mainframe and minicomputers use probability-weighted outcomes. When the program prepares to offer advice about a particular course of action, it has been told by its designers that the possible courses of action to be followed by the user are not equally probable. The program, therefore, first follows a path previously designated as the one leading to the most likely solution. If the course of action is rejected for some reason, the computer returns to the point at which it made the probabilistic decision, selects the next most likely course, and pursues it.

Expert systems on micros will typically not employ probability-weighted outcomes. Systems that do not incorporate such probabilistic alternative selection are probably less efficient than those that do. This is because they are more likely to encounter "blind alleys" from which recovery is not easy. But to argue that they are, therefore, less "expert" is to judge computers differently from the way we judge human experts. After all, we wouldn't conclude that of two experts in a particular area, the one who is able to reach his conclusions more rapidly is more expert. There are simply different ways of reaching conclusions and analyzing problems.

Another criticism of microcomputer implementation of AI programs has to do with the issue of whether an expert system can "explain" how it reached its conclusion. Some AI specialists demand that the program be able to "remember" and report the steps it went through in the decision-making process. The issue is more one of form than of substance. It is similar to the long-running argument in schools over whether students should be given credit for correct answers to math problems regardless of the process used in getting there. It becomes a question of objectives. If an expert system teaches us how to think and analyze a problem, then an inability to explain its course of analysis is certainly a major drawback. If, on the other hand, we are interested in expert advice, how a program gets to the point of giving us mostly correct advice becomes merely academic.

The last definitional problem with expert system design on microcomputers is the most difficult. The issue is one of knowledge acquisition: How does the expert system get its expertise? In most micro-based systems, the expert system is involved with a person who may be called a knowledge engineer who creates an original knowledge base, testing it in real-world or simulated situations and modifying it until it has reached a certain state. The knowledge base then produces advice. New facts, even those that may emerge from a person's use of the system, are not automatically integrated into the knowledge base. This inability to learn easily is clearly a problem, and one that people who design software for expert systems on micros must overcome before they can produce a true artificially intelligent expert system. The current argument, however, may be purely semantic.

Jeff Perrone, founder and president of the only exclusively AI and expert system software distributorship, grew tired of arguing about the issue and substitutes the term, "advisory systems." These are expert systems that are not self-extending or capable of "learning" without human assistance.

For people seeking advice, an expert system or a Perrone advisory system providing that advice is valuable.

Bringing AI to Micros

There are some difficulties to be faced in implementing AI on microcomputers in the next five years. Technical barriers will certainly be overcome during this time, opening a path for the 1990's of the advent of such programs on many home systems.

On the whole, larger and more difficult obstacles to implementing AI-based systems on microcomputers are similar to those of

AI research in general. They are, in fact, really obstacles to AI's realization in *any* hardware environment.

Some obstacles are software issues involving language selection, data structuring, retrieval methods, and the very way computers are designed and operate. The language disagreement that currently occupies AI workers' minds focuses on the issue of whether LISP, the traditional AI programming language, should be replaced by a more recent innovation, a language called Prolog. The conflict affects the implementation of AI-based systems on microcomputers.

There are three schools of thought on the subject of languages and their appropriateness to AI applications. (Actually, that is something of an oversimplification, but it will suffice for our purposes.) The first approach teaches that a procedure-oriented language is needed, the second says a non-procedural language is required, and the third view states that the language is not important enough to be worth fighting about. Another variation on this third alternative is the school of thought that says using language at all constitutes reinventing the wheel; what we should be using, these people would argue, are tools that make the language transparent. This is the position taken, for example, by Perrone.

The procedure-oriented school is easily the dominant one at this time. Most of its adherents argue that LISP, (which stands for LISt Processing) is the best language in which to develop AI applications. Procedural languages like LISP (and many others) provide a strict sequence of steps the computer must follow to solve a particular problem or class of problems. The languages define or describe the solution in increasingly smaller steps, or blocks, and their programs look like collections of procedures.

Non-procedural language supporters, on the other hand, generally line up behind a relatively recent arrival on the AI programming language scene called Prolog. A very popular language in Europe, Prolog has also been chosen by the Japanese for the implementation of their highly touted fifth generation (artificially intelligent) supercomputer systems.

Prolog is a non-procedural language in which the problem itself is defined and described, and the language "figures out" how to solve the problem. No particular sequence of procedures is involved; instead, the Prolog program is set up as a description of the rules and parameters of the problems to be solved.

As is always the case in such black-or-white discussions, there is no right answer to the dilemma.

Procedural languages are easier to design and write programs in (at least most people think so) because they can be neatly structured, divided into small pieces, and given to lots of different programmers to work on. They are, therefore, efficient. Non-procedural languages, on the other hand, are more effective—they are more flexible and adaptable to the needs of an AI or expert system application where the parameters and circumstances change continually. Non-procedural languages are also, at least arguably, easier to learn since they have a far smaller reliance on syntax rules and other language artificialities.

The third school of thought on AI languages tends to react with boredom to the whole conflict. Industry observer Esther Dyson publishes a newsletter, *RELease 1.0,* read by thousands of people every month. She claims the issue boils down to the relatively uninteresting question of which language the AI systems are prototyped in, not which language they are implemented and sold in.

"There won't be a bunch of LISP-based machines in the real world marketplace," she says. "Instead, AI programs will be developed in LISP or some other language and then implemented in Pascal or C on the microcomputer."

We agree.

The discussion about which programming language is best suited to AI program development is not so significant to potential users of AI systems as a casual reading of articles in the trade press might lead one to believe. The fact is, any programming language *can* be used to develop an AI application or an expert system. Even the much maligned BASIC and the highly structured Pascal—to say nothing of the cultic language FORTH—have been used to design and develop expert systems. And a great many such programs have been designed and implemented in FORTRAN, a language that was originally intended to be used to manipulate mathematical formulas. The question, therefore, is not which language *can* be used for AI, but rather which is *preferable*. The answer, as is often the case, is not absolute.

Organizing Knowledge: A Key Issue

There is, however, an issue larger than language. It is not, precisely speaking, a software issue, but appears most definable in the discussion of software. The question concerns how we organize knowledge. A computer program that stores information about a company's employees, for example, can permit access to that data a number of ways. We can get fairly sophisticated reports out of such a properly designed system. For example, we can find the name, age, and home address of every employee in the company who has a certain job title or level of education. But the information we can extract from such a system is limited by the amount and kinds of data we provided to the program at the beginning. For example, we couldn't find out how many blonde-haired men work in marketing support (without physically counting them ourselves, of course) unless we've told the computer system about hair color.

The problem becomes even more difficult if we want something *really* useful and complex from the system. What if, for example, we want the computer to "recommend" an employee for a new position we have open in Djakarta, Indonesia? We'd like to be able to say to the computer, "Please find me an employee with a good background in chemistry who is likely to adapt well to a new culture and is free to travel for a year or two on company reassignment." This request requires the computer to make some value judgments. At this point, our known data base retrieval systems break down. They can regurgitate information to us, but they cannot extrapolate from it.

Finding new, intelligent ways for such information to be stored and retrieved is a major challenge for the AI community. But this challenge must clearly be met and overcome if we are to make highly flexible use of intelligent systems. All the "experts" tell us we will indeed be doing that in the next couple of years.

The technological problems related to making AI products available on all computers in general, and moving AI products to microcomputers in particular, are serious. Behind these, however, lies a deeper, almost philosophical problem.

Phillip A. Kaufman, president of Silicon Compilers Incorporated,

San Jose, California, says, "We can't talk about artificial intelligence until we know what real intelligence is." Austin Henderson of Xerox's prestigious Palo Alto Research Center says his team spends most of its time trying to " . . . understand understanding."

We humans know remarkably little about how our most important and impressive organ—our brain—works. (See What Makes Thinking So Difficult?) Many AI theorists believe the real work in the next decade or so must be focused in psychology, philosophy, and communications theory, not in computer science or programming. As a group, these disciplines have recently been collected together under the title Cognitive Science. This research gap, or better, chasm, will dictate that the near-term future of "true" AI products on microcomputers will not consist of a flurry of products but rather of a series of simulations of AI activities on microcomputers. In short, according to these people, we may believe we are dealing with systems that are artificially intelligent but we won't in fact be using such systems for another 10 years.

Because of AI's unique nature as a computer discipline, new kinds of development tools will provide for the revolution in AI-based products. In fact, in the next two to three years, the major new products introduced to a market eagerly anticipating intelligent software will be development tools aimed at programmers who are willing to respond to that anticipation.

We have dwelt at length on the issues behind the implementation of expert systems on microcomputers primarily because we must make decisions about careers and strategies. This requires a framework within which to make value judgments about such ideas.

The press is filled with skepticism about AI and its promise. Noted AI authorities question whether a "real" AI system can run on today's relatively limited microcomputer systems. The non-technical observer might conclude that expert systems are too far off to be of any practical use to him or her.

Dispelling that feeling is part of the reason for this elaboration of the underlying issues. It would not be enough, in the face of rampant skepticism, merely to *assert* the presence of an error.

Practical Proof

But beyond the underlying issues, the question of whether expert systems with real value can be achieved on microcomputer systems can best be answered by examining real-life applications that have already been developed and by looking more closely at the tools available for developing such systems.

First Step: Micro Tools

The computer itself is an uninteresting, useless object. Only when given instructions in the form of a program does the computer take on value and meaning. And those programs must be written in languages that use tools such as editors, interpreters, compilers, and operating systems. The microcomputer would have remained an engineering curiosity had it not been for an important fact: at some point early in its life, enterprising people developed *tools* that made it possible for other entrepreneurs to develop computer *programs*.

For the most part, those who developed the early microcomputer programming languages and tools did not do well economically. During a brief flourishing period the rest of the microcomputer industry seemed to camp on their doorstep, eagerly waiting pearls of wisdom to drop from their keyboards. But when many applications were available on the market, other people developed other tools and languages, and pretty soon the early pioneers were not so necessary or mysterious.

This scenario will repeat itself as AI emerges as an important application area for microcomputers during the end of the eighties and comes into its own in the 1990's. Right now, an absence of usable, meaningful, and flexible programming aids and tools is the bottleneck to development. Lack of these aids discourages those who would otherwise attempt to overcome obstacles to the development of real AI applications. In the next several years, a number of new and existing companies will prepare and market languages, editors, and other programming aids aimed specifically at the AI program developer.

Like their predecessors in microcomputer language development, AI tool creators won't become instant millionaires. And also like those predecessors, the new toolmakers will find themselves, sooner rather than later, fighting for survival in an increasingly competitive and crowded marketplace. AI development tools is, therefore, not a long-term growth industry. But the next few years will provide a crucial link in the chain bringing intelligence to home computer systems.

The New Toolmakers

Already, a surprisingly large number of companies are attempting to carve out a niche in the emerging AI development tool business. Some products have already been introduced, and in the months ahead more and smarter tools will quickly make their appearance.

One product that has been on the market for some time is a program called Expert-Ease (see Expert-Ease: Expert Systems for Everyman?). This program was built by Professor Donald Michie of the University of Edinburgh, Scotland to run on the IBM PC. At its price of under $700, Expert-Ease has gained the interest of a number of people interested in the development of AI-based software for the micro world. "It is the lowest priced way of getting your feet wet in the AI business," one software entrepreneur said as he placed his order for the product. "Even if it turns out I can't develop a complete AI system using Expert-Ease, I'll be able to find out how such a development project ought to look and be managed."

Expert-Ease is marketed in the western United States by Jeffrey Perrone and Associates, Inc., of San Francisco and published in the United States by Human Edge Software of Palo Alto, California. Perrone, an AI enthusiast with a marketing flair, freely admits that Expert-Ease ". . .isn't the final answer." Perrone's group handles several other AI development tools for microcomputers, including one called Insight, which sells for the remarkably low price of under $100, and another product that will permit the millions of owners of Apple, Atari, Commodore, and other "older" personal computers to undertake reasonable expert system design using limited numbers of rules.

A number of expert system development tools and programming languages were explored in depth in a Spring 1985 issue of the widely read *PC Magazine* as the publication devoted a special issue to the subject of expert systems on IBM PC's. The mere appearance of such an issue in a magazine catering to a relatively traditional business user speaks to the rapidly gaining acceptance of the field among microcomputer owners.

Expert-Ease was the only micro-based expert system development tool we could find that claimed a major success in a real-life application, and the success was of substantial size. Robert Barry, who directs AI projects at one of Westinghouse's plants in Pittsburgh said his company increased its business volume at that plant by $10 million per year using Expert-Ease on an IBM PC to solve a problem that had stubbornly refused to yield to more conventional methods of analysis and solution.

Another knowledge worker, Evlin Kinney, reportedly has developed two relatively sophisticated but practical expert systems using Expert-Ease. The first is called Chest Pains and it helps diagnose possible origins and treatments of chest pains. The other is as yet unnamed, but deals with predicting the likelihood of a blood clot that will lead to a serious heart problem called an embolism. Neither product is yet in commercial use at this writing.

Teknowledge, a Palo Alto firm, is also in the micro AI development tool business with a product called M.1. An easy-to-understand demonstration program that accompanies the program simulates the decision-making process of a wine connoisseur in selecting a beverage for a specific combination of meal ingredients and personal preferences.

San Francisco-based Intellicorp has introduced a product known as KEE, an acronym for Knowledge Engineering Environment. KEE does not run on microcomputers but on the more classical LISP and AI systems supplied by companies like Xerox and Symbolics, Inc. These latter are dedicated systems with huge amounts of storage and fast response times. AI developers who are serious about getting into the commercial marketplace with a system have used these machines for the past several years. These large, complex systems are also used in AI research by universities and think tanks like Stanford Research Institute. Their price tags—in the $30,000 and up category—put them out of the reach of many innovative-thinking entrepreneurs who would like to develop an AI product for home or small business use.

Another entrant into this field, Texas Instruments, introduced its Explorer AI tool and its Personal Consultant applications generator for its IBM PC look-alike units in late 1984 and early 1985.

Interestingly enough, a number of people, including this author, who have attempted to discover how much real effort was being expended on the design of expert system development tools in the United States have found that more work of this type is originating in Europe, and particularly in Great Britain, than in this country. We have mentioned Expert-Ease, which is of Scottish origin.

A pair of companion compatible programs from British-based Isis Systems Ltd. called Micro Expert and Macro Expert, will allegedly permit the development of expert systems on any computer from the popular Apple II to a huge DEC or an IBM mainframe system. The tools support probabilistic approaches to decision-making. The knowledge base is built using any text processor outside the expert system tool, which then operates on the information contained in the knowledge base.

Sage is the name given to another expert system generator that originates in England. SPL International has introduced this tool and described it as a "model-building language." Like Micro/Macro Expert, Sage permits the use of probabilities in its decision-making structure and processes. One key feature of this new system appears to be a highly interactive development environment in which the expert system designer can set up part of the structure, ask the system to indicate how it will respond if a certain answer is given to a certain question, and then return immediately to the system development process to modify the design accordingly.

The first commercially available expert system development tool written in Prolog appears to be ES/P Advisor, a product of yet another British company, Expert Systems Ltd. ES/P Advisor is designed exclusively for complex text-based applications such as those where the decision-making process involves complex rules, regulations, standards, and procedures. The knowledge base used by ES/P Advisor is created using a word processor. ES/P Advisor is available for the IBM PC and a number of other 16-bit personal computers running IBM's MS-DOS or PC-DOS, as well as systems running CP/M-86.

SRI International, of Palo Alto, has also created a general-purpose expert system generator that is capable of being run on an IBM PC computer. The product is called SeRIES-PC—a complicated acronym for SRI Expert System-Personal Computer. It carries a hefty $15,000 price tag, but that figure includes the creation by SRI International experts of a custom knowledge base for use by the system.

A few companies have attempted to bring expert systems development capability to the millions of people who own less expensive 8-bit machines like Apples and Commodore C-64s. One such product has enjoyed a modicum of success. It is called Superforth 64 + AI and is published by Parsec Research of Fremont, California. The product was developed in large part by AI aficionado and FORTH programming guru Jack Park of Sacramento. The product sells for less than $100, but is not for the fainthearted. FORTH is a peculiar cult language which, while quite powerful and known for very fast execution, is almost always seen by students as quite difficult to learn.

This list is not exhaustive, and there will be many more companies entering this market as time goes along.

ExperTelligence's Mac Tool

ExperTelligence of Santa Barbara, California is preparing a product for the Apple Macintosh family of microcomputers rather than for the otherwise dominant IBM PC. (See Expert Tool for the Mac.) This news is exciting for several reasons. First, the Mac, with its built-in graphics capability, use of pull-down menus, various windows, and a mouse controller, closely resembles the approach used on the more traditional Xerox and Symbolics machines. Thus, programmers who are interested in spinning out of existing AI product houses—always a fertile source of talent for forming a new industry—will have a preference for the ExperTelligence product.

A second significant reason for the ExperTelligence decision to use the Mac environment is the departure it represents from the IBM PC world known affectionately as "Big Blue."

ExperTelligence president Denny Bollay (see Denny Bollay's Excitement Started in School), is a true AI aficionado. He is designing a tool that will permit any business user to develop an artificially intelligent program to deal with his or her own need for expertise and "consulting" help in managing his business.

In mid-1985, ExperTelligence, seeking to establish itself as *the* Macintosh AI group, introduced a complete implementation of a very popular mainframe expert system language, OPS5, under the name (surprise!) ExperOPS5. The product was met with immediate enthusiasm by a number of expert systems developers.

Bollay indicated that his company will also introduce an expert system development tool on the Mac, which he called ". . .an incredibly powerful and flexible environment within which to develop expert systems."

AI tool development for microcomputer-based AI products in the short-term will involve a number of other companies, start-ups and established AI firms alike. As such companies proliferate, before 1990 we will begin reading and talking about a "shakeout" in the industry. Such a shakeout, when it comes, will have serious implications for companies that have adopted the particular AI program development technology produced by that company.

The ideas and concepts underlying AI development are imprecise—far less sharply defined than, say, a general ledger or word processing program or even a flexible data base manager. Many layers of complexity are involved in the knowledge bases from which they will operate. For these reasons, the sudden disappearance of a company that has walked a particular line on some of the fuzzier issues could have disastrous results for the companies who relied on that particular expert viewpoint. This will be a far more serious problem in the final years of the 1980's than the software publisher shakeout that occurred in the middle two years of the decade.

Applications Packages

The development tools we have been discussing will spawn applications packages in the next five years that will make desktop advisors or experts available in a number of areas of professional endeavor. Before 1990, a limited number of such packages will be available for home use, particularly when expert system development tools begin to be bought by owners of the long-popular eight-bit microcomputer systems like the Apple II, Commodore 64, and Atari 800 series.

Applications packages are being developed today on micros, but are being used primarily inside large and medium-sized organizations to solve specific problems. There are companies, which prefer not to be identified for competitive reasons, which use expert systems to do such things as assist customers and dealers in troubleshooting computers, make preliminary evaluations of complex loan applications, predict the profitability of a particular type of legal case, and plan recombinant DNA (genetic) experiments and projects.

Financial analysis tools are potentially fertile areas for the early application of micro-based AI products. Syntelligence, a small Palo Alto firm which, like many other AI companies, spun off from a university (in this case Stanford) reportedly soon plans to introduce a sophisticated expert system aimed at bankers. One company with ambitious plans in this arena is Palladian, of Cambridge, Massachusetts. Palladian plans to offer interconnected expert systems in the areas of manufacturing capacity planning and capital budgeting, two long-term issues that affect many companies.

A series of applications-oriented expert systems has been recently introduced by London-based Helix. This company designed the Nexus expert system generator for use on large systems. Now it uses Nexus to design and implement expert systems that run on an IBM PC. The expert systems packages the firm has already introduced include Investment Adviser (helps in selecting appropriate investment portfolios), Financial Adviser (analyzes the financial performance of companies and recommends appropriate remedial action if it finds problems or deficiencies), and Company Tax Adviser (suggests strategies for minimizing corporate tax liabilities).

SRI International has for the past two years been building a group of in-house consultants, headed by Sandra Cook, in its Financial Expert Systems Program. Ms. Cook believes that "...expert systems will invade the financial community" in the near future. She sees particularly fertile ground in some areas, including international bank loan evaluations, commercial loan assessment, financial planning, insurance underwriting, financial product sales, and insurance claims processing.

SRI International's first real product in this arena plays the role of an international banking expert in loans. It will ultimately be developed so to run on an IBM PC, though it presently does not. The program interacts with the user in a friendly, professional dialogue using terms that such a person would normally be expected to use and understand. It helps assess the lender's advantages, the risks involved, and the resources and credibility of the prospective borrower.

Perhaps the biggest AI *publishing* news of 1985 came in mid-year when Lotus Development announced a deal with AI pioneer and researcher S. Jerrold Kaplan. While Lotus and Kaplan were mum about the specific products they would develop together, it doesn't take a genius to look at Lotus' expertise in financial analysis software to conclude it is in that arena that the first products will almost certainly appear. Lotus thus became the first major national publisher of microcomputer software to make an overt move into AI; others are undoubtedly pursuing similar tactics on a *sub rosa* basis.

These companies are reluctant to discuss their specific future plans. In fact, their representatives refuse to reveal whether they intend to make their products available on microcomputers or not. From that reticence, we conclude they *do* so intend. Therefore, these companies will join the ranks of those who give the lie to the widespread viewpoint that no "real" expert system will be available on a micro before 1990.

Intelligent Arenas

The companies that will emerge as the big winners in the marketplace of the applied expert systems are either not yet formed or are in very embryonic stages. This is more true than in any other aspect of the industry examined in this book. The next few pages will, therefore, not attempt to look at many specific companies but will focus on some areas of life and business that may be among the first to see the marketing of real-life micro-based expert systems applications on the market.

One company—ODS, Inc. (the letters are an acronym for Organization Development Software)—introduced a product that at least gave the appearance and feel of an expert system in mid-1985. The product is called ods/CONSULTANT. Co-developer Dan Tagliere and his partner Jon Tegethoff spent more than a decade as organizational consultants. At some point, they decided to try to reduce their expertise—or as much of it as lent itself to such a product—to a software program that would enable non-clients to think through problems with consulting help available from the computer rather than from a high-paid human consultant.

The product is very Mac-like, meaning it uses pull-down menus, windows, and lots of icons for intuitive ease of use. Their developers refer to ods/CONSULTANT as a "consulting expert system" to differentiate it slightly from more general expert systems. It is designed to assist users with creative (often referred to in popular psychology articles as "right brain") thinking, critical ("left-brain") thinking, planning, evaluation, and problem analysis. All of this the company gathers under the newly coined rubric "Computer Assisted Thinking."

"A good consultant doesn't tell his clients what to do, but guides them through the process of thinking about the problem and its solution," Tagliere maintains. "We designed ods/CONSULTANT with that consulting model in mind. It doesn't know about specific kinds of companies or problems, but it does understand general problem analysis and solution techniques. It guides the user through this process using very English-like, relatively unstructured approaches where feasible."

One feature of the program enables the user to enter a whole list of criteria that will go into making a decision, then rating them, and having the program do the calculations, comparisons and analyses to assist him in resolving the issue.

Another company taking a somewhat similar approach is the Palo Alto-based AI Mentor, Inc. This company was founded by several psychologists and consultants who had been assisting other companies in solving personnel management problems. Putting their expertise into a knowledge base, these people designed a product called Performance Mentor that takes a manager through the process of conducting effective performance appraisals. "Unlike many other personnel management products, Performance Mentor does not help the user *do* the review but rather teaches him or her the *techniques* and *processes* involved, using AI techniques," co-founder Dr. Nancy Nygreen points out.

The company planned to ship its first products in late 1985.

Therein Lies a Trend

Performance Mentor and ods/CONSULTANT share an interesting characteristic: Both are expert systems of one sort or another developed not by software houses, but by people with expertise to share with others. This trend toward knowledge engineering originating where the knowledge is as opposed to where the engineering is will certainly continue and accelerate as the 1980's draw to a close and the 1990's dawn.

"Intelligent" Data Base Management

We should mention at least briefly another area of AI applications that began to emerge in the market in the last few months of 1985. Symantec of Palo Alto introduced a product called Q&A (for Question and Answer) that said it would boast a "natural-language interface" so that users could get information from their data bases without having to learn any specific command syntax or formats.

Micro Data Base Systems (MDBS) of Lafayette, Indiana, in early 1986 released a new product called, tantalizingly enough, Guru. This system combined the usual integrated software (data base management, spreadsheets, business graphics, text processing, and telecommunications) with an expert system building tool and a natural language processing interface. The company says it is trying to create a new business work tool environment in which developers can move from one type of application to another with little or no thought to the underlying structure (unlike, e.g., Symphony and Framework where the underlying structure is critical to understanding what is going on).

Guru permits the user to make relatively normal-sounding, English language inquiries of the system. Such queries are not limited to the data base management component but can be applied equally to the spreadsheet or the expert system. An expert system can be completely and transparently integrated into the spreadsheet so that the expert system itself need not ask the user for specific data but may merely "grab" it from the information placed into the spreadsheet and/or data base manager and draw expert conclusions from that information. First evaluations of the product were very favorable despite its relatively high price tag ($2,995). Guru works on an IBM PC.

The arena of data management seems destined to be one of great AI and expert systems activity during the next few years.

When Is a Problem Suited to AI?

Only a certain class of problems lends itself to expert system assistance. Clues to the makeup of this class are found by looking again at the program Expert-Ease, which comes equipped with a demonstrator program called PROBLEMS. This program, which is in reality a very small expert system, provides the person who uses it with experience in examining and using expert systems. Let's look at the questions it asks and see if we can gain some clues and insights into what kinds of problems might lend themselves best to expert systems approaches.

When we run the expert system PROBLEMS, the silicon expert first asks, "Are the answers to your problem or your decisions determined at random?" If we answer yes, then Expert-Ease will say, "We would advise you to not use Expert-Ease for this problem. Expert-Ease cannot spot patterns which do not exist."

This is our first clue to the class of problems that lend themselves to expert system assistance: The solutions or answers to the problems we ask the system to deal with must be predictable. This is not to say that the problems must be obvious or easy; in fact, spotting patterns in a collection of dozens or even hundreds of examples is one of the most challenging tasks we humans face, which is why such problems often appear on intelligence and achievement examinations. Expert-Ease can handle large problems that require the examination of a broad range of defined issues and look at answers to all of them before determining a course of action. No expert system, however, can help solve a problem whose solution may be different from time to time under identical circumstances.

A problem we could not expect an expert system on a computer to solve for us then would involve things such as subjective judgments. Predicting whether people will like a particular piece of art, for example, would be incredibly difficult for an expert system because the factors are not predictable. Many factors that are not intrinsic to the painting or to our taste in art per se go into the decision: what we had to eat for lunch, whether we like purple or not, the time of day, how we are getting along with our boss. . . .

On the other hand, *if* a group of people could articulate, say, 57 things they look for in a painting, and if those things could be quantified (described in objective terms) and if we recorded the reactions of these people to enough paintings, then we could use those criteria, perhaps, to construct an expert system that could predict with some accuracy whether this group would be likely or unlikely to react positively to a given piece of art.

If we respond to the first question the system PROBLEMS asks us by indicating there *is* a pattern to the answers, then another question is asked: "How complete is the set of examples describing your problem or decision?" Here, we are given a choice from four possible answers, ranging from "100% complete" to "only a small number." If we indicate we have a set of examples that is 100% complete, we will be advised to use Expert-Ease. But if we say we have defined something less than 100% of our examples, the computer asks us, "How important is accuracy in the answers or decisions? What is the consequence of a wrong answer or decision?" Again, we have a range of choices, this time three of them, from "I need total accuracy" to "I can tolerate initial errors as long as I can adapt the system to new or changing circumstances."

The advice process has become a bit more complex, hasn't it? For example, if we say we have only a small number of the possible situations that could occur in our example base but we need 100% accuracy, we will be advised not to use Expert-Ease. A message will tell us, "You will get an unacceptable level of wrong answers because your examples do not cover enough situations." If, on the other hand, we indicate that even though we have only a small number of the possibilities in our knowledge base, we are able to tolerate errors if they can be adjusted for, then the system patiently asks us another question: "How well will the people who will use the system be able to detect wrong answers?" Here, we have two choices: They can spot errors and compensate for them or they will not be able to do so. Based on our answer to that question, the system will advise us whether or not to use Expert-Ease in this particular situation.

By way of summary, then, this small expert system bases its advice about whether to use Expert-Ease to solve a particular problem on four criteria: predictability of answers, importance of accuracy, completeness of our example set, and the ability of users of the system to monitor it for wrong advice.

We could add a great many other factors. As a matter of fact, in the course of learning Expert-Ease, we added another dozen or so factors and several additional levels of advice to the example system the publishers of Expert-Ease furnished us. But the principles remain the same.

An expert system may be used then in a situation where the problem to be solved or the question to be answered is characterized by:

- predictability
- repetitiveness (designing a full expert system to answer a one-time question might be valuable, but most of the time it probably will not be)
- necessity of a consistent solution
- need for accuracy
- quick decisions
- reliance on one or a small group of often inaccessible experts in the organization
- relatively thorough understanding of the problem
- an appropriate degree of understanding of the problem by the user of the system (a level near zero could be accommodated if the other factors were right).

Obviously, not all problems have all these characteristics; in fact, probably very few have a substantial number of them. But classes of problems that are characterized by many of these traits are probably good candidates to consider for application of an expert system.

Understanding these limitations, what can we say about the

domains in which AI might be profitably applied in the next few years? There are dozens, but we will focus on a few as examples where expert systems will play a role in our lives in the near future.

Some Early Products are Already Successful

AI has already been successfully applied to the field of oil and mineral exploration. Experts can predict where a company is likely to find oil or other valuable natural resources by using a relatively straightforward, though complex, set of quantifiable criteria. Dozens of factors, like shape of the ground, geologic nature of the soil, and results of sonic soundings conducted in the area, can be plugged into a system that will then predict with a fair degree of accuracy whether minerals might be found in the particular location.

In late 1983, an expert system was developed by SRI International and named, appropriately enough, PROSPECTOR. The system predicted a rich deposit of a valuable mineral, molybdenum, in eastern Washington state. Human prospectors then explored the area around Mount Tolman and discovered several large deposits of the mineral precisely where the program predicted they would be. Based on geological, geophysical and geochemical information fed into the system from digitized maps and other sources, a computer had located a substantial mineral deposit.

An expert system soon will help discover a major oil strike, an event that will catapult micro-based expert systems into the news headlines and make even more of us aware of the awesome potential residing in this technology.

We have already mentioned banking and financial planning as areas of interest among expert systems developers. The factors to be taken into account in these fields, while complex and myriad, are nonetheless definable and quantifiable. It is not likely that two people could consistently agree, for example, on whether particular companies engaged in pioneering research and product development would be a good investment.

On the other hand, we could decide that companies should be evaluated against a particular set of criteria—like years of experience of founders, number of previous successes, percentage of completion of current projects, number of competitors, and potential profit (which in turn is judged by a whole sub-set of criteria). We then would be able to design an expert system which, when evaluating two similar sets of data, would consistently reach the same conclusions about such potential investments.

Similarly, decisions about loans, construction projections, interest rate determinations, and a host of other relatively quantifiable aspects of banking and finance lend themselves quite well to such analysis by a computer-based expert system.

Another area to which AI and expert systems design will surely be applied through the rest of the 1980's is engineering. During the first half of this decade, major strides took place in the development of Computer-Aided Design (CAD) and Computer-Assisted Engineering (CAE) tools. These products improve the efficiency of designers of other electronic products.

In a sense, such tools are incestuous; their use breeds more products that put more demand on the need for engineering talent, resulting in increased demand for more engineering tools, and so on, *ad infinitum*. Many aspects of an engineer's job can be automated. Still others lend themselves to expert system and analysis. As the integrated circuit ("chip") industry moves to larger scales of integration (see Hardware Development, page 201) it becomes possible to enable designers of new highly complex electronic products to use high-level design tools to assist them in their work.

Silicon Compilers Incorporated is a San Jose-based company that manufactures dedicated computers and workstations for system designers to use in developing new integrated circuits to handle complex electronic circuitry demands. The company recognizes expert systems as a strong future trend. SCI president Phil Kaufman told us, "We expect to see more and more application of intelligence on the part of the design tools in the next few years."

Telecommunications (see Broadening Our Community, page 66) is an area where AI is being applied, not as an expert system but as problem-solving programs. The programs require no human intervention and provide no information. Instead, AI-like programs will be installed inside forthcoming computer-telephone links. The programs will enable us to use ordinary telephone lines for very high-speed communication of computer data without the fear of losing valuable information in the "noise" that is an inherent part of the transmission lines themselves.

Modem pioneers like Lee Hearn of Santa Cruz, California, will introduce more such intelligent circuitry in the rest of the decade. "There's already a lot of smarts inside a high-quality modem," Hearn says. "Filtering out unwanted parts of the signals coming across the phone links to the computers is an important area for research and new product development and introduction as we move into the 1990's."

Education and training are other areas in which AI programs will play an important role in the last half of the 1980's and beyond. Computers have become familiar members of the teaching community and have been integrated into its processes of learning and teaching to a significant degree in the past ten years. But when AI techniques dedicated to helping *humans* learn better are applied to computers, exciting things will happen. The computer will suddenly become an active participant in the learning process.

For example, the computer will constantly monitor the student's responses to particular questions, integrate what it "learns" of the student's understanding into its own knowledge base and will then tailor the learning experience in specific ways for that student in order to maximize the effectiveness and efficiency of the learning event. The educational process is fertile ground for AI research; much of the early work in the field took place in the educational arena and a great deal of the research being undertaken today happens in educational environments, primarily universities and colleges.

An Educational "Game" About AI

One of the earliest programs introduced for Apple's Macintosh computer was an AI learning game in disguise. ChipWits, from Brainworks, Inc., turned out to be a popular and intriguing design.

A ChipWits participant—the word "player" seems somehow not to fit—programs a robot by using a collection of graphic symbols that have meanings like "turn right", "look for a wall," "see if the floor has disappeared," "search for food," and other similar activities. He arranges these programming steps in a layout form and then watches as his robot carries out the commands in different artificially created environments. The objective is to design a robot that will thrive in each environment, with the requirements varying from one "room" of the ChipWits layout to another.

The program is ingenious and well-received by people of all ages. It is animated, graphic, includes sound effects, but most importantly is an effective and quality teaching aid to assist people who are interested in AI to learn more about how the processes and programs work on a functional level.

Teaching and engineering are not the only professions to be affected by the coming revolution in AI and expert systems. In fact, the more traditional professions such as medicine and law have already seen some startling developments begin to take place.

In the field of medicine, books have been written on the application of AI and expert systems techniques to the design of systems that enable physicians to make faster, more accurate diagnoses, gain quick access to hard-to-find information in time-critical situations, and generally function on a more creative and effective level. Diagnosis has been a particularly fertile ground for new research in AI and expert systems in the past several years. It will continue to be so for the foreseeable future.

Perhaps best known of the medical AI systems is Stanford University's MYCIN, which carries on a dialogue with a physician, helps the doctor diagnose patients with bacteria or meningitis infections, and recommends courses of therapy for such patients. Not only can it do all this, but it can explain its reasons. This system was developed during the mid-1970's and has been in active use both as a real-life tool and as a model for expert systems researchers ever since.

MYCIN embodies several hundred rules that represent the human-level expertise about the subjects with which it deals. It also incorporates a *knowledge-acquisition system*, by means of which its knowledge base can be updated as new information on the subjects of its expertise becomes available.

Attention has recently been focused on the work of The Rand Institute of southern California and others in applying AI to the practice of law. Dr. Donald Waterman of that prestigious think tank has been involved in developing a package known as LDS that assists in the process of analyzing and estimating damages in cases involving product liability. If you bought a can of a chemical that was supposed to kill the weeds in your lawn and your neighbor became ill from it and sued the company that made it, you'd be involved in a product liability case. Dr. Waterman's package could help the attorneys involved evaluate the extent of probable damages the injured party could expect to be awarded by a court, given all of the very complex circumstances.

Dr. Waterman and his team are at work on a more specialized version of the same package, designed to assist in the analysis of cases where the product at fault was asbestos.

Dr. Waterman firmly believes that micros will be important in the AI and expert systems worlds in the next few years. Even though increased memory capacities of the small machines is important to their becoming really useful in real-life situations, he points out that memory costs are declining and the ability of the central processors in such machines to handle millions of characters of storage is increasing to a point where. . ."Full-blown expert systems on micros are inevitable and a lot closer than many people think," he says.

A number of researchers are working on other aspects of applying expert systems technology to the practice of law. Dean Schlobohm, a San Francisco attorney and partner in a small software firm, recently won a national prize for an expert system he developed that assists attorneys in dealing with a particularly troublesome aspect of tax law.

Before leaving this section, let's ask whether expert systems will be used in the home and in small business environments in the next five years. The answer is yes. There will be *some* systems available before the 1990's. However, widespread use of home expert systems will not take place until the 1990's or later for several reasons.

First, the hardware available to most people on their home systems is capable of supporting only small knowledge bases and expert systems programs. Second, the number of areas in which most people consult experts in their homes is not very large—even expanding the definition of the word "expert" to encompass reference books and library resources. Finally, the precipitous decline in the home computer software market that took place in 1982-84 is not one from which many companies will rebound with great enthusiasm in the next few years.

An Assessment of the Near-Term Future of AI and Expert Systems

The main issue in AI for the next few years will be knowledge acquisition. This will be so for both micro-based expert systems and their "Big Brothers" the mainframe and minicomputer systems. In other words, we're going to have to answer the question, "How do we get all of this knowledge into a system so we can use it?" The question is related in significant ways to the deep question of how we humans get usable information into *our* systems.

The crossovers among computer science, psychology, and philosophy help explain why current AI research is such a morass. Yet issues associated with the nature of intelligence and the processes of learning are fundamental and important to understand if we are to assess intelligently where AI is headed in the next few years.

Stanford University professor, and author Edward Feigenbaum speaks about the "knowledge acquisition bottleneck." His description seems particularly appropriate. Pick any subject area in which you would like an expert system's help and you will find a glut of knowledge and information that must be fed into the system before the program can *begin* to function. Multiply this glut by a factor equal to the number of areas of human endeavor in which we would like to design expert systems and you get some idea of the breadth and depth of Feigenbaum's bottleneck.

The discussion is carried on both on a conceptual level and on a practical or technological one.

Conceptually, the issue focuses upon the question of how human learning takes place. From this we might, for example, devise an effective teaching machine. Essentially, the debate concerning computer learning comes down to a question of whether human experts provide the machines with information in the form of a set of rules about the behavior being modeled or with a collection of examples of previous decisions made by the human expert. In the latter case, the machine will infer a rule or set of rules from the data we provide. (For a discussion of this aspect of the debate, see Teaching by Rules vs. Teaching by Example.)

A deeper issue underlies the technical debate over rule-based vs. example-driven learning systems. Recounting the complex theories involved is beyond the scope of this book. A nodding acquaintance with the essentials of the debate, however, will clarify the issues behind the question concerning the best way to "teach" machines about subjects.

There are at least four ideas about what it means for a machine to learn about something. When we talk about machine learning in the context of expert systems, we almost always mean by "learning" the process of "acquiring specific knowledge." The definition is adequate for a limited purpose, but viewed in the broader context of machine intelligence, we would have to consider the possibility that a machine is learning when it improves its performance, acquires or improves existing *skills*, or formulates new theories. All of these are valid ways of looking at the subject, and none is necessarily "better" than the others.

The Problems of Information Transfer

The technological aspect of the problem is less controversial and far more grounded in traditional issues of data entry. It does, however, have one interesting twist.

Broadly speaking, the question of knowledge acquisition by a computer system is only part of the question of how we move any information from one point to another. AI researcher and author, Pierre Bierre says, "Everyone involved in AI agrees that knowledge is the key to intelligence." It follows, then, that in moving knowledge from a human's brain to a computer's memory banks and disks we are providing the system with the basis for future intelligent analysis and behavior.

Bierre has developed an unusual and challenging concept of machine learning. His idea is to build what he calls a "sensory learning machine."

Conceptually, Bierre points out, knowledge falls into a seemingly endless chain of what he calls prerequisite knowledge. As he puts it, "If Knowledge X depends on being expressed in terms of its prerequisite Knowledge Xp, and *that* knowledge in turn depends for its expression on prerequisite Knowledge (Xp)p, and (Xp)p has to be written in terms of ((Xp)p)p, and so on, then where does the process begin, and with what kind of knowledge does it start?"

This, of course, crystalizes the fundamental philosophical issues underlying much of current AI research: What is the deepest level to which meaning can be traced? Or even more philosophically, where (or what) is the source of all knowledge?

What Bierre sees happening in the AI community (see Learning vs. Performing) is a subtle shift from systems that *perform* some task, which is clearly where virtually all current expert systems can be positioned, to those that *learn* about how to perform tasks. The difference is subtle, but important.

Bierre offers elaborate and convincing proof that all knowledge is sensory in its essential nature. The world, he argues, can be pictured as a giant computer spewing out billions and billions of pieces of information that can become knowledge if we can capture it for later recovery and use. It is the conceptualization, design, and ultimate fabrication of a machine to accomplish this awesome task that is the *raison d'etre* of Bierre's company, aptly named Clairvoyant Systems.

He envisions the ultimate use of video technology—in some form well advanced beyond where it is today—with sophisticated cameras tied into sophisticated computer systems that capture, analyze and "represent" (computerese for giving internal importance or meaning to something) this information in very compact and usable ways. In fact, the idea of the representation of knowledge (ROFK in Bierre's defined AI parlance) is at the core of what Clairvoyant Systems plans to do over the next five to ten years.

"It's not particularly easy to describe what a sensory learning machine will be or look like," Bierre says, "but I can tell you what it will *do*. It will permit us to grab data (that) is streaming past us all the time, in quantities even our brains can't deal with on a level of which we are aware, and will process and store that information for our later use." Bierre speaks about an electronic ". . .library-of-the-future, a distributed knowledge base, offering *universal* accessibility and *open-ended* extensibility."

Bierre admits development of a product is "at least five years away." Whatever he may ultimately accomplish in the way of products, Pierre Bierre will have an impact in the short term on how we think and talk about the representation and transmission of knowledge. These ideas are so fundamental to AI as a research subject that defining and extending them may well become an important development in the next few years.

A great deal of the knowledge in the world is already recorded in forms that a computer could use without a great deal of our help. For example, information printed on book pages could be retrieved by attaching an OCR (optical character reader) to a computer and having someone put page after page of information through the OCR into the computer so that it literally "reads" the information into its memory. That would be one way of getting a lot of data, or knowledge, into a computer system.

Another way is the one we have discussed in connection with Expert-Ease. We explicitly tell the computer system—in a structured way—the material we want it to learn. We do this by typing in answers to questions it poses, filling out structures it presents to us, and going through an iterative refinement process until the system is finally able to deal with the breadth of knowledge we need it to have to solve our problems or answer our questions.

The two methods of teaching machines about subjects are both similar and different from one another. They are similar in that both provide the expert system with explicit information, observable data, about the subject. In the first instance, the system receives what someone has written about the subject and in the second it obtains what someone specifically prepares for the system's use.

The difference between the two methods of knowledge acquisition lies in the structure of the information. In the case of OCR entry, the computer system ends up with an undigested mass of words, characters, and symbols that lack any particular inherent arrangement or structure by which the computer can later retrieve the data. A step is missing. At some point a human being must intervene in the process and organize the information given to the system. The information typed into the system by the expert in the second case, on the other hand, is quite explicitly organized, along the precise lines required by the program's way of looking at the problem. The information is immediately usable.

Both methods have a serious drawback. In the case of the books and journal articles being "read" by the computer, the need for someone to organize it all later is a major obstacle to getting information into an expert system. In the case of human-entered, explicitly defined information, the quantity of information that can be fed into the system for analysis will be limited by the availability and stamina of human users. If the problem being solved is large and the mass of data needed is extensive and dynamic, neither approach will be very satisfactory.

This is where the concept of automatic knowledge acquisition comes in. Significant advances will take place in this area in the next few years, and there will be an explosion of approaches and solutions in the early 1990's. Automatic knowledge acquisition happens when the system we are using on a computer "learns" by "watching" what we do as we use the computer. This can happen either by running the expert system program itself or by running some other program with which the expert system is designed to help us. A specific example may help to clarify what we mean here.

If you were the user of a data base management program such as dBase II or an integrated software package like Lotus's Symphony package on a microcomputer, you might have found yourself in the situation where you were trying to enter information into a data base designed by someone else and running into problems and errors trying to do so. In the absence of a clear picture of the total structure of the data base and the underlying programming languages and concepts that comprise the data base manager's systematic approach, you might be hard pressed to figure out what you are doing wrong and how to correct the problem.

But if we designed an expert system that could run in the computer at the same time as the data base program and "knew" about the structure and syntax of the system as well as the needs of your application, the situation could be made much more manageable. This feat of having a program in "background" has been achieved in recent months with a great many programs on the

IBM PC, and other micros. (The Mediator, a program discussed in Software Advances later in this book, has some of the earmarks of this kind of program.)

For example, if you were trying to enter the sex of a new employee into the system and every time you typed "F" or "M" the computer beeped and refused to go on, you might not know precisely what to do. But if the background expert system were a kind of automatic "helper," it could tell that the area in which you were trying to enter the sex needed a value that was a number instead of a letter (because some programmer decided 0 should stand for male and 1 for female). It could, in fact, interrupt your work and pop a new window onto your computer screen that would say something like, "I know you're trying to enter this employee's sex as a letter, but the program is looking for a number—either 1 or 0."

At the same time, the program could store the fact that this is a problem you have frequent trouble with, which might save it time next time you encounter the same situation. It could come to your rescue sooner and more efficiently.

Another level of automated knowledge acquisition could take place while running an expert system itself. Take the example of the sample Expert-Ease system called PROBLEMS, discussed above, which helps determine if the program Expert-Ease would be a useful tool for solving a particular type of problem. If we made the process far more complex, we could conceivably have a number of combinations of attributes for which no solution had been provided in setting up the system. If PROBLEMS could "watch" how we deal with such situations, it could theoretically update its own knowledge base to account for the new information. The next time it encountered a similar set of facts, it could solve the problem we had previously failed to tell it how to handle by way of an explicit example.

All this is of more than passing interest. Until the questions of knowledge acquisition are solved so that those of us who own microcomputers can gain access to significant expert systems, their use will be limited to small, manageable sets of problems for which, it could be argued, we do not need an expert system in the first place.

Tying it Together

At the beginning of our discussion we said our primary premise is that computers will, in the next few years, become more human and more humane. Perhaps nowhere is the truth of this thesis more clearly visible than in the exploration of artificial intelligence. In fact, it can be argued that until computers are imbued with a semblance of human intelligence—even the mere simulation of such intelligence—the process of making computers more human, *or* more humane, will necessarily be slowed.

As a result of the preceeding discussion, we trust you can see the ways in which a microcomputer no more powerful than one you can buy today for a few thousand dollars can become an ally, a problem-solver, a counselor, and a consultant whose advice is precise and useful.

In providing microcomputer systems with the ability to assist us in daily living, we will make great strides toward computer systems that are more human and humane than those with which we are now able to work.

Opportunities, Strategies, and Decisions

We have reviewed the current and near-term future state of the art in artificial intelligence and expert systems as it affects and applies to the world of microcomputing. We now question what value all of this has for us.

The implications of changes in this field are serious and far-reaching.

Careers If you are reading this book because you want to be in on the ground floor of a new career opportunity, consider the exploding field of knowledge engineering. A major need will arise in the next few years for people trained in helping companies build the knowledge bases on which the systems will operate.

If you are more interested in secondary fields of endeavor, be aware that the first careers to be impacted by the explosion in expert systems expected in the early 1990's will be those that require professional expertise of a type that is easily codified and classified.

Prepare to gain more than a passing acquaintance with the subject of expert systems since many jobs in North America will be affected, altered, and even abolished by the emergence of this new technology. We have traditionally believed that blue-collar jobs would be the first to yield to automation. To some degree this has happened as robots have moved into factories in this country and abroad. But people have underestimated the degree to which white-collar positions, particularly those involving decision-making in controlled and quantifiable situations, will be impacted by the emergence of expert systems. Christopher Evans, in his popular book *Micro Millennium*, predicted just that kind of move in the early 1980's. He was right.

Investment   If you're interested in making ground-floor investments in high technology companies, look at your plans from two perspectives. First, if you are interested in high-technology investments for short-term growth, look at companies that engage in manufacturing development tools for other AI users. For longer term growth though, find companies that are in their early career curves and intend to apply AI and expert systems ideas to specific vertical markets. The more narrowly the company defines its niche, the less likely it is to suffer from competition from major companies moving into this field in the late 1980's and early 1990's when it becomes "safe" to do so.

If your investment strategy includes purchasing stock in more traditional, less high-tech companies, keep an eye on how the use of expert systems impacts the companies in which your key investments are located. Clearly the companies that learn to capitalize on this new emerging technology will be better positioned to be efficient and productive as the decade unfolds.

Management   If you are approaching this book from a manager's perspective, begin now to explore expert systems and think about how they apply to your industry in general and to your company in particular. For example, do you have a senior consulting person in your firm whose knowledge of a particular subject area is crucial to your firm's continued success? Consider beginning the process of having him convert the knowledge he has gained into an expert system. As we have seen, this can be done without the heavy expense of programmers by using such systems as

Expert-Ease, Insight, Series-PC, and others, though you'll probably want to hire a consultant to help you determine the best course of action.

Perhaps you can use your own desktop micro to implement some of the decision-making processes you go through to improve your own efficiency. In any event, keep AI and expert systems high on your list of areas to keep informed about. Read popular journals and books on the subject. Think about AI and expert systems and how they can help you work more productively and profitably.

Denny Bollay's Excitement
Started in (of all Places) School!

The 32-year-old Denison ("Denny") Bollay is founder and president of ExperTelligence in Santa Barbara, California. He traces his interest in computers to a high school with a vision of the future. "I went to school in Santa Barbara," he recalls. "The school had some experimental terminals with which students and faculty could get access to a GE computer system. At some point, funding for those terminals ran out, but GE and the school together found a way for members of a newly formed computer club to go to GE's facilities and use their mainframe systems."

The educational establishment sometimes questions the ultimate value of introducing microcomputers into the classroom. Some of the arguments are quite persuasive. Denny Bollay is glad that the voices of early opponents of micros in education didn't carry the day in Santa Barbara. If they had, his life would have been vastly different.

We are removed by more than a decade in time from the events. It is easy even now, however, to detect the sense of awe and wonder that was a part of who the younger Denny Bollay was.

"They had a GE 235 timesharing system, an IBM 704 with about a zillion tubes and another system or two as I recall," Denny says. "It was one of only about 15 or 20 installations in the country that had such a super-computer installed." Bollay played with BASIC and remembers the first time an engineer from GE let him experiment with a modification to BASIC that the engineer had made to permit the then-primitive language to handle strings. "I was in seventh heaven!" Bollay says.

Early AI Programmer

After graduating with an engineering degree from Harvey Mudd College in nearby Claremont, Bollay spent several years working as a computer programmer and developer. In the mid-1970's Bollay worked on a project that applied AI techniques to the real-time analysis of Chicago Board of Options and New York

Stock Exchange quotations, pointing out to the system's user "spread situations" worth investigating. "It was about 10 years ahead of its time," he says, as he looks back on the experience, "but it was a good moneymaker for about two years and then the option market shifted and the system became obsolete."

His next major task involved applying AI concepts to signal processing in a project where he worked with Frank Lehan and George Mueller of Systems Development Corp. Bollay, like many of his co-workers and contemporaries, remembers Mueller as "the man who put us on the moon." Bollay says that many of the things he worked on during that stint as a consultant were forward thinking. . ."even by today's standards."

In fact, it was during his work in signal processing that Bollay helped develop the idea of combined forward and backward chaining in AI system design. This idea lies at the heart of his company's soon-to-be-introduced expert system development environment (see page 50).

The Great Computer Camp Leap

In 1980, Bollay made a giant career leap from AI programmer and designer to founding the Original Computer Camp organization. "The camps grew out of a desire to share the excitement and the experience of my early teen years," Bollay says. "It was so exciting to think about what could be done with a small computer that the idea was just too good not to want to pass it on to the next generation."

From 1980 until mid-1983, the computer camps were the main focus of Bollay's life. The camps grossed $800,000 in 1983. "But I kept drifting back to AI and its implications," he says as his voice trails off as if lost in some personal fantasy. In July 1983, he set up a company called Original Computer Camps, but later that year gave formal recognition to his AI itch by renaming the organization ExperTelligence.

Bollay wrote his "first expert system in the traditional sense" on a Symbolics machine at ExperTelligence. In the process he learned how to apply his earlier AI concepts to the newly emerging world of micro-based AI and expert systems for general use.

"Its domain," he says, "is a toy problem, much like most of the early AI experiments were and tend still to be. But we learned a lot in the process of creating it, including a great deal about the *process* of expert system creation."

When Apple introduced the Macintosh in 1984, the last piece of the puzzle fell into place for Bollay to be able to make his company's next product decision. "Here was a machine that had sufficient memory potential, a sophisticated processor, a dynamite human interface, and all the tools and hooks to permit us to build a real and useful expert system development tool," he says.

And that's what he intends ExperTelligence to undertake as its next major project.

To get there, though, Bollay first had to create a LISP language interpreter. As a result of that development, his company introduced in early 1985 the first compiled Logo language ever made available for any computer system. Shortly thereafter, the company introduced a compiled LISP for a microcomputer—the Mac, naturally enough. In several months this will be followed by a full-blown expert system generator (see Expert Tool for the Mac).

What's Next for Denny?

Bollay is not the kind of guy who can be pinned down easily as to his future plans. Certainly they seem likely to support his career-long belief in AI as the next major wave in computer technology.

Learning vs. Performing: Pierre Bierre's Insights

Pierre Bierre of Clairvoyant Systems is championing an auditory-visual sensory learning machine. He is wagering that the AI community will shift emphasis from problem-solving systems to learning systems in the last half of the 1980's.

"Problem-solving systems do some functions in a particular environment," he says. "Learning systems expand both the function and the environment."

Bierre, 35, traces his development as an AI scientist and futurist to a problem he began thinking about during his undergraduate days at Stony Brook. "I was a rocker and a physics student. My first synthesizer was a signal generator. I was annoyed by the limited repertoire and fatiguing sound quality of such oscillators, borrowed from the physics lab. I used to doodle synthesizer designs during class, and soon began wondering how to design a universal synthesizer, or one that could produce any sound producable by any other sound source, including natural sounds, music, and speech."

Learning, Not Designing, Your Way Out of a Paper Bag

Every attempt Pierre made to design his universal synthesizer ran up against unacceptable flaws. The programs would grow to unmanageable size and be unacceptably slow. Also, the machine was complex and difficult to learn how to operate.

As a student at the University of Colorado, Bierre discovered that his problems with the synthesizers were problems people had with software.

It dawned on Bierre that the way to construct the universal synthesizer was to "bring samples of the sounds you want to the machine and let the machine teach itself about the sounds." Bierre dubbed the device an "auditory learning machine." It was the forerunner of his present work on the audiovisual learning machine. "Throwing in the visual channel makes it a universal graphics animation synthesizer with sound, as well as adding visual communication as a means of instructing the machine."

Bierre sees the movement toward high-bandwidth, sensory learning beginning to take shape, as evidenced by the current marriage of videodisc and microcomputers in education and marketing applications.

He predicts that we will pass through a seven to ten year phase where video and audio will be handled mechanically as files of data retrieved by pressing buttons and typing commands. Following that, we'll arrive at the point where there is just one lifelong, continuous-running stream of input. The machine will break it up into "things" and decide "what goes with what." Memory retrieval will be accomplished by communicating requests naturally through the machine's vision and hearing. Clairvoyant fits into the niche in which audio-video "files" will be leap-frogged and work will proceed straight-ahead on automatic representation of sensory experience. With adequate research capitalization, Bierre thinks American computer companies can begin offering learning machines commercially by the late 1990's.

Already Bierre has outlined the scientific principles guiding sensory learning research in his paper, "The Professor's Challenge," published in the prestigious *AI Magazine*, the official journal of the American Association for Artificial Intelligence (AAAI). The article appeared in the Winter 1985 edition and drew much attention in the AI community.

Unraveling the "Spaghetti Theory"

Bierre's emerging role as a respected AI theorist came as no surprise to his father, Malcolm Beers, who is a systems architect at Eastman Kodak Company in Rochester, New York. "During the formative years we enjoyed wildly speculative discussions around the dinner table about artificial intelligence," Bierre remembers. He said, "Dad would be very good at defining the problem, trying to state it as meticulously as possible, then I'd come out with some outlandish theory comparing intelligence to a long strand of spaghetti that grows on one end and keeps winding back through itself into a great blob. I learned a lot about computers, electronics, information theory, and AI by a very pleasant process of osmosis within my early family life."

Pierre was born Peter Beers but changed his name when a college friend translated his name into French. "It had a good pattern to it, and I adopted it later as a performing rock synthesizist for a stage name, and finally had it legally changed. Now, it fits well with my AI learning research which directly concerns patterns and the ease with which they are remembered.

"Besides," he points out, "I can refresh contacts as infrequently as every couple of years. . . . Nobody ever forgets my name."

Expert-Ease: Expert Systems for Everyman?

The world of expert systems has plenty of Cadillacs—systems costing thousands of dollars and usually requiring expensive, large-scale computer systems. At present there's a dearth of Plymouths. One of these is a product called Expert-Ease, designed by Scottish AI researcher Donald Michie. Expert-Ease is sold in the western United States by Jeffrey Perrone of San Francisco.

Expert-Ease began its life in American markets priced at $2,000, but in late 1984 the price was lowered to $695. Expert-Ease provides an expert system generating tool that operates on an IBM PC with at least 128K of memory and one floppy disk drive (though more memory would certainly be advisable for developing "real" systems).

Example-Driven "Apprentice"

Some AI purists argue that a product like Expert-Ease is not a "true" expert system generator because the program at the heart of the product is not driven according to sets of rigid rules. The designer of an expert system will usually spell out rules underlying decision-making by the system in necessarily great detail. The Expert-Ease program does something very different: It infers the rules for decision-making from examples provided during the process of "teaching" the system the expertise needed for a particular application. The first method is very time-consuming and, therefore, expensive. The second method is swift and cheap.

Expert-Ease uses the example-driven apprenticeship model very effectively. For example, to teach Expert-Ease how to diagnose a problem in a jet engine, a jet engine mechanic would sit at the computer, crank up Expert-Ease and then provide the computer with questions and answers that he would ask himself during the process of troubleshooting and repairing a jet engine. "Does the engine start?" "No." "Is there electricity getting to the gizwidget node?" "Yes."

In the process of analyzing these question-answer combinations, the program deduces the rules being followed by an expert in decision-making processes, which it then applies to other, related decisions about which it has not yet learned.

The Expert-Ease program automatically checks for conflicts or clashes as data is being entered into the system. For example, if the hypothetical jet-engine mechanic rules out electrical malfunctions when encountering a particular test result in one case, but retains electrical malfunctions as a possibility when encountering the same result in another, the program will call attention to the discrepancy and insist on getting some resolution of the difficulty.

The program is also smart enough to know when it lacks necessary information in some areas. It tells the user in those cases that it doesn't know the answer. (In this sense, at least, artificial intelligence is more intelligent than some of the human intelligences we have met.)

"I don't think there's any question that Expert-Ease is an artificially intelligent program," Perrone says. "Professor Michie (who designed the program) is, after all, one of the foremost AI authorities in the world. The system design may not conform to some people's ideas about what AI really is, but any system that can learn and expand as it gains experience with a set of problems, and draw inferences on the basis of that learning, is intelligent. But who cares? The question shouldn't be, 'Is the program really AI?' but rather, 'Is this program useful and will it expand as my needs and knowledge expand?' Viewed in that light, Expert-Ease is a solid contribution to the world of software."

One thing is certain: Expert-Ease at the very least provides an inexpensive and easy-to-learn way of finding out about expert systems and what they can (and, incidentally, cannot) do. In that sense it stands out as a product to be reckoned with as interest in expert systems develops during the rest of the decade.

Expert Tool for the Mac

ExperTelligence has introduced a new development tool that will enable us to design and implement full-blown expert systems on Apple's Macintosh computer. The product will provide one more good reason for people to jump on the Expert System bandwagon. The tool is called the EXPEROPS5.

ExperTelligence president Denny Bollay (see Denny Bollay's Excitement Started in (of all Places) School!) provided a glimpse of what the product does and how it does it.

Controls and Gauges

The system, of course, incorporates all of the Mac-like tools that users of Apple's once-revolutionary system have come to expect: mice, windows, pull-down menus, icons, and sophisticated graphics. But ExperTelligence betters Apple itself in using graphics to adapt the Mac to the world of expert systems.

There are several unique ways of getting mechanical and simulation information into and out of the system. These methods involve simulated gauges on the screen.

For example, suppose the user is trying to develop an expert system to manage a chemical process that requires certain temperature and pressure controls over time. On-screen gauges could be used both to enter information about the constraints into the system and to read the simulated performance of the system out for the user to monitor and analyze.

Combined Chaining

Another aspect of the EXPEROPS5 worthy of note is that it implements an unusual combination of forward and backward chaining of data elements and symbols that make up the knowledge base. The combination is seen by Bollay and his development team at ExperTelligence as crucial to designing really useful expert system generators on microcomputers.

On large computers with plenty of memory, high-speed processors, and lots of I/O control, single-direction implementation of

AI control structures is adequate. But Bollay believes that in adapting AI to the world of microcomputers combining both methods is essential to optimum system performance. This is particularly true, in his view, if one's purpose is to design a "generalized expert system development tool," which is how he characterizes his company's Macintosh AI product.

Meta-Rules and Probabilities

Two other widely used AI techniques are also incorporated into ExperTelligence's development tool: probabilities and meta-rules (rules about how to think about rules). The former technique allows users to attain statistical accuracy more easily and efficiently than routine mathematical manipulation permits.

According to Bollay, "If the expert system you are designing requires you to choose among several alternatives, probability weighting of the various courses of action can save a great deal of time. It can also increase the likelihood of being right the first time through the decision node."

On the other hand, "If the probability technique is designed so that it self-adapts as it gains experience with the system, it becomes an even more powerful tool in making the expert system generator more effective and efficient in the microcomputer implementation, As a result of this, it is capable of developing more powerful expert systems."

ExperTelligence has great hopes for its new product. It certainly has a revolutionary potential!

What is Artificial Intelligence?
Don't Ask the Experts!

When readers, both serious and casual, wade into the waters of artificial intelligence (AI) for the first few times, they may find themselves swept away into a sea lacking clear navigational boundaries. It may occur to readers, after a fairly brief exposure to the subject, that the definition of AI is multitudinous or, perhaps, non-existent. Faced with such a problem, readers might appreciate an opportunity to ask the experts in AI what their discipline is all about. That, however, would be a mistake.

To make the point more clear—and perhaps at the same time shed light on the subject—we've gathered basic definitions of AI from practitioners of this new art-science. After reading and ruminating on the definitions, we will find ourselves no closer to a concise and universal definition of AI. We will, however, have learned something about intelligence.

Focus on Intelligence

Donald Michie suggests that AI should be defined broadly as "the development of a systematic theory of intellectual processes." He argued that where these processes are found—in man, machine, or system—is immaterial to the definition. Another European, J. P. Hays, offered the succinct observation: "AI is the study of intelligence as computation."

Strictly an Engineering Problem

N. J. Nilsson, among others, would prefer to think of AI as primarily involving technological problems like programming and system design; his definition describes AI as an ". . .engineering discipline."

Broad and Nebulous Meaning

Perhaps the most intriguing attempt at a definition of AI was made by Marvin L. Minsky, a pioneer in the field, in the late 1960's when he said, "Artificial intelligence is the science of making machines do things that would require intelligence if done by men." A problem here is the crux of the definitional issue: There is virtually no agreement of what constitutes *human* intelligence. Assuming, then, that AI is an attempt to translate human intelligence into a machine or system, how will we know when we've done it? We can't define what we are trying to get the machine to imitate.

Margaret Boden wrote one of the most literate and comprehensive introductions to the subject we've seen in years of researching. Her 1977 work, *Artificial Intelligence and Natural Man*, offers this definition:

"By 'artificial intelligence' I mean the use of computer programs and programming techniques to cast light on the principles of intelligence in general and human thought in particular. In other words, I use the expression. . .to cover all machine research that is somehow relevant to human knowledge and psychology. . . ."

The emphasis on computers and computer programs, which seems to tread closely to the purely engineering definition offered by Nilsson above, may turn out to haunt Ms. Boden in years to come.

Avron Burr and Stanford University's Edward Feigenbaum, in the introduction to the three-volume *Artificial Intelligence Handbook* that they edited, offer a more formalistic definition of the subject at hand. "Artificial Intelligence (AI)," they assert, ". . .is the part of computer science concerned with designing intelligent computer systems, that is, systems that exhibit the characteristics we associate with intelligence in human behavior—understanding languages, reasoning, solving problems, and so on."

A Popular Writer's View

Michael Crichton, author of *The Andromeda Strain* and more recently of a delightfully irreverent little book called *Electronic Life: How to Think About Computers*, offers a more succinct definition. "AI is a branch of human psychology. It will remain a field of study devoted to understanding human behavior—at least for the foreseeable future."

Many other writers and researchers have observed, with Crichton, that the limitations on AI in the near-term future will be a function of how little we know about how human intelligence works more than about how little computers can do.

Britain's Geoff Simons, chief editor of the National Computer Center in Manchester, would agree with fellow author Crichton. "There is a clear sense in which artificial intelligence is concerned with *minds:* It illuminates ideas about what may be considered to be the 'mental attributes' of artifacts and in turn helps us to understand the mental equipment of human beings."

Turing's Tantalizing Test

A. M. Turing, an early thinker in the field of AI, suggested that trying to answer the question, "Do machines think?" was a waste of time. Instead, he proposed as early as 1950 setting up a verifiable and repeatable experiment to answer the question. This "Turing Test" has been the subject of more debates, objections, clarifications, and discussions than perhaps any other single contribution to the literature of AI.

Turing suggests that the experiment consist of a human being who communicates with another human being and with a computer, both via a terminal, and without being able to see them. By asking questions, posing problems, and probing answers, the human operator's task is to determine which of the other two participants is the human and which the machine. The machine's program will be designed to react in such a human way that it might even, for example, make mistakes in arithmetic! If we could design such a machine and program, Turing suggests, then we will have devised an artificially intelligent machine, a feat Turing believed would be attained by the end of this century.

The End of This Line

This confusing—and perhaps somewhat illuminating—discussion leads, it seems, to one conclusion: AI cannot be defined, at least not yet, because its field is broad, its age young, and its practitioners zealous. Technical and popular definitions of AI will continue to evolve in the coming few years as the principles involved in programming and systems that effect and are affected by the issues of machine intelligence are applied to an ever-widening circle of human experience and need.

What Makes Thinking So Difficult?

Think about being in the fourth grade. Your teacher tells you the following story.

"A woman goes into a restaurant. She orders a steak dinner. After an hour of waiting, the dinner arrives. The steak is badly overdone and the potatoes raw. She becomes angry and leaves the restaurant without paying for her meal or tipping the waiter."

Now the teacher asks a question. "Did the woman eat the steak dinner?"

How long do you suppose it would take you to answer? In a couple seconds you would shout, "No way, teacher. She didn't like the dinner so she didn't eat it!"

What's Involved Here?

This example provides an opportunity to demonstrate why emulating in a machine or system the thinking and reasoning processes of human beings is so difficult a task that it has been attempted constantly for more than two decades without being accomplished.

If a computer program and system could "listen" (electronically or audibly) to the same story and as quickly come to the same conclusion, we would be well on our way to satisfying Turing's Test (see What Is Artificial Intelligence? Don't Ask the Experts!) of a truly intelligent machine.

Before we could design such a system, though, we'd have to define all of the things the system would have to "know" to understand our story well enough to answer such non-obvious questions as, "Did she eat the steak?" First, it would have to understand about restaurants—that they are places where people go to eat, that waiters work in such places and have certain definable roles and tasks, that one customarily orders, is brought a meal, eats the meal, pays for the meal, and leaves a gratuity for the waiter who brought it.

Each of these bits of knowledge will, in turn, require myriad additional bits of stored information. For example, it may be necessary for the system to understand the concepts of money, payment, change, and even credit cards to be able to deal with the example in a complete way. The collection of all of this data is often referred to in discussion of AI as a "script."

Intuition and the System

"But," you might argue, "I intuitively know about all of those things but I don't think about them when I find myself faced with the story and the question."

Precisely. Aside from the arguable issue of whether people actually do gain or use "intuitive" knowledge, the fact is that we make a great many decisions and take a great many actions based on thought processes that would be difficult to verbalize. This difficulty of verbalizing patterns in thought and reasoning makes designing artificially intelligent machines difficult. Because if we can't describe, in great detail, how we do make decisions, how will we teach a machine with no human frames of reference enough information that it can figure out that the woman did not eat the meal?

So That's *Why Progress is Slow!*

Semi-automatic thought processing and decision-making are at the heart of what makes us intelligent, at least in terms of behavior selection. These semi-automatic mental processes make programming a computer to make decisions a slow and imprecise process. Some AI experts believe that AI is more a problem of learning how we humans think than it is about teaching machines to emulate or faithfully duplicate the processes involved.

Intuition, or semi-automatic thought, is not only a difficult matter, but is one of the more interesting issues involved in AI. Intuition concerns the aspects of any decision that are hidden, subconscious, or even inborn. These are the most difficult matters to program a computer to handle. We humans have difficulty, even when consciously trying to do so, in outlining in detail all of the steps and prior knowledge that make up a particular action.

A brief example will help to clarify what we mean.

Starting a Car

Pretend for a moment we are teaching an interplanetary visitor how to start an automobile. The first part of the dialogue might go something like this:

Earthling (that's us): Now we are going to learn to start a car.

Quarkian (that's "it"): I don't process the word "car."

Earthling: A car is a thing with four wheels that we use to travel from one place to another.

Quarkian: I have seen you move from many places to many others inside this environment called "home," but I have not seen you use a four-wheeled thing to do that. What is the difference?

Earthling: We use a car outside the home to travel from here to places more distant than the next room.

Quarkian: Okay. I understand. What is the first step to starting the car?

Earthling: We first have to get the key.

Quarkian: But I thought you said the car was a physical object, not an idea.

Earthling: It is a physical object.

Quarkian: I thought you told me yesterday that a "key" is a way of getting at the main idea in a thought.

Earthling: It is. But another meaning for the word key—

Quarkian: You mean you have words with more than one meaning?!

Earthling: Oh, yes, lots of them!

Quarkian: (shaking his heads) I may never get used to this Earth talk. What does this new key do?

Earthling: It lets us get into our car and turn it on so that we can use it.

Quarkian: I think I follow you. Let's go ahead and try to start the car.

Earthling: (Sigh of relief) Okay. Let's go outside.

(The two of them go out the door to the driveway. Earthling points to his new BMW and starts to move toward it.)

Earthling: This is a car.

Quarkian: (Bewildered) Where are its wings?

Earthling: It doesn't have wings. It travels on the ground, not through the air. Now open the door over on the other side of the car.

Quarkian: I don't think I can do that.

Earthling: Why not?

Quarkian: Because there's no doorknob over here that I can see. All the doors I can open have doorknobs on them.

Earthling: These doors have on them something called a "handle" that acts like a doorknob but is not turned. Instead, you pull out and up on the handle and the door will open.

You get the idea. Teaching a machine about a car and how to start it would be even more complex than teaching a "Quarkian." A computer wouldn't even know about doorknobs, wings, keys as things that unlock ideas, or many other subtle, unconscious things that are second nature to us in our daily lives.

Obviously, our Quarkian friend has had some experiences on our planet and has considerable previous knowledge on which to build. For example, when the earthling said, "Let's go outside," the Quarkian understood immediately. The sentence contains a number of concepts with which a computer would have an awful time.

Fuzzy Speech and Fuzzy Thinking

One of the most important and frustrating (for both the Earthling and the Quarkian!) exchanges took place over the definition of the word "key," which turned out to have two widely differing meanings. The English language is full of such ambiguous or ambivalent meanings for words. From the context, we humans know which meaning is intended, at least most of the time. We would find it peculiar for a friend to say, for example, "The key to the whole philosophical question is hanging on a ring in my pocket." That may be true in the sense in which our Quarkian friend had first heard the use of the word "key," but it is not likely to be; we know that. A machine has to be awfully smart to pick up on the idea. Imprecise ideas and ambiguous meanings are things we learn to deal with every day but they are inimical to a computer.

This ambiguity may be described as the context-based interpretation of ideas. It requires an ability to think outside rigid channels of intent. It is the biggest challenge facing AI researchers in the next half decade and beyond. Some very interesting work is being done in this area but AI still has far to go.

Teaching by Rules vs. Teaching by Example

A crucial issue in AI research focuses on the question of how artificially intelligent programs should gain the knowledge they use to make decisions and give advice. Two basic possibilities are: explicitly telling systems about knowledge bases, and providing information from which to infer an understanding of knowledge bases. The distinction is significant.

A few examples dealing with human beings and how they learn various things may clarify the issue and its significance.

You are the parent of a young teen-ager who seems bent on a path of self-destruction at school. She pays little attention to her studies, does a minimum amount of homework, prefers to spend all of her time on the telephone with her friends, and is generally irresponsible. Being a forward-thinking person, you wish to help her focus attention on the future impact of her current choices. If you were using a rule-based method of instruction, you would simply say, "We have a rule about how people who act like you end up in life. That rule says. . . ." And then you articulate a rule that imposes the set of values you wish your daughter to have. If, on the other hand, you wished to use an example-driven or apprenticeship model, you would approach the subject by saying things like, "I had a friend in high school who had some of the same kinds of attitudes and problems you have, and he ended up in San Quentin. I had another friend who did really well in school and had very few friends and he ended up a college professor, but a lonely man. Another friend of mine. . . ." You get the idea.

An important question, of course, is which of the two methods may produce more lasting and valuable learning.

Now let's move to a more direct teaching situation. Let's hypothesize that you are a top-flight jet engine mechanic on the verge of retiring from your company. You're so good that every jet engine mechanic in the company at one time or another needs to seek your advice about sticky or elusive problems. Your boss is really worried that when you retire the firm's planes will not be so easy to maintain and he wants you to teach someone else all you know about jet engine repair. Using a rule-based approach, you would simply sit down and go through the process of jet engine repair a step at a time, carefully following each branch in situations where more than one course of action is possible or likely. "First, I remove the cowling. Second, I open up the turbine chamber. Next. . . ." If, on the other hand, you were a follower of the apprenticeship method of teaching, you'd say, "Come on. Watch me while I work on a few dozen engines, ask questions where you don't understand what I'm doing, and we'll get you so you're a real expert on these things."

Now let's translate what we've just read into how we can and should "teach" an expert system about the subject in which we want it to be expert.

Teaching a Computer

Earlier, we described how Expert-Ease's sample demonstration program called PROBLEMS operates. The program advises us whether to use Expert-Ease to solve a particular type of problem. The use of the program is straightforward enough, but how does the computer know which course of action to take in each situation? The short answer is that it follows a set of rules it "knows" about the decision process.

But how do the rules get into its system in the first place? Again, we have two basic alternatives. We might choose a development tool like "Insight" that requires us to state the rules about our decision process explicitly. Depending on the language and syntax required, we might type in something like this:

```
if random=no and examples=complete use-it1
```

This cryptic-looking sentence simply says that if the user has said the problem's solutions are not random and he has a 100% complete set of examples to work with, just advise him to use the expert-system tool by printing a message labeled "use-it1." The system contains additional rules needed for it to draw conclusions from data we give it. Thus, we would have a rule that might look like this:

```
if random=no and examples=incomplete or examples=fair and
  accuracy=tolerant use-it3
```

It is possible, of course, to design a rule-based program that would help you through the process of entering the rules explicitly rather than simply expecting us to memorize a new "language." The point, however, remains: To teach an expert system in a rule-based way, we must enter each rule individually and explicitly. The program is smart enough to check to be sure we don't enter conflicting or confusing rules and that we follow *its* rules about rules.

The Expert-Ease product takes care of a big problem that many other expert system tools struggle with, often unsuccessfully: While there is much evidence to indicate that people think in a rule-based way, it is clear that most of us don't think *consciously* about the rules with which we operate and make decisions. A gap exists between the apprenticeship method of learning—in which we learn by watching someone else perform the desired task and inferring from the examples we see how the process works—and the rule-based method. This gap has created what Stanford's Ed Feigenbaum called "the knowledge acquisition bottleneck." Experts are not generally conscious of the rules they use in solving problems, therefore it is difficult or impossible for them to codify and state those rules in such a way that a computer system can learn and apply them to solving new problems.

One problem with this approach is that we may not know all the rules relevant to a particular decision-making process. If we leave out a factor, of course, the computer system will never become aware of the omission. But what if we put in a number of factors and some combination the system wasn't prepared for? An example would be something like when questions 1, 3, 5, and 11 are answered with an *a* and question 48 is answered with a *true*, but the user has skipped question 27 and not answered it. The system has no idea what to do in those circumstances. The problem isn't fatal; in other words, the computer isn't likely to explode or anything, but the system has failed to do what we expected it to do.

An example-driven or apprenticeship model of training would approach the problem quite differently. Each expert system generating tool, of course, is different from the others. Let's look again at Expert-Ease and see how we would set up an apprenticeship program using our computer as the student.

The first thing we would do is to define the "attributes" of the problem—in other words, select the parameters and their possible contents or values. In Expert-Ease, this process is a great deal like using a spreadsheet program. In fact, in its earliest introductions to the United States a few years ago, the marketers of Expert-Ease (not the current ones) called it a "decision spreadsheet." The user simply defines each factor to be taken into account—in this case, random, accuracy, examples, and judgment—and then places under each factor the various values that it may have during any run of the program. Each outcome or solution is defined under a heading like "Answer."

In the process of doing this, we can also define full-text explanations, questions, and evaluations of the information being put into the expert system. That way we can live with one of the rules—that attributes cannot be arbitrarily long—and still let the person using our expert system be able to answer nice human-language questions and prompts.

Having defined as many of the criteria and possible values as we can think of, and having set up full screens of text for the questioning process that is at the heart of the *user's* view of the system, we next furnish the system with examples of how we respond to certain situations. We do that by filling in yet another matrix that looks very much like a spreadsheet.

When we've entered our examples, we take a very powerful step: We instruct the program to "infer" a set of rules from what we've told it about criteria and examples. After a pause that can be quite long (if we have many examples involving many criteria), the computer sets up a "decision tree" that we can then examine to see how it structured the logic of what we told it in our examples. This process of inference uses a very intelligent piece of software that AI people call an "inference engine." This is the "brains" of the outfit. Once the decision tree has been developed, we can run the program, answer the various questions different ways, and note the result.

Sometimes, the values of one or more attributes won't concern us. An example is when we tell the program PROBLEMS that our solutions tend to be somewhat random. The system "understands" in that situation that no more questions are needed; Expert-Ease just isn't the answer. Expert-Ease permits us to identify places where we don't care what the value of a particular attribute is; we just put an asterisk in that place.

If we run the program we've created and we give the system a combination of answers for which we haven't defined a solution, the program informs us of that fact. We, therefore, can learn better how to solve problems of the class involved in the program and can add yet another example to the knowledge base. Then we run another inference cycle and the rules change, if needed, to accommodate the new knowledge the system has learned.

Which is Better?

Advantages and disadvantages of both approaches to "knowledge engineering" should be fairly clear. The rule-based method seems a bit cumbersome and requires us to think precisely through the rules, but the number of rules involved is at least potentially capable of being kept to a minimum. The apprentice, or example, method, on the other hand, lets us work without really having to know the rules at all, just the criteria we look for and the possible values the criteria can have. However, a catalog of examples big enough to permit the computer to infer a really meaningful expert system might be too large to be useful in a micro and is certainly going to take a great deal of time to type into the system in the first place.

Like many things in life, neither of these approaches is inherently better than the other. They are different. They work in different situations and settings. Each has its place.

Thinking About What You Just Thought

Most AI-based programs implement forward chaining. This process links each node in the decision tree to the next node(s) in the chain in a forward direction. ("Node" here means "branch intersection." It's the place where two or more possible courses of action separate from one another.) If a forward path leads to a solution to the underlying problem the AI system is to solve, this approach works fine. In fact, the manner in which most problems are defined and the way in which solutions are arrived at ensure that forward chaining will be sufficient.

But what if the problem reaches a dead end or a node where the appropriate decision for the program to make is to reverse its path and return to a node, say, three levels earlier in the decision tree? In a forward-only chaining system, such a retracing of steps is inefficient since the program must begin again at some previously stored node location and trace the steps forward until it arrives at the node where a new decision should be tried. To solve the problem, many AI designs implement backward chaining.

As with forward chaining, backward chaining is sufficient all by itself to solve a particular problem or class of problems. In such a system, each node to which we send program flow "remembers" by association the nodes from which it could have emanated and links back to them. If retracing to a specific previous node is needed, therefore, the retracing is easily implemented.

2
Broadening Our Community

Telecommunications literally means communicating on the telephone. The term "computer telecommunications," therefore, refers to sending and receiving data with a computer over telephone lines. It doesn't sound earthshaking, but the technology of computer telecommunications is creating an information culture and is changing the way business, research, and even thinking goes on in our society. As the young hero of the movie *WarGames* showed, telecommunications may be used to change a student's grades—or to manage a global conflict.

One easily ignored reality of the telecommunications experience is that it is so disarmingly simple! In a little-known essay, nineteenth century American scientist James C. Maxwell made the following observation about the telephone, which had just been introduced a few years earlier: "When at last this little instrument appeared, consisting, as it does, of parts every one of which is familiar to us, and capable of being put together by an amateur, the disappointment arising from its humble appearance was only partially relieved on finding that it was really able to talk."

Modern telecommunications employing, as it does, personal computers and ordinary telephones, often produces a similar "Is that all there is?" reaction in people. We will see, however, that telecommunications will be an important area of advancement in the development and application of computer technology. In the next several years telecommunications will affect most American personal computer owners—and a great many people who *don't* own computers as well.

To a large extent, our reaction to the increased importance (intrusion?) of telecommunications in the last half of the 1980's will be a function of our feelings about global community. The realization of the long-awaited global village of the late R. Buckminster Fuller has been brought dramatically nearer by the marriage currently being consummated of the stodgy, old telephone with the glamorous, young personal computer.

Distorting Time and Place

The computer takes the revolution started by the telephone to heights Alexander Graham Bell could not have envisioned. The telephone bridged vast distances, but did very little to overcome time barriers. A business manager in a company's corporate headquarters in New York, for example, could pick up the handy instrument on her desk and, by dialing a few numbers, make connection with her sales manager in San Francisco. If, however, the New York manager had the bad manners to attempt the connection before lunchtime in Manhattan, it was unlikely she would receive a human response on the other end. In fact, before the appearance of the ubiquitous answering machine, any response at all would have been surprising.

Time-dependence comes about, of course, because voice telephone communications are *attended* interchanges; there must be a live person on both ends of the hook-up to *attend* to the mechanics before two-way communication can take place.

Computer telecommunications, on the other hand, are not only *possible* in unattended situations, but are probably most often engaged in that way.

If the hypothetical sales manager maintained a current, "on-line" record of transactions, the business manager in New York could contact that data base in San Francisco and find out, for example, how much income was generated by the Donnaly account during the past six-month period and the total costs charged against that account during the same period of time. She can get that information more quickly and accurately by computer than she probably could by quizzing the sales manager— especially at 5 A.M. And it makes no difference to her if it is 5 A.M. California time and the sales manager is still in bed. The business manager is engaging in an *unattended* telecommunications event. As a result, bridging time with the computer is as easy as communicating from New York to San Francisco with the telephone.

Obviously, this time-and-distance-bridging technology makes computers more humane by allowing *us* to choose when and how to work in interaction with other people and their computers.

Telecommunications Today

Every evening, tens of thousands of Americans sit down at desks, dining room tables, and breakfast nooks all over the country and turn their usually introspective computer screens into windows on the world. These people are "users," not of drugs, but of vast information services that are on the verge of becoming major utilities. Individuals from all walks of life engage in this use of information—Lockheed's enormous collection of electronic data bases include *seven* data bases dedicated to the subject of agriculture and life sciences!

There are no reliable figures that reveal how many people in this country operate personal computers on-line, or of how many hours per week they spend hooked up to a massive computer, or to someone else's microcomputer system, in a tangled web of networking that defies even a broad-brushed attempt at definition. The largest on-line services boast more than 200,000 subscribers. One fact, however, which points indirectly to the growing use of telecommunications, is the increasing sales of modems—the little devices that connect the computer to the telephone. Home and personal computer users generally purchase low-speed modems. Sales of these modems topped 500,000 units in 1983 and exceeded 600,000 units in 1984, according to several reliable estimates.

Telecommunications, which is growing at an annual rate of more than 15%, has become a $250 million per year business in the United States. Eight million modems will have been sold to home computer owners before 1989. Today, there are certainly more than one million people who use their personal computers to engage in some form of telecommunications interaction.

The burgeoning growth of the industry has proved a gold mine to companies ready to take advantage of the situation. CompuServe, an Akron, Ohio-based company, operates the most widely used information services utility in the United States. Though Compu-Serve officials are intentionally vague about the number of users or subscribers they have, reliable estimates place the number at more than 200,000 subscribers and upwards of 50,000 "regulars"— people who log on to the system at least weekly. We'll take a closer look at a few of CompuServe's more innovative offerings and groups later in this section. People who subscribe to CompuServe gain access to a wide range of information and services, the shared expertise of many other people, and interaction unexcelled in any other easily accessible medium with the possible exception of a well-run major city library.

So what are these modern-day armchair explorers up to during the long evenings of pounding at keyboards and staring at endless streams of words sliding from their phone lines onto their computer displays? That's not an easy question to answer, primarily because of the variety of things they can choose from when they decide to go on-line. Let's look at some options commonly available to people with modems.

The first decision is whether to be a little fish in a big pond, a big fish in a little pond or a whale in a private lake.

Telecommunications Services Available Now

It's easy, with telecommunications, to be a little fish in a big pond—with thousands of other users, tons of information, and dozens of choices of things to learn, do, talk about, and explore. You'll probably log onto CompuServe or The Source or, perhaps, one of the lesser known but upcoming national information utilities. There, you can join a special interest group ("SIG" for short; people who hang out in them are called "SIGgers") that caters to your particular interest.

The range of these groups is incredibly broad, encompassing, for example, pilots, war game players, writers, artists, lawyers, and people whose common thread is the ownership of a particular brand or model of computer.

The national on-line subscriber organizations also provide up-to-the-minute news from syndicated news and financial services. Need some information about a particular topic? Try browsing through the electronic edition of Grolier's *Academic American Encyclopedia,* a research tool that never goes out of date because it is updated at least monthly. (See Who Knows? Anybody Who Wants To!)

If being a big fish in a little pond is more your style, you'll probably plug into a local "bulletin board system." Local BBS's, as these systems are called, typically have one incoming line hooked to a microcomputer, often in someone's home. The BBS's contrast with national organizations that operate huge computer systems to which you simply connect over telephone lines and become one of several thousand simultaneous users.

BBS's provide channels for interactive communication. Each BBS takes on the personality and flavor of the person who operates it (the "SYSOp," shorthand for "System Operator") and of those who frequent it. Some BBS's are devoted to owners of a particular brand of computer, others to a single topic, such as politics. In fact, one US Senator uses a BBS to communicate his thoughts and plans to his constituency, as well as listen to their ideas and feedback. Other BBS's, on the other hand, offer broad opportunities for communication on any subject the users dictate.

Finally, if you're *really* hooked on the telecommunications experience, you may want to play "Whale in the Lake" and open your *own* BBS (or some other home-run telecommunications facility like a Fantasy Plaza, discussed shortly). Then *you* dictate the topics of discussion, determine who can use the system and who can't (within some rather broad constraints), and generally get to play a major role in shaping the telecom experiences of at least a small number of people.

A totally different approach to the marriage of computer and telephone has been taken by several companies, one of which is Dialectron of Mountain View, California. This company has produced a plug-in printed circuit board for the IBM PC which, when used with some accompanying software, creates a Smart Answering Machine (whose acronym, SAM, is the product's name).

SAM combines digitized voice stored on computer disks with a well-designed human interface to automate all of the features of the most sophisticated small answering machines, plus a great many other activities. (See SAM Brings New Meaning to Answering the Phone.) Not useful in computer-to-computer communications, the idea behind SAM and similar products from other companies is to make the computer a more practical tool during the vast majority of the time it is sitting alone in a room while its owner is off taking care of business.

From the availability of a computerized answering service like SAM it is a long but not impossible leap to a system envisioned by Alan Kay.

Kay, a widely known visionary and computer industry guru who gets paid to think of new products for the not-too-distant future, suggests that a computer could be trained to recognize the voice of the caller, remember that he had called in earlier in the day and deal appropriately with various common business telephone situations. Such a product could also respond to the owner's voice prompts over a telephone line to retrieve messages, answer intelligent questions ("Was it important?", which the computer answers by seeking for words like "important" or "critical" or "emergency" in the text it has received) and change the system's method of dealing with specific callers' needs.

Kay actually showed a videodisc of such a product at a recent computer conference.

A Glimpse Ahead

Let's explore the world of telecommunications today. These few paragraphs can only give you a flavor for the myriad number and variety of activities you can choose from and the environments from which you can make such selections. The rapid expansion of home computers will reach new heights of importance in the daily lives of millions of Americans in the next few years.

Three things will cause this rapid growth. First, the price of modems will be continually reduced as higher-speed devices (see Chapter 5 on hardware for details) move onto dealer shelves and the volume of sales reaches a level where cost reductions are feasible. Before the end of the decade, it will be possible to buy a modem that transmits and receives at the rate of 1200 baud for under $100. A modem capable of 2400 baud communications will cost less than $300 by the end of 1987. And a 4800 baud device—assuming some other problems with telephone line quality can be resolved—for less than $1,000 ought to be obtainable by the end of the decade.

Second, the suppliers of such services will become far more innovative than they have been in determining the kinds of products people will be willing to spend extra time and money purchasing from them. This product expansion, more than the availability of inexpensive modems, will excite and motivate more and more people to get into the telecommunications game.

Finally, telecommunications facilities will become easier to use. Two new companies recently launched services designed to permit access to more than one information utility without users having to know a great deal, learn about the technology, or even necessarily have their own subscriptions. These companies are Business Computer Network of Denver, and Easynet from Telebase Systems in Narberth, Pennsylvania.

Business Computer Network allows users to pick from any of several available services and then automatically gets the subscriber signed on and hooked up to that service. Easynet, on the other hand, has another degree of "smarts," being capable of deciding which data base will be most helpful in a particular situation and then automatically transferring the user to that data base.

Both in making more rational and people-directed choices about telecommunications-based products to be offered and by providing easier-to-understand "front ends" for telecom interfaces, these people and companies will be bringing computers one step closer to a human and humane role.

Business Leading the Way

Two major uses to which telecommunications power is being put today by business foreshadow ways in which consumers may find the service useful in the future. These are electronic mail (also known as E-Mail) and bibliographic data base research.

Industry observers estimate that more than a million electronic "mailboxes" are in use throughout the United States, most of them by businesses. The electronic mail business probably grossed about

$200 million in the last year. Experts predict growth rates upward of 60% per year in this exploding area of the microcomputer business.

Electronic mail has many manifestations. In the most widely used situations, central computers act as the depository. These may be owned by the company or by an information utility like Compu-Serve. All electronic mail correspondents have access to the system. Correspondents can retrieve messages left for them by other users of the network and leave messages for other people—or even designated lists of other people. Federal Express came up with a new twist on that idea with Zap Mail, which requires neither the sender nor the recipient of electronic mail to *have* a computer, let alone use one. There are other variations on the theme as well.

A recent study concluded that the cost of sending an electronic mail message was eighty-six cents (most of that cost is time), as compared to an average cost of between eight and ten dollars to send a letter via the land mail. And electronic mail is faster, arguably more reliable, and more convenient (no scheduled pick-ups or deliveries are needed).

Although most electronic mail users today are businesses, more and more individuals sign up for the services as a means of making their own communication easier, less expensive, and more convenient. Such consumer uses of electronic mail as catalog ordering, communication with legislators, family emergency notification, and other day-to-day activities will serve as a springboard to greatly increased everyday use of electronic mail.

Another increasingly useful aspect of telecommunications is the on-line bibliographic data base. Services such as Lockheed's DIA-LOG, a broad-based system that comprises hundreds of individual collections of data on a myriad of subjects, help businesses find answers to critical marketing, financial, and other decisions in an instant. Services like Lockheed's are relatively easy to access and use (see An Out-of-this-World Solution to Down-to-Earth Problems). They provide access to more information than all but the very largest corporations can afford to keep in any other form.

CompuServe's on-line electronic encyclopedia is a variation on that theme. More such services are bound to be offered as an information-hungry society searches for faster and more effective means of getting the data it needs to conduct its living, working, and studying.

Two Phones in Every Home?

The telecommunications explosion will greatly benefit the various telephone companies in the United States (along with, of course, their estranged mother, Bell). Since anyone calling your home while you are on line with CompuServe or your local BBS cooking school will get a busy signal, many families will see the need to have two telephones in their homes; many already do.

Gregg Collins, a young entrepreneur in Burbank, California, who set up the first BBS to be sold to others as a moneymaking idea, says, "I picture just about everyone having two telephone numbers, their voice number and their data number, businesses included." He believes this will begin within the next half-decade and be a fact of life within ten or so years.

Setting up two phone lines in one house, though, costs money, and people will be unlikely to undertake such a task unless they see real, tangible returns for their investment. The key to the home telecommunications revolution is far less a problem of technology than it is one of appropriate products. It is a matter of offering the right mix of services and products to a public ready for the convenience of obtaining those services from the comfort, convenience, and safety of their own homes.

Graphic Communications

Peter Black of Xiphias in Marina Del Rey, California, is one of a number of people who believe that significant increases in the use of telecommunications await yet one further development. Today, with only a few minor exceptions, we can send only words and numbers over telephone lines. "So long as people look at the display on their computer and think 'TV set,' they're going to be less than blown away by words marching across the screen," Black says.

Black could be wrong. He is, however, one of the foremost experts in graphics on computers, and is one of a handful of people involved in assisting Apple Computer, Inc., develop its next generation machine, a system about which little else is known other than that it will be even more graphic than the breakthrough Macintosh computer of 1983.

Peter Black is, however, not a lone voice in the textual wilderness crying for pictures. A combine of Sears, CBS, and IBM is at work on a new information service called Trintex, which will allegedly be able to transmit graphics. If those three companies decide to establish a standard for the transmission of non-textual information, they will be able to do so with virtually no more effort required than to introduce it and make it work.

There is still much to be done, but the possibility of sending what Black refers to as "medium resolution graphics" (by which he *means* what microcomputer people call *high* resolution graphics) will greatly expand the kinds of data available to users of telecommunications facilities as well as attracting more people to their use.

One CompuServe group took a major and intriguing step in the direction of graphic telecommunications in late 1985. A CompuServe SIG called MAUG (for Micro-networked Apple User's Group) contains a group of Macintosh Users known as MACUS. One of the members of MACUS is Bob Perez, who developed a program called VMCO (Visual/Vocal MAUG Conferencing Utility.)

Perez contributed his program to the public domain and numerous conferences have been held by MACUS members. In a VMCO conference, a graphic depiction of a conference table is surrounded by user-created faces representing the participants. Each user can have up to nine faces (representing, for example, different moods or reactions or a desire to speak). The effect is incredibly like a real-world conference and users quickly work through the computer interface as if it weren't there and they actually were all together in one conference room!

(As if the graphic interface weren't enough, VMCO also uses an Apple-supplied program called, imaginatively enough, Mac-In-Talk, to enable the participants to hear the comments of other users read by a software-driven voice synthesizer in their own Macintosh.)

At this point, of course, the VMCO facility is limited to people who own Macintosh systems. But other computer aficionados like Perez will follow his lead and develop such programs for the IBM PC and perhaps for Amiga and Atari's new ST "Jackintosh" computers as well. It may be a slightly long step to on-line televised conferences where we see each other's *real* faces, but it is a fascinating development nonetheless.

By permitting the transfer of visual images, people and companies who make progress in this burgeoning new area of telecommunications will make the computer process somewhat like the more familiar television world in which most of us have grown up. In so doing, they will, of course, make the machines and their software more like us in the way they present information to us and transfer our information to others.

Telecommuting and the Electronic Cottage

There's a group of people called variously telecommuters, tele-workers, or electronic cottagers (after Alvin Toffler's chapter in his 1980 best-seller *The Third Wave*). They are in the forefront of a movement of people working from their homes either full time or part time.

At present, most of these people are independent consultants and self-employed service workers. In the future, thousands of workers in jobs involving the management of information will spend all or much of their work time at home, where they can largely schedule their own time, work around other time demands, take advantage of creativity as it occurs, and generally be more productive.

In July 1985, *Personal Computing* magazine conducted a survey of a random sample of its readers. The survey uncovered some interesting facts about telecommuters. Among those tidbits were the following:

- Over half of the people who worked at home said they did so to enable them to work at their own pace, while 45.6% said it increased their productivity and only 18% indicated they were interested in reducing commute time (respondents gave multiple answers to this question).
- While the vast majority of these telecommuters said the primary use of their computer was word processing, three other activities—data entry, planning and forecasting, and budgeting —tied for second place.
- In excess of half of the respondents who work at home said they were "very satisfied" working there.
- There was a very even distribution of occupations among telecommuters, with professor-researchers, programmer-analysts, consultants, teachers, accountants, administrators, data processing consultants, engineers, secretaries, and sales people all representing between 3.8 and 7.8% of the total respondents who worked from their homes.

The "electronic cottage" is not, of course, all roses; a number of people and groups, notably the AFL-CIO and a national women's group known as "Nine to Five," have expressed concern or opposition to the trend.

The state of California recently undertook a study to determine what kinds of workers will be most effectively used in work-at-home situations. A report on that study is expected to produce a recommendation to proceed to a more intensive test of the concept for state workers. Some state workers then might well work from home or in satellite office centers well removed from the concentrations of people, traffic, information, and noise in the big cities.

The idea of working from home has already caught on sufficiently that it has spawned its own group. Paul and Sarah Edwards of southern California have become known informally as the "Ambassadors for the Electronic Cottage" for their pioneering work in this field. We'll look more closely at that group—and at the opportunities it both sees and presents—later in this section.

The last several pages have presented viewpoints on where the growth of telecommunications as a home phenomenon is taking us. Now let's be more specific. It's time to meet Dr. Robert Lindamood, a computerized counselor with a vision of using computers to help people in need, and Gregg Collins, a young man who wants to move computing from shopping for a mate to shopping for the things you'd like to give your mate, and finally Paul and Sarah Edwards who gave up promising and lucrative careers in law and management to pursue their vision of a national network of independent entrepreneurs working from their homes, linked by a web of personal computers.

The visions of the next wave in personal telecommunications will inevitably come from people such as these.

Here Today, Expanding Tomorrow

This section will look at three up-and-coming ideas that use telecommunications to broaden the community's horizons. We could, of course, discuss many more ideas than three; hundreds of concepts and products lurk in the minds of people who are plugged in to the newly broadened community we have been examining. These three will, however, give you a feel for the growing potential in the field.

Dr. Bob Lindamood's On-Line Counseling Service

Karen, a single mother in rural Iowa, is having a problem with her teenage daughter, Sarah. Sarah has lost her appetite and her weight has declined dramatically. The weight loss is a problem that is growing increasingly worrisome to Sarah's mother. The family physician, while helpful as far as he can be, lacks the expertise to deal with such situations. Sarah can be helped—if Karen can get her to a specialist in Des Moines, a two-hour drive away. Even then, it's possible the problem will require expertise that only a few specialists in the country really possess. It would be difficult to get Sarah to one of these specialists and, of course, impossible to get one of them to Sarah. If only effective consultation could be carried out at a distance!

Steve and Gina Roberti have taken their two children, Angie, 16, and Douglas, 15, on a Caribbean cruise. Douglas, who has been in therapy for problems related to the death of his younger brother, begins developing signs of emotional problems. The therapist who has been counseling Douglas and his family in their home town of Los Angeles happens also to be on vacation—in Vail, Colorado. If there were just some way for Douglas, the therapist, and the Robertis to confer together concerning Douglas's condition!

Intergalactic Software Moving and Storage Company wants to promote three managers to vice-presidential slots at the home office in Shreveport, Louisiana. The idea has met with strong resistance in all three of the managers' households, for similar reasons. The company's staff psychologist believes the problems could be resolved if the three families could be gathered together in one place for group counseling and discussion. Unfortunately, the families are located in Detroit, Atlanta, and Honolulu. The expense of all 12 people traveling to a central location is out of the question. If they could only somehow *get* together without actually *being* together!

These situations are disguised accounts of three actual events. In each case a computerized, on-line counseling service known as dataFamiliae came to the rescue and provided the help needed where traditional means of delivering such support would not work.

DataFamiliae is the brainchild of Dr. Robert Lindamood (see Dr.

Bob Lindamood: Information 'for Cheaps') formerly of Columbus, Ohio, which is, not coincidentally, near the Akron base of Compu-Serve Information Systems. At present, Dr. Lindamood resides in Hobbs, New Mexico. This proves that geography is no barrier in the telecommunications age. DataFamiliae is a prime example of using phone lines and computers to bridge the time and distance gaps that separate us from one another and narrow our sense of community.

Strangely enough, dataFamiliae started as a book. "I had written a book on parenting strategy," Lindamood, a soft-spoken but enthusiastic man, recalls. "In effect, I decided to publish it electronically by breaking it into pieces that were easily digested and putting them all into the CompuServe computer system where anyone who wanted to know more about a particular subject in the field of parenting could get at the appropriate piece." From that beginning as a small data base for people interested in parenting skills, dataFamiliae grew into the extensive service it is today.

DataFamiliae, until early 1985, was available to any Compu-Serve subscriber. CompuServe, however, has since dropped it because the service wasn't generating enough revenues. Lindamood plans to resurrect the service in the near future.

DataFamiliae consists of three primary components:

1. Narrative modules covering such topics as cognitive development, emotional development, communication, nutrition, wellness, individual roles, charting family history, decision-making, and familial stages;
2. Short courses for self-paced study; and,
3. Interactive on-line consultation sessions with experts in various aspects of family life. These and other topic areas are divided into five clusters, each of which is managed by an expert in the specific area. The experts then work with and through the dataFamiliae staff headed by Dr. Lindamood.

Dr. Lindamood candidly admits, "The system has created a great deal of experimental activity but has not yet become economically viable," even though he says the service has a nearly 100% rate of collecting its bills from counselees. "What's needed," he believes, "is for companies to recognize the value of this kind of thing as an employee benefit and to sponsor it as a fringe."

Actually, beyond this acceptance step, Dr. Lindamood sees five additional steps the industry will take that will provide data-Familiae with the ability to reach a significant portion of the families in the United States. He lists these steps as:

1. Reduced prices for hardware, software and networking link-ups.
2. Reduced professional resistance on the part of counselors.
3. Increased emphasis on preventive psychological care.
4. Increased numbers of professional counselors and potential clients trained in and comfortable with the use of computers.
5. Funding for such activities by possible client companies or research facilities.

Dr. Lindamood understands "preventative care" to be not only of a psychological nature, but of any type. Dr. Lindamood has specialists scattered throughout the country dealing with five areas of specialization. His ultimate goal is to end up with one specialist for each of 16 essential areas of parenting and family life. Dr. Lindamood has initiated a creative program of training for staff development and management training for the purpose of developing the skills his associates will need in meeting the challenges of the dataFamiliae service.

Dr. Lindamood says that he and his dataFamiliae colleagues have " . . . begun delineating a host of factors that clarify the strengths and weaknesses of this channel of communication" in an effort to present the method to fellow psychologists and counselors in ways that won't result in immediate dismissal or difficult-to-overcome resistance. He is adamant about increasing the emphasis on preventive psychological care: "We cannot afford to do otherwise, quite apart from the issue of the computer and its potential. People must learn to connect information, knowledge and education with preventive techniques and take advantage of prevention when it's available to them."

Beyond the implications for counseling and therapy, Dr. Lindamood has a broader vision of where the telecommunications era is taking us.

"I have a dream that through this medium, many millions of people will have access to vast storehouses of information, knowledge and skills garnered by experts and stored for their use as they need it and as they see fit.

Telecommunications has the potential to decentralize knowledge and put it, with its concomitant power, into the hands of people in ways we haven't even begun to think about yet."

Gregg Collins's Fantasy Plaza

Some ways in which knowledge leads to the power Bob Linda-mood speaks about so fervently are obvious. One of these will undoubtedly be the power of the marketplace. Even early science fiction writers and cartoonists predicted that shopping by "remote control" would become a major factor in the future way of life. The first inklings of the coming boom in computerized shopping have now appeared. If Gregg Collins, a young entrepreneur from Burbank has his way, your local mall may soon join the dozen or so national retailers who invite you to browse electronically through their "catalogs" at your leisure and in your home.

Let us take a quick look at the issue of electronic shopping: where it is today, what its image is, and what Gregg Collins thinks will happen to it next.

Electronic shopping is still very experimental. But some of the names one encounters when shopping via keyboard and modem assure the future of this new way to coax dollars out of the pockets of modern consumers.

Sears, Roebuck, J. C. Penney, the Knight Ridder publishing chain, Saks Fifth Avenue, I. Magnin, and Bank of America are among the established commercial giants one can already find experimenting in this fertile new area. In fact, Bank of America is but one of more than 1,000 banking organizations in the United States experimenting with at-home banking of one form or another, though only a small handful of banks have currently adopted a full-blown, commercially available program.

Perhaps nowhere is the surge in interest in at-home electronic browsing and buying more evident than on CompuServe, the main electronic information utility in the United States. Five distinct shopping services are already available on-line, with more being added monthly. The service extends from Comp-U-Store, a 60,000-item discount home shopping service managed by Compu-Card International of Stamford, Connecticut, to the Music Information Service set up and operated by Shoemaker's Music, Inc., of Ft. Lauderdale and Hollywood, Florida.

Most products being offered in these "micro-malls" are obviously aimed at the upscale professionals who make up the vast majority of CompuServe's subscriber base of nearly 200,000 people.

A difficulty exists in heavily promoting marketing services to people who may resent paying money for on-line subscriber time and then being forced to read "commercials" from the host service. Marketing services on a general-use system like CompuServe cannot be allowed to intrude too seriously upon the attention of people who are on-line for other purposes. This problem has limited early acceptance of the idea of electronic shopping on CompuServe. The appeal of telecommunications and of electronic malls will broaden as on-line marketing services become less expensive (or even free), cover more widely demanded products, and use marketing methods that are not obtrusive but still permit easy, instant access to the services.

The public is interested in on-line shopping. A study completed in early 1984 by Booz, Allen, and Hamilton, Inc., a New York consulting firm, and published in CompuServe's subscriber magazine *Online Today*, indicated that as many as *60%* of American households would do at least half of their shopping for "consumer durable goods" electronically if quality and prices were competitive with those offered in stores.

The high proportion of people willing to buy products sight unseen by computer should cause small and medium-size retailers to sit up and take notice. So far, they haven't done so. But with retailing giants like Sears, Penneys, and I. Magnin testing the waters, the "little guys" are going to have to jump in soon or be left behind and, quite possibly, wiped out as the information society's march continues.

Consumers will find it far easier to do comparison shopping if they can "visit" five or six competitive stores in one brief period at the keyboard. Comparison shopping almost always leads to big stores and major discount chains making inroads into specialty and neighborhood stores. For an example of competitive shopping, we turn once again to CompuServe.

The CompuServe program called AutoNet offers potential new car buyers opportunities to do a detailed, on-line comparison of new car features and specifications in more categories than most of us would think to ask about in the dealer's showroom. More than 250 cars, foreign and domestic, are compared in categories like equipment (standard and options), fuel economy, roominess, and recommended price.

Armed with information from just 30 minutes spent in the AutoNet section of CompuServe—at a total cost of less than $5—a friend of ours recently purchased a new, hard-to-find mini-van, and did so at a savings of close to 20% over the best deal he had been offered before "shopping" the electronic mall!

Besides giving retailers an opportunity to have their products "examined" by a select group of upscale computer-owning people who are definitely in "buy mode," electronic shopping set-ups offer another marketing edge to those who use them to sell goods—immediacy.

Consider this example: Retailer A and Retailer B both sell appliances in Cincinnati, Ohio. This afternoon, a local distributor for a line of microwave ovens calls and offers them both an excellent buy on some products being liquidated by the manufacturer as a model close-out. He needs their orders within 48 hours.

Retailer A, a traditionalist, calls in his advertising agency, briefs them on the product and the pricing strategy, and then waits for them to produce a suitable advertising layout; a process that will almost inevitably take at least a full day and perhaps several days, depending on how elaborate the ad message is. The agency or the store owner will then call or visit the local newspaper and have an advertisement inserted into the paper's next edition. If lucky, he can get his message on the street in three days; more likely, it will be five days or longer. Retailer A either misses the buying opportunity or he purchases a block of goods on speculation in the hope he can find buyers for them.

Meanwhile, his competitor, Retailer B, hangs up the phone after talking to the distributor, flicks on his personal computer, dials up the electronic mall where he's a regular, and leaves a few well-chosen words about product availability and price. Within minutes, thousands, perhaps tens of thousands, of potential buyers have seen his message; some have been interested and placed orders. By the second day, when his deadline for ordering is upon him, Retailer B has already received solid orders from a few dozen buyers—and he's done it in far less time and for less advertising cost, than his competitor, which means he can probably also offer a lower price.

The scenario oversimplifies a number of elements. The cost per thousand people reached with electronic advertising may be relatively high, electronic shopping reaches a more limited audience, and electronic words do not permit buyers to see, let alone test, the product. But the basic idea is sound—getting out early with a message to a selected audience is good retailing. The microcomputer will bring power in ways beyond our present imagination to people who sell things.

The Corner Computer

All of which brings us to Gregg Collins. His idea for on-line marketing is called Fantasy Plaza.

Gregg was one of the earliest entrants into the computerized dating business. His approach differed from the normal strategy, however. Rather than set up a matchmaking service bureau himself, Collins designed and sold software that would enable anyone to set up a matchmaking service in his or her own home. Through the software, men and women interested in meeting members of the opposite sex could access a data bank of information about such people.

Collins's product was the widely publicized Dial-Your-Match program, of which he sold a modest 150 or so units at a price of less than $150 each. But even that relatively small success spurred Collins on. "I think everybody wants to bring these services into the reach of millions of people," he says. According to Collins, many of the SysOps who ran Dial-Your-Match programs on their home Apple or Commodore systems received as many as 100 calls per day.

Dial-Your-Match convinced Collins he ought to continue mining the vein of home telecommunications as a business. That led him to electronic shopping and to Fantasy Plaza.

Collins set up Fantasy Plaza to simulate a trip though an exclusive mall, whisking electro-shoppers around the many-floored center by an electronic elevator.

Customers spend $399 for the package, which includes instructions on how to run the software and how to start a business. The package also includes the franchise right to use the software and the name "Fantasy Plaza." With a Commodore 64 computer and peripherals, anyone can get into the business of setting up local electronic shopping centers for less than $1,000—emphasize the "local." The local orientation makes Collins's Fantasy Plaza idea different. The local emphasis, he hopes, will ultimately help it to succeed in a world of retailing and information utility giants like Sears and CompuServe.

Collins is in good company in maintaining that hope. Gary Arlen is an industry analyst who publishes the widely read and respected *Videotex/Teletext News.* Arlan considers the local angle "very important," particularly in the supplying of news and information. "People are always interested in local information— whether it's where they can buy things from local merchants or what the local weather will be," he says confidently.

The people who buy Collins's new shopping package may sign up local stores in the program. They may even *be* local stores who wish to set up their own in-house electronic shopping system. "I expect to see both kinds of buyers in the near term," Collins says, "though I think the independent entrepreneur who is not in the retailing business full-time will be the best bets for early placements."

Whoever the buyers are, they will be able to set up a store that has up to 12 shops on each of a number of floors limited only by disk capacity. The total system can accommodate 300 items with full-blown descriptions, or 3,000 items with minimal information about each, or any combination of fully described and simply listed items. The system produces, on cassette tape, all the ordering information from which it will also print invoices and shipping labels.

The descendants of Fantasy Plaza will one day replace the store on the corner of the block with a computer in the corner of a room.

Working At Home, But Not Alone

One reason Collins believes Fantasy Plaza and other electronic shopping centers will fare well in the next five years is because, "The work force will decentralize and people will spend more time at home. Many of the needs people have can be met through on-line services and this aspect will spur the acceptance of this new way of living."

Collins's theory about more people working from home in the

future is, of course, not a startling revelation. Discussion of the idea of "telecommuting" has been going on for many years. It was, however, spurred to great heights of credibility and public awareness by Alvin Toffler in his book, *The Third Wave*. In that book, Toffler, the renowned futurist, referred to the coming of the "electronic cottage." Through application of technology, working from home will become a dominant theme of American life as the information society emerges.

The following sections will focus on the state of working at home and telecommuting today, the problems and potentials inherent in the movement, and the recent emergence of a national AEC (Association of Electronic Cottagers), a "product" with roots in trade unions and a future in independent associations of a type previously unknown in American society.

The world of working at home consists of two kinds of people: independent contractors who are self-employed and do most of their work from home, and company employees who do some or all of their work from home using computer terminals and other tools while drawing regular paychecks. It is certain that the former far outnumber the latter. It is also certain that, in the next few years, the situation will reverse itself.

Access to a personal computer and a modem can bring economic independence within grasp. Obviously, as more people have such access, more people will be able to choose economic independence by becoming entrepreneurs and self-employed workers. We want to look at people who are working from home using personal computers as a main means of either income production or linkage with the world.

There are about 2,000 members of CompuServe Information Service's on-line Working From Home Forum who use micros in their day-to-day livelihoods. A recent perusal of the Forum'smembership list reveals dozens of people working in at-home information brokering, some already beginning to specialize in law, medicine, or high-technology research. One New Yorker, who identifies himself only as "John," is undertaking the highly specialized business of conducting on-line theater research!

Problems and Promise

Several factors keep the number of independent workers of all kinds at a relatively low level—the fear of going into business and losing job security, the difficulty of marketing, lack of start-up capital, pressure from family and colleagues, and a simple lack of motivation. Other factors, however, are unique to computer-directed undertakings. One of these is the relatively low penetration level of computers in society at large, which leads to questions about the viability of a market for, say, in-home word processing work. Another limiting factor is the lack of standardization in hardware and software. Often contractors might be willing and qualified to do a particular task for a particular customer, but they have the wrong computer system. A third factor limiting the start-up of work-at-home businesses using computers is the relative expense required to purchase a microcomputer system suitable for day-to-day high-volume usage in a business.

An area of concern to home workers is the development of more "up to date" zoning ordinances. In some cities, workers who operate out of their homes are in at least technical violation of zoning laws aimed at businesses of a more traditional kind. Zoning is an area that most work-at-home groups focus upon as organization begins.

Gil Gordon publishes the first newsletter in the nation dedicated to analyzing and serving telecommuters. This newsletter, in its inaugural issue, carried a piece on the subject of zoning. Fran O'Neill, chairperson of the zoning committee of the National Alliance of Homebased Businesswomen (NAHB), was among the interviewees. Her group drafted a model ordinance that emphasizes what they call "performance criteria" for zoning considerations rather than delineating specific occupations or activities that are prohibited.

Gordon admits zoning " . . . hasn't become a major issue yet for home workers, perhaps because our numbers are small or perhaps because, as we believe, our impact on neighborhoods is relatively invisible." On the other hand, a number of workers expressed concern that zoning ordinances aimed at cutting down traffic, noise, nuisance, and pollution problems in neighborhoods could be a "time bomb" that local governments will call into use if working from home becomes a threat to some established interest group.

Solutions are being found for these problems. There is, for example, a growing micro-industry made up of people who present themselves as "information brokers." For a fee, these people will conduct on-line research for corporations, law firms, or even writers interested in the latest information about a particular topic. The level of computer penetration in society isn't an issue, since the customer is buying data, information that can be used for some purpose. And since most publicly available information utilities are accessible with almost any kind of hardware, the standardization issue doesn't rear its ugly head, either.

Similarly, in-home word processing or secretarial work *can* work in spite of compatibility issues, provided the customer wants a finished printed copy and doesn't care in what disk format the material is stored. Often, however, clients want such outside services to supplement in-house efforts and will insist that the documents be provided on disks, which of course raises again the issue of machine compatibility.

On the employee side of the telecommuting coin, there is an increase in interest on the part of many companies in having some kinds of employees work out of their homes. The employees use computer equipment to do their work and perhaps to stay in touch with the home office.

The U.S. Department of Education recently funded a research project called "At Home In The Office," headed by a University of Tennessee professor, Sheila Webster McCullough. Part of the study involved university clerical workers working from home for nine months.

"Companies are interested in the potential of telecommuting primarily because it can save money," Gordon of *The Gordon Report* says. "The direct and indirect costs of office space are staggering. In suburban office parks, space is often simply not available at any price. Secondarily, but very high on the list of reasons for the interest we're seeing in this subject, companies are having a difficult time finding certain kinds of employees, most of whom are needed for information-oriented jobs. They're willing to try to see if they can find a few more workers by making working from home available as an option."

A development in recent years on the office space front shows vacancy rates in downtown centers are going up, while suburban office parks are filling faster than developers can build them. "It's interesting," Gordon muses, "to speculate on a scenario for reversed land use: What if people moved *back* into the cities into lower cost housing (in converted office buildings?) and commuted or telecommuted to the suburban office? They'd have the best of both worlds, some would say." Some of this already taking place in and around New York City.

Working from home will significantly change another aspect of job patterns in America. In recent years, there has been a movement toward a concept of "job sharing." Pairs of people, both of whom want to work part-time, share single positions, allowing them to have what they want and employers to have the full-time employees they might have otherwise had a difficult time recruiting.

Someday soon it will be common for people to work from home part-time for an employer and part-time building their own businesses. Other people will also work part-time for two or more employers, each of whom needs less than full-time support in a particular job function. It is easy to see how this idea of job-sharing fits neatly into the concept of multiple-career lives, which will be, as we have said earlier, a watchword of the next two or three decades.

As employers become increasingly willing—even eager—to have workers do some or all of their work from home, more and more workers will take advantage of the freedom and flexibility that come with such an arrangement. An increase in entrepreneurship will be a byproduct of telecommuting. Some of the problems mentioned earlier that deter more people from going into their own businesses today must still be addressed; the issues that stand apart from those directly related to the computer.

Association of Electronic Cottagers

Enter Paul and Sarah Edwards. They left their budding careers to set up their own business—from home, naturally. Paul was a practicing attorney and top-level business executive, and his wife Sarah was a former training director and psychotherapist. About ten years ago they concluded that working from home was the life style and work style they wanted. After years of study and after answering hundreds of questions about how to do this, they decided to help people who wanted to undertake working from home but weren't quite sure how to go about it.

Now, five years and hundreds of seminars, radio shows, TV interviews, lectures, tapes, and a couple of books later, the Edwards are known in many circles as the "Ambassadors for the Electronic Cottage." They have helped thousands of people start their own businesses at home, most of the recent ones setting up businesses that use microcomputer systems. And they are the SYSOps or hosts of the CompuServe Working From Home Forum.

"We see a huge need for in-home workers in the data processing end of industry and business," Paul says. He parallels his latest enterprise, the Association of Electronic Cottagers (see Electronic Togetherness for Home Workers) to the hundreds of temporary placement agencies that have sprung up in business in the past decade.

A Whole New Model for the Global Village

Working from home is particularly appealing to several identifiable groups: rising lower-middle managers facing a shrinking management opportunity chain; retired or semi-retired individuals interested in income supplementation; single parents who wish to work from home to stay with children; couples seeking a second income; burned-out executives seeking a more relaxed life style; and people home-bound with physical disabilities.

One other group of people will become especially significant in this movement in the next half decade: people who wish to escape suburbia and live in remote or inaccessible places. One of these places, Telluride, Colorado, is one of the most difficult-to-reach places on the American map.

In Telluride, people are building a whole new town focused on the information society. The innovations will provide inspiration for architectural and environmental planners and designers well into the next century.

The Telluride Project

The chief architect, planner, and thinker behind the Telluride project, known as Mesa-Z, is London-born architect-composer John Lifton (see John Lifton's Parallel Worlds). Lifton's dream is to convert an 1100-acre plot of uniquely positioned and contoured ground in the spectacular Colorado Rockies into an enclave for people who have used the emergence of the information society to catapult themselves into a position where they can live where they want, independent of physical links to society.

Around the Mesa-Z project, Lifton and some of his colleagues, including his wife, painter and science fiction author Pamela Zoline, have formed a private non-profit foundation that has attracted futurologist John Naisbitt and his wife, Patricia Aburdene, to the board of directors of Telluride Institute, along with Canadian author John Clute and others. The Institute recently launched a planned series of annual Telluride Ideas Festivals under the theme "Reinventing Work."

But the Mesa-Z project itself holds for Lifton the greatest long-term interest. The objective: to build a totally self-contained, energy-efficient information community in a place people will want to live.

"If someone wanted to sit in his Jacuzzi at night and carry out transactions through electronic links to the Hong Kong stock exchange, that will be possible from the Mesa-Z town," Lifton says. He maintains that the idea isn't as far-fetched as it might seem. "We had a man here a year or so ago who was doing something similar with transactions on the Chicago exchange," he says.

In the course of designing the new town outside Telluride at Mesa-Z, Lifton is returning to the once-abandoned architectural career that is his first love. He says, though, that the quest for artistic excellence in architectural design has taken a new twist for him. "I'm always going to be trying to deal with the question of how an intelligent house should behave," he says with not a hint of whimsy or irony in his voice.

A business park, retail stores, a soon-to-be-completed airport, and planned recreational facilities to complement the wintertime skiing round out the Mesa-Z project plan. Some of these projects are being undertaken by people other than Lifton and his colleagues and family.

Summing up his reasons for continuing to be involved with the Telluride dream that is Mesa-Z, Lifton says soberly, "The environment is ceasing to be purely physical and is becoming equally informational in nature. Architecture, along with all of the other useful art forms, must respond to that change in meaningful and practical ways if it is to continue to be relevant to a rapidly changing society."

Around the Next Corner

The discussion so far in this chapter has been directed toward an analysis of products and ideas that are on the verge of reality today, or are already real but are just emerging as significant. Now we will look at products and ideas that are in a stage of experimentation similar to those we've been discussing but will require more intense development, or face more difficult barriers to acceptance or fruition.

The final segment of this discussion will look at some far-out ideas that are just concepts on drawing boards or in people's minds today—and some that may not even have progressed that far—but will possibly have a great impact on society.

Peter Black's Encyclopedia Electronica

Peter Black, the 34-year-old founder and president of Xiphias Systems in Marina del Rey, California, has become one of the leaders of computer graphics in the past three years. (See Peter Black: The Sanskrit Connection.) His company began by pioneering in the area of computer-generated graphics for use by television stations, then moved to developing more broadly based video graphic software for microcomputers.

Among Black's marketing triumphs was the sale of a graphic package for creating short-turnaround business graphics and institutional video graphics. The sale was made in late 1984 to ChartPak, the nation's largest graphic arts product company, which until recently was a subsidiary of Times-Mirror, but has been acquired by Brentwood Associates, a leading West Coast venture capital firm with a long history of investment in computer graphics.

Black has a vision, and that's why we're interested in him here. He has imagined a software product called Encyclopedia Electronica. The resemblance between that name and the revolutionary *Encyclopedia Britannica 3* is no mistake; Black sees the *Britannica's* organizational structure of hierarchical levels of information detail and depth as significant. Just as *Britannica 3* is organized into three main modules, each of which offers a different depth and view of the subjects covered by the books, so Encyclopedia Electronica would consist of three tiers: two static, non-perishable data bases containing information about topics that are not subject to constant change, and one a changeable, dynamic data base that can be continually updated as knowledge expands.

The new key features of this encyclopedia, Black believes are "TV-quality graphics, and an immense information medium that is both high in content and extremely transportable (see Extendable Encyclopedia on the Horizon?). His faith in this product design grows out of his strong belief that there is a new political constituency emerging in the United States. The belief was built by years of activist involvement during which he served, among other things, as the national public relations director for Transcendental Meditation.

"I see men and women in the 30-year-old age bracket—call them baby boomers or yuppies, if you like—who are very interested in education," he says, "not in the classic sense but in the sense of imparting values, priorities, and knowledge and wisdom to their children. The children will lead the revolution by taking control of education into their own hands." He sees the computer gaining the power to carry out this high ideal, and believes this will happen as the computer undergoes a "fundamental transformation." Its strong graphics orientation will be modeled around ideas and concepts originating early in our formal educational processes. In other words, computers will become more suited to the ways children learn and therefore more apt at becoming powerful tools for carrying out that learning process.

Group Writing: Cooperatives of the Word Processor Set

During the era just prior to the time when Black's new political constituency began to grow into adulthood, it was "in" to belong to a cooperative or a commune. Residents of these alternative familial environments shared many things, including the burdens of work and opportunities for creativity. A 1980's equivalent of the commune will be communal creative projects, made possible by the widespread availability of telecommunications.

On CompuServe's Literary Forum, for example, a number of authors have contributed chapters to a growing science fiction fantasy saga. The writers work under some fairly loose rules, among which is a prohibition against one writer killing off a character created by another writer. Would-be collaborators read the story as it has progressed to this point, then write their own contributed chapters, which they then transmit to the forum for addition to the area containing the work.

Beyond its novelty value, this method of collaborative working has the real-life potential advantage of pulling together writers of several different creative bents, located in widely dispersed places on the map, on one creative project. This "instant access" to varieties of expertise may have huge and unexpected payoffs in society.

For example, what is the legal responsibility of system operators (SYSOps) for the content of messages "posted" on their electronic bulletin board systems (BBS's)?

This recent legal problem brought national prominence to a young southern California BBS SYSOp named Tom Tcimpidis. The situation led to an opportunity for more than a dozen attorneys and law students from as many states to assist in the legal research, discuss potential defense strategies, kick around ideas about ways of approaching needed legal reform, and generally brainstorm about the best way to handle the case, all without any of the principals meeting one another face-to-face. Paul Bernstein of Chicago, a lawyer with some experience as a SYSOp himself and knowledgeable in telecommunications law jumped into the middle of the defense and coordinated everyone's efforts to avoid duplication of work and research. All of the hard work paid off when Tcimpidis saw charges against him dropped by state and local authorities, a precedent many legal observers believe will be important in coming years as government regulators struggle with the unique problems posed by this technology.

Building cooperative ventures among people who might otherwise never have "met" will become a more and more frequent occurrence as telecommunications expands in the next five years. Fears on the part of sociologists and social psychologists that computer users will somehow lose the ability to relate interpersonally will prove ill-founded and completely off the mark of actual experience. Computers, especially when linked via telecommunications technologies, will create unprecedented opportunities for humans to be more human in relationships with one another.

University Without Boundaries

Nationwide group collaboration will be one result of the boom in telecommunications facilities and their use.

Education will also be a frontier on which new developments will be established. The question of values—whether or not the computer *should* be used in education—is beyond the scope of this book and probably has no "right" answer. Right or wrong, telecommunications will have a major impact on education in the next half decade.

Microcomputers have already become as commonplace as movie projectors in elementary and secondary schools, and some of the most innovative work with computers has been done by students who are not yet out of high school but who have been weaned on microcomputers and their associated technologies. All of this seems somehow remote to most of us—even those of us who have children perched in front of a Macintosh computer two or three hours each week improving their math skills.

One San Francisco-based company, TeleLearning Systems, Inc., has started a university without walls. TeleLearning Systems is counting on the fact that courses by computer will be the next revolutionary move in the practical use of home systems.

The chairman of the board, Ron Gordon, has named the new school the Electronic University. It offers computer-aided instruction courses and the obligatory "electronic library" (which looks like a mini-DIALOG data base).

According to a recent catalog, college courses for credit are offered in such diverse subject areas as literary analysis, "Bio-ethical Problems in Biology and Medicine," self-improvement programs from memory training techniques (using the famed book by Harry Lorayne and ex-basketball star Jerry Lucas), and "The California Wine Connoisseur," hosted by Greg Malone of California's wine country, a founder of one of the nation's most prestigious wine tasting and judging organizations.

For students interested in pursuing a non-resident college degree, The Electronic University offers counseling services in selecting the right college and course plan, preparing for college-level credit examinations, and planning for combining class attendance with The Electronic University's on-line courses to satisfy degree requirements.

The school's current curriculum includes four undergraduate programs as well as three MBA's—a general degree, a degree in individual financial planning, and a degree in managing hi-tech programs.

The current enrollment is 15,000 plus. This represents a 100% increase over last year. Chairman of the board, Ron Gordon, expects the number of students to increase to 100,000 by next year. One source of relatively phenomenal growth is expected to be from companies that will offer to reimburse their workers for tuition paid for course work in The Electronic University. One large company, Pac-Tel, is already doing this and others are expected to follow suit shortly.

It is no secret that adult education studies have proven time and time again that the way humans learn is far better in a self-paced environment than in a forced classroom situation. So TeleLearning Systems and its successors and imitators will have a great deal to say about the ways in which microcomputers become more able to serve our human needs in the years lying just ahead of us.

Two-Way Video Telephones

Science fiction stories and scripts often incorporate the idea that, at some future time, we will use our telephones not only to *talk* to one another, but also to *see* each other during those conversations.

It is unlikely that such a scenario will be commonplace, or even possible, in any but the wealthiest of American homes by 1990.

Use of such technology in the world of business, however, is already commonplace. In fact, the current increased sophistication of video teleconferencing would have astounded even Dick Tracy with his two-way video wrist communicator.

During 1986, there will be close to 1,500 video teleconferences in America—and many will involve international communications. Of course, this is minor when compared to the billions of telephone conversations that take place every day in the world. Technical problems (see Video Teleconferencing), only now being overcome, have limited expansion of this otherwise excellent alternative to expensive and time-consuming travel—which used to be required for a group to communicate face-to-face.

Assessing the Near Term

During the next five years most of the momentum in telecommunications at the personal level will take place in the form of rapidly expanding services made available to a slowly growing number of people with access to the equipment and software required to take advantage of the medium. In many ways, the rise of the technology parallels television's early days. As television emerged, very few people could afford the receivers. As a result, audiences were small, and programming was limited and of poor quality, even when judged by the standard media communications of the day, radio. Because programming was limited and poor, few people felt a need or desire to buy sets.

The dilemma was not solved by a technological breakthrough. In fact, television changed very little from its inception to the late 1950's when color was introduced. The formation of networks capable of producing large quantities and varieties of programs for mass consumption contributed more than any other single factor to the success of television as a medium. Despite a Federal freeze on new stations in the late 1940's that wasn't completely lifted until 1952, national networks developed and more than 10 million TV sets were sold.

A similar development in telecommunications will break the cycle in which computers are not perceived by many people as being sufficiently useful to justify the expenditure and the low installed base of computers is not enough to justify spending huge sums on developing new programs to make computers useful. Someone or some company will eventually be willing to sink money into the medium in a way comparable to the expenditures of the television networks during the pioneering days of that medium. When that happens—and it *will* happen—computers and software and telecommunications will take off as fast as the television set did in the late 1950's. The increased use of computers for telecommunications, to get access to information, education, and recreational facilities outside the immediate physical reach of one's home town, will be at the forefront of this product breakthrough.

Faint Signals: An Assessment of the Mid-Term Future

What can we expect to see from telecommunications in the next several years? Among the trends that now are faint lights on the horizon, three have unusual potential: "smart" communications, graphics, and non-telephonic links using satellite and/or radio communications.

Applying AI to Telecommunications

The next few years will see the creation of a new family of AI products for the telecommunications area. The products will be intelligent interface programs that will permit users of microcomputers to set up new data bases of knowledge.

Users will later be able to access these data bases without regard to form and format. The programs will then "learn," over time, how the individual user uniquely asks for information.

A program will learn, for example, that when you say, "Tell me the cheapest place to buy tires," it should translate that to mean "search your list of retail commodity prices for a supplier of automobiles tires, preferably radial-4ply, size 155sr13, by a reputable manufacturer, within 20 miles of our present location."

The program would be able to do this because it knew what

kind of car you drove, what you could afford to pay, and how far you were willing to drive for certain kinds of purchases. In short, it would do so because it had become at once more human and more humane.

As the system and the user gain more and more experience together, the computer will be able to do more and more of the decision-making and searching without direction from the human operator.

Fully intelligent interfaces will be designed for data base programs, for large bibliographic services, and for information utilities like CompuServe, The Source, and Lockheed's DIALOG Information System. This development will ensure that millions of people who are in need of information and knowledge about particular subjects will find themselves compelled to plug into the computers available via a home microcomputer system and a modem.

Rudimentary products with artificial intelligence-like features have already begun to appear. In 1983, a company called Excalibur introduced a plug-in printed circuit board and a complex software program for the Apple II family of computers. The product, known as Savvy, was designed to permit English language design and use of data bases. It fell far short of that goal, but the idea was sufficiently on track that the company parlayed the concept into a public stock offering that raised a huge amount of money for a company with virtually no sales at the time of the offering.

Several other products for similar purposes are on the market at this time. They claim intelligence, although the claims are in need of qualifications by our standards. (For a more thorough discussion of this subject, see Chapter 1, Expanding Our Minds.)

Graphic Transmission

Within ten years, the ability to transmit pictures of objects under discussion, photos of items offered for sale, and live images of people involved in computer-to-computer linkups will be commonplace. There are, to be sure, technological problems. One of these is a little item called "bandwidth." Broad bandwidths are currently required for real-time visual graphic image translation and transmission. (See An Out-of-This-World Solution to Down-to-Earth Problems)

Nonetheless, the obstacles will be overcome. Combines like the Trintex system and a lesser known product called Viewtron, which uses expensive AT&T color graphic terminals, are in experimental use. Dozens of other companies and people are at work on one phase or another of developing a system capable of such transmission and reception.

An early improvement in the technology will be the emergence of a standard to which all such transmission will conform. The industry is currently faced with the untenable situation of having to receive and interpret many different kinds of signals. This is roughly equivalent to needing a different TV set or antenna for each channel we want to watch!

Eliminate the Phone Lines

One way to get both broader bandwidth communication and more accessible channels of communication is to find an alternative to telephone lines for carrying data transmissions between computer systems. A secondary advantage is that alternate channels of communication would eliminate the need to have at least two phones for every house and business. This will quickly bring access to the telecommunications tools we have been discussing within the perceived grasp of many more people.

Two alternate communications channels will develop in the next few years: radio waves and satellite communications. Satellite communications will probably combine with some form of telephone or radio hook-up at one or both ends of the chain.

Amateur radio operators, known colloquially as "hams," are among the early adopters of such gadgetry as computers and modems. And being hobbyists, hams tend to be fairly experimental and irreverent when it comes to tinkering with the technologies presented to them. This band of electronics lovers already has available repeater stations that can be used as intermediate message-sending points in many places. Sending a lot of data through the airwaves by telemetry (radio) is a common engineering feat.

When a computer user wishing to access CompuServe can simply switch on a small transmitting device connected to his computer and start typing, a major barrier to widespread acceptance and use of the technology will melt away—the necessity for phone lines. That is, the phone line barriers will melt when such alternate devices become inexpensive, reliable, and designed so that the user doesn't have to understand them.

In the last few months of 1985, three developments took place that tend to indicate a major movement toward radio signals being used as data communications links will occur in the next few years. Lotus Development Co., the almost overnight software giant that introduced 1-2-3 and Symphony to the world of personal computers and made a lot of money in the process, announced a new product called Alert, which is aimed at personal computer users with an interest in the stock market. This product, a plug-in circuit board for an IBM PC and some software, intercepts radio signals to which the user subscribes, decodes them, and determines which are of interest to the user. It then captures the relevant data and can plug this information (naturally enough) into 1-2-3 or Symphony to generate analytical reports and graphs.

The second development was the announcement of a joint venture among American Broadcasting Companies (ABC), Epson, and a small Mountain View, California, company called Indesys (an acronym for Information Delivery System). The group plans to offer a $250 expansion board for an IBM PC permitting the system to receive electronic mail by radio waves and store them for later retrieval and reading. Alternatively, those who don't own an IBM PC can buy a similar, slightly higher-priced, apparatus for their Epson printer and have the messages printed out, a kind of poor man's Telex.

The final new development in 1985 in the marriage of radio and computers was the debut of a software distribution technique dubbed by its developers Softcasting™. Softcast Corporation and its sister organization National Digital Radio Network, of Redmond, Washington, began transmitting public-domain (translation: free) software over FM radio bands. The signals can be received by anyone who buys a $70 decoding device from the organization. Transmission takes place at 1200 baud. A 2400-baud version for cable TV outlets is being tested with one cable supplier and planned for release in 1986. According to George Ure, Vice President of Softcast, by the fall of 1985 the company had 16 radio outlets in cities from San Francisco to Portland, Maine, and from West Palm Beach, Florida, to Minneapolis-St. Paul transmitting the software.

Softcast's ultimate idea is advertiser-supported software. One format they use for softcasting involves a 30-minute sponsored radio show that is interrupted four or five times for software transmission. It takes about 20 seconds to send a program of 16K bytes size over the radio waves using their technology.

Other companies are attempting radio delivery of software, many of them using sub-carrier signals, in other words, a sideband that is sent with the regular FM radio signal but is not audible on the listener's end. Such systems require the user to buy a special receiver for $100 to $200 in addition to whatever decoding device the transmitting service requires. Ure is convinced that using the mainband channel will be more attractive to users and advertisers.

"What would have happened to TV," Ure asks, "if the only way to receive programs was on video cassettes or video discs costing anywhere from $5 to $500 each? Not many TV sets would be sold." It is clearly possible such new delivery techniques that involve advertising will result in a surge in computer sales. Ure resists the temptation to make such a claim, and so do we, but radio telecasting of software will be a significant trend in the next few years.

The use of communication satellites and ground stations will also free users in the future from depending upon the telephone system for computer telecommunications. Satellite communications are in widespread use today in intercontinental communications, teleconferencing, and document transmission.

An application of technology to one-way communication that will continue its explosive growth is the placing of parabolic antennas in backyards, on top of roofs, on top of campers, etc., so people may receive TV programs directly from satellites. Total two-way communication via satellite is currently a reality for governments and many businesses; the only current limiting factor is the dedication of insufficient resources to the problem of designing and building a practical, reliable, and inexpensive means of accessing the channels.

One other technology should be mentioned: the electronic

transmission of words as mass communication with TV signals. This technology is called teletext and has been around for a few years. Though its one-way limitation makes it unsuitable for the kind of telecommunications we've been discussing, it does have its own particular uses.

Our friends in Great Britain have made extensive use of Teletext as a way, for example, of transmitting programs over the airwaves to personal computer users. The high-speed, low-cost dissemination of a great deal of digitally stored information may be expedited this way in the United Kingdom in the next few years.

Basically, teletext takes advantage of some unused portions of a standard broadcast TV signal to transmit textual information at a very high speed. The technology requires only two of the 525 scan lines of graphic image being transmitted to our TV antennas or receivers. Transmission rates of 25,000 baud—or about 20 times faster than the fastest modems in widespread home use—are possible with this method.

As indicated, teletext cannot be used to access services like CompuServe or BBS's. It will, however, be used for one-way communications such as program downloading. Teletext will extract a program from a remote computer, transmit it as a TV signal, and store it into your computer while your family watches the news. When that application is developed, the technology will also tie in with information utilities. People will then use interactive telephone, satellite, or radio hook-ups at their relatively slow speeds for conducting searches, identifying information to be transmitted and the like. They will then switch over to teletext to receive the needed data being transmitted in high-speed "bursts." That could significantly unclog phone links and make telecommunications accessible to more people.

Widespread application of teletext may be a while in developing. A year of research turned up little or no serious work currently being done in this area. Unless someone with sufficient resources to make the required technical improvements takes an interest in it, teletext may never fulfill its destiny by becoming an important ingredient in the telecommunications picture in the United States.

Opportunities, Strategies, and Decisions

Let's turn our attention for a moment to the way the telecommunications developments we've been addressing in this section will have an impact upon you and your life. Regardless of your perspective—career-oriented, investor, or business manager—you *will* be impacted by what will take place in this arena in the last half of the 1980's.

Careers To a career-oriented person, the emergence of widespread computer telecommunications will have at least two major potential impacts. First, examine the question of whether being directly involved in the telecommunications revolution is a good idea. More and more engineers, programmers, customer support technicians, data base organizers, repair personnel, and marketing experts are going to be called for in this exploding industry. If you already have one of these skills but are stuck in a field that does not seem to be expanding rapidly enough to suit your career objectives, consider moving to a modem company or to one of the providers of such services . . . or of starting your own.

The revolution also has career implications in opening avenues of freedom for you in the *way* and the *place* that you work, almost regardless of career. Thus you may be able to give serious consideration to a career field that a few years ago would have been of no interest to you because it called for working in an office environment with the usual restrictions.

Investment Soon there will be an explosion in the number of companies offering on-line services of various kinds, a la CompuServe and The Source. There is, to be sure, big competition there already, but there is plenty of room for smaller companies that can find a solid vertical market niche is being ignored or served poorly by the "big boys."

There will be hundreds of opportunities. You might consider starting a small bulletin board system, local Fantasy Plaza or similar operation in which you turn your house and your home computer into a moneymaking enterprise by taking advantage of telecommunications.

One final point—at the very least, if you are an investor, you should gain direct, first-hand access to stock, bond, commodity, and other financial data so that you can better shape your own investment destiny and rely less on brokers and others.

Management Managers should immediately begin to examine the potential impact of work-at-home on their company or group. Can you benefit from it right now? Could you be more effective, efficient, profitable with it today? Is there a key employee (perhaps several) who would be more likely to stay with the company longer if he or she could work from home a substantial part of the time?

Beyond employee relations issues, managers should also definitely investigate the availability of on-line information services and how they might help the job get done more expertly. Answers to many of the questions you face every day in your job are available from outlets like DIALOG. Their instant accessibility could make the difference between success and second place (or failure) in the difficult years ahead.

Bob Lindamood: Information "for Cheaps"

In the early 1960's, Bob Lindamood, then a young Presbyterian minister dealing with New York City street kids, had a vision. In his words: "I got a passion for vast numbers of people getting vast amounts of information for cheaps." He has spent the last 20-plus years chasing that dream and has seen the day come when the home computer provides what he characterizes as the "ideal tool and best method" for accomplishing it.

Lindamood, 53, lives with his wife, Judy, in the little town of Hobbs, New Mexico, where she teaches at New Mexico Junior College and he consults, counsels, and dreams. And dreams. And dreams.

Like all dreamers, his visions are occasionally shattered. That happened in the midst of our discussions concerning this book. CompuServe, which had sponsored his original on-line counseling service for a little over two years, decided, after a change in management, that dataFamiliae didn't make business sense any longer and terminated the relationship with Lindamood.

Dealing with an illusion-shattering experience like that might not be easy, even for a skilled professional counselor, but for the fact that he had been steeled for the situation by continually encountering a wall of professional resistance to his ideas that he calls "amazing, amusing and tragic."

Access is the Key

Lindamood saw CompuServe and its ability to link home computers to a central collection of information and wisdom as a way of overcoming one of the tragedies of life he had seen in his more than two decades as a counselor. "I saw families in Brooklyn," he recalls, "fumbling around ignorantly trying to deal with a problem when the information, knowledge, or skills they needed were available. They didn't have access. Ever since, I have been getting people access to what they need—when they need it in center city, suburb, Haiti, Ecuador, and small-town America."

Bob Lindamood has been involved with very large-scale programs, including a three-year stint as executive director of the State of Ohio's Commission for Children and Families, an organization that inventoried and analyzed more than 150 federal, state, and local programs aimed at providing services to families with children. That experience followed six years as a deputy in Columbus, Ohio's Franklin County Children's Services department. So Lindamood learned to think big, and it is not surprising that, as a result, he thinks big about on-line counseling services.

"On-line counseling and all of its benefits could literally be available to any employee of any company who wanted to provide it as a fringe benefit for an incredibly small number of dollars—perhaps as low as two to five dollars per month per employee—today," Lindamood declares.

Lindamood may have found his "sponsor" for such a corporate introduction of the idea in a New Mexico banking chain for which he is completing work on a computer-assisted on-line learning program. "If they like what we do with the training program," says the upbeat Lindamood, "they've promised to take a look at the on-line psychological counseling service to see if it's a potentially attractive fringe benefit."

A People Guy

All of this would probably come as no surprise at all to people who have known Dr. Lindamood since the mid-1950's when, armed with a fresh B.S. Degree in business and history from Marietta (Ohio) College, he stepped into a slot as director of personnel administration at Broughtons, Inc., a local dairy food products company. He spent two years there, taking the company through its first unionization experience, before moving into the preaching and counseling ministry.

Logically enough for a business grad, he started his ministerial life as an administrator in a Methodist church in Columbus. Having tasted this different kind of people involvement, Lindamood decided he liked it well enough to make a career of it. He moved to New York City where he attended Union Theological Seminary while he worked as a street minister at Brooklyn's First Presbyterian Church.

A year later, he completed a second master's degree in education and counseling psychology at Columbia University before moving back to his native Ohio, where he was involved in federal, state, and local programs aimed at providing services to families and children.

A Liking for Radicals

Spending most of his adult life dealing with people and their problems and needs has kept Lindamood a young-thinking quasi-radical, a trait that still shows in his hobbies. He lists his main interests outside his counseling activity as backpacking and music.

Dr. Lindamood, by belief and practice, holds that service for others can be extended to a specific business in an industry-specific setting. He is working on his dataFamiliae project from that point of view. That is the reason for his move to the Southwest. He is pursuing three industry-related projects at this time.

He and his wife and their two sons are avid outdoors people who have spent many hours hiking Ohio trails and, more recently, climbing mountains in New Mexico's central "spine." But Dr. Lindamood is not a solitary man. "I have a passionate regard for people," he says. "Especially, I like to work with those for whom there is no hope of 'making it.' " Like many of the people in this book, Dr. Lindamood is also attracted to music, where, he says, "my tastes run from Beethoven to Thelonious Monk." Quite a range, considering he once considered a professional music career. In his youth, in fact, he headed up a local rock group known (no kidding!) as Bobby's Little Bee-Bop Boys.

Allan Barker and Dialectron:
A Case of Curiosity

A few years ago, Allan Barker was a researcher for Xerox's famed Palo Alto Research Center (PARC) in the esoteric area of plasma etching for semiconductor fabrication. He decided he'd like to find out if anyone called him while he was away from home, which he was a lot of the time. So he rigged a gadget that connected the phone jack to his personal computer. All it did was count the number of times new telephone calls came in. "I was just curious whether an answering machine might be a good idea, if I was missing a lot of calls," Barker says.

"One evening, I thought to myself, 'Hey, I could hook up a digitized voice synthesizer to this telephone call system.' So I did it. That evening." Within a few hours of having the idea, Barker had the first working model of what was to develop into the Smart Answering Machine—SAM for short.

A few months later, a friend who owned a software company saw Barker's product and urged him to take it to market. Within a few weeks, he had decided to abandon his job as a research manager in what he called a "frustrating and deteriorating situation" at PARC, and start his own company. He's never looked back or regretted the decision. "To me, this is what's fulfilling," he says as his alert eyes scan the array of computers, test gear, and paperwork surrounding him in one bedroom of his Mountain View, California, apartment.

In fact, life has been so fulfilling that he and his partner, Richard Herrold, are planning to write a book called something like *The One-Minute Guide to Starting Your Own Company.* "We have the chapter titles worked out. For example, the first one is, 'Talk is Cheap'. Because we found out it *really* is!"

Barker, later joined by Herrold, went through a few false starts, a bad hiring decision or two and some funding gaps before making it to market with SAM in the spring of 1985. For Barker, it was the culmination of a lifelong interest in science and technology brought to bear in a tangible way. "I'd always been fascinated by science," the Ph.D. in chemistry says. "I guess that was partly because my father was a chemist. But it turned out I missed the mark when I went into chemistry; I belonged in electronics." So electronics, and more specifically computers, became a hobby that turned into a serious avocation and later became his profession.

Barker expects to spend the next couple of years helping keep Dialectron on target during a rapid growth phase that began in the fall of 1985 when publicity about SAM began to appear in the trade press.

Barker has a love for the outdoors. "I'd really like to be lying on a beach in Maui," he says only half-joking. He considers the possibility he might someday end up in a university as a professor and finds the idea intriguing " . . . once I'm done with this company and am no longer needed."

Barker likes simplification in his life. And it was that idea that became the driving force behind the SAM product. "Our objective was to make a product so inexpensive that no one would try to duplicate it or compete with us at the low end of voice compression and digitizing systems for telephone management," Barker says. "We've done that. We are so far under the price of comparable systems on the market that we constantly amaze people." When told about his price—just $295 and destined to come down to about $200 this year—many prospective buyers ask, "And how much extra is the board?" Of course, the board is included.

Barker is proud of that question. He's also proud that many users comment that the SAM software is some of the best-written programming they've seen. "A lot of hair-tearing and analysis and sweat went into that code," he says. "It had better be good."

Peter Black: The Sanskrit Connection

If someone walked up to you and said, "In classic Vedic, culture was conveyed orally from memory," you'd probably conclude either: (a) that you were on the campus of some obscure college in some obscure town time had forgotten; or (b) the person to whom you were speaking was so firmly rooted in the past that the idea of electricity might be a foreign one to him. But if the speaker were Peter Black, you'd be wrong on both counts—and probably on several others as well.

Black, founder and president of Xiphias of Marina del Rey, California, is inventor of the Encyclopedia Electronica. He is a very modern thinker, a practically oriented product developer, and a businessman who just happens to have a master's degree in Sanskrit and South and Southeast Asian Studies.

The Sound of Knowledge

"In Sanskrit," Black says (and who am *I* to argue with an expert?), "there is a fundamental link between knowledge and the *sound* of knowledge. The text or content is linked to the melody is linked to the rhythm." This audio link made it possible for early Hindu leaders to memorize hundreds of pages of religious texts (called "Vedas," which is where the word "Vedic" originates) with great precision. "It was essential that in conveying the religion and culture of a people from one generation to the next, consistency should prevail," Black explains.

Black's interest in Sanskrit, Hindu culture, and Asian studies is inextricably linked to his experience in the 1960's as a teacher of Transcendental Meditation (TM). "Lots of people who don't do it," Black says somewhat defensively, . . . see it strictly as an anti-intellectual or merely passive approach to the world. Not so. Maharishi Mahesh Yogi—he's the man who led the TM teacher training courses—spent a great deal of time and energy looking at human knowledge and experience in ways that are vastly different from the Western world's way of examining those subjects."

Interestingly enough, Black is just one of several ex-TM instructors and devotees who are making their marks in the microcomputer industry, perhaps the best-known of whom is Mitch Kapor, founder and president of the phenomenally successful Lotus Development Corporation.

Black sees a strong tie among his educational pursuits, his TM experience, and his current interest in tying graphics and microcomputers together in ways that extend man's access to knowledge. He is concerned about how knowledge looks, graphically, and how knowledge *sounds*.

As a bridge from the very ancient past to the very distant future, Black may be an unusual, if not unique, participant in the electronics revolution. Keeping an eye on where he and his company go in the next few years could be a pastime with great dividends.

John Lifton's Parallel Worlds

John Lifton, creator and designer of the Mesa-Z project, a new information society town high in the Colorado Rockies, has seen two pairs of parallel worlds converge in his latest project. This is a confluence that may propel Lifton into the ranks of the leading visionaries in the world in the next 10 years. His London upbringing and his wife's Colorado roots have merged to bring him to the physical place where the project is feasible. Also, an interest in architecture, once forsaken, and its complementary replacement, animated computer art, team up to give John the technical and design background to pull off the ambitious project of building a new city uniquely suited to the information society.

How Do You Get to Telluride, Colorado?

Lifton started his professional life as the youngest licensed architect in Great Britain. Less than two months into a promising career as a designer of buildings, he chucked it because "I was dissatisfied with what architecture was doing in practice as opposed to what I wanted it to do in dealing with the emerging information society."

Lifton moved from architecture to interactive computer art and quickly rose to prominence in Great Britain in the late 1960's. A pioneer, he was a founder of the prestigious Computer Art Society of London. He helped put together the first Computer Art Laboratories project that offered free timesharing computer facilities to artists. He also set up large warehouses as bases of operation for large-scale computer art projects in London.

In the early 1970's, Lifton found himself with three jobs, all at the well-known Royal College of Art in London. Two of the jobs involved teaching art, but the third was the one that was to catapult him into his present position of opportunity. "I was given a research project to use the computer to simulate the cognitive processes engaged in by an architect early in the conception of a building design," he explains. This project combined fledgling research in artificial intelligence (see Chapter 1) with explorations of how a creative mind works.

"It was," he says, "in a word, fascinating. I became entranced with the questions of how we could get to a place where we could delegate high-level creative judgments to machines."

No Snow Winter

Somewhere along the way, John met Pamela Zoline, a transplanted American who was studying art in London. "We don't even remember when or how we met," he laughs. "We knew each other for a long time before we got together and became more than friends."

Pamela, an accomplished artist and a published science fiction author, had family in the Telluride, Colorado, area, where they had started the ski resort.

"We always told them that if they needed us to come over and help out for a bit, just to let us know," Lifton remembers. In the winter of 1977, Rocky Mountain ski resorts from Tahoe to Wyoming were hit hard by an unusually snow-free weather pattern. Pamela's parents had to lay off the resort staff. "They called and asked us to come and help and we came gladly, intending to stay only one year to help them get through to the next winter," he says. That was nine years ago.

"Shortly after we arrived, her parents had conversations with some local businessmen in a nearby town and they bought the resort. They asked me to stay on and build a new project, Telluride Mountain Village, to serve and support the resort. I couldn't resist. By this time, my interest in architecture had been rekindled, and the challenge of building a whole new town is not something one expects to have dropped into one's lap more than once in a lifetime. So we stayed."

John and his wife have been there ever since. They have three children ranging in age from 3 to 9 years. Although they have no hobbies—"We do lots of things," he laughs, "but we take them all quite seriously!"—John is presently at work creating an opera in which the singers' movements and actions control the synthesizer that generates the music. "I am intrigued by the idea of putting the instruments under the control of the artists in the performance," Lifton says. He traces his interest in such a compositional concept to his work in London with interactive computer art.

"If there's one thread which runs through my life," he says reflectively, "it is the idea of interaction and control. It's the main idea behind the Mesa-Z project and it's the main thrust behind this new opera." Lifton has certainly interacted with and gained control of a huge piece of his own environment and, if he is successful with his Mesa-Z dream, he will make the same kind of interaction and control available to hundreds of other people.

Electronic Togetherness for Home Workers

An early sign of the growing strength of the work-from-home movement is the formation of the Association of Electronic Cottagers (AEC). The AEC offers a support group for anybody working from home on a computer, whether connected over the phone lines to a company computer, working as an independent contractor, or self-employed. Two levels of membership are available in the AEC: national and local. National members pay $75 per year dues and are basically eligible for all of the benefits of AEC membership except local job placement. Local members will pay about $250 per year and qualify for job placement with companies in their area looking for their particular kinds of expertise.

The Edwards plan to manage the enterprise through the first 50 local memberships. They will offer members a number of benefits, including:

- network of computer dealers who offer help and discounts;
- support contact with other members for overload and emergency back-up help;
- special equipment packages designed and tailored for home workers;
- discounts on things like courier services, computer equipment, business management consultation, seminars, books, tapes, and supplies;
- electronic banking to speed payment of bills by AEC to members for work performed;
- a CompuServe Information Service membership;
- a business start-up kit;
- optional group health and life insurance packages;
- subscription to a monthly news magazine called *Electronic Cottage News;*
- lobbying support on issues affecting electronic cottage workers.

On the last point, the AEC got its feet wet early—and got some premature national publicity in the process. They jumped into the fray when organizers became aware that the AFL-CIO, the largest union organization in the United States, had gone on record as opposing electronic cottage arrangements. The union argued that management would use the non-traditional methods to exploit workers, as it once had exploited workers through work-at-home spinning and knitting piecework contracts—paying for piece work, cutting salaries, taking work out of the labor-negotiated mainstream, and other tactics.

Efforts were successful as the federal government rejected the idea of curbing such arrangements. The victory clearly did not belong entirely to the AEC organizers and electronic cottage members of the CompuServe Forum, but it is partly because of them. The controversy was highlighted on the popular CBS news program *60 Minutes* and in several national newspapers and news magazines.

Electronic cottaging is a concept whose time has come. "Some of our research indicates that, for example, in the Los Angeles area, companies are looking for 15 times as many data-related temporary office workers as the placement agencies can locate and place," Paul Edwards says. "That's an opportunity you can drive a truck through."

By combining placement services with consulting support for the potential worker-at-home, AEC plans to put tens of thousands of new enterprising workers into their own home-based businesses in the next five years. By the end of the first year, the Edwards' plan to have 250 in-home personnel turning out 10,000 hours per month of at-home labor on behalf of hundreds of clients in the Los Angeles area. From there, a franchise-based national organization is planned.

"One big service we furnish," Sarah Edwards points out, "is to drastically reduce or even eliminate the need for electronic cottagers to do their own marketing. The other main service is support: quick rental of machines in the case of equipment failures and other, similar kinds of support that will help keep a one- or two-person operation going during a difficult time or unanticipated problem."

For every 50 members recruited, AEC will have two staff people, one assigned to the tasks of marketing and placement, and the other to service support. The latter, armed with a lap-sized portable computer and a telecommunications link, will work from their homes and provide technical and referral back-up for the workers "placed" in various jobs in their homes.

"What we're building," Paul says, "is a new institution, similar in some ways to temporary job placement services, but radically different in terms of the kinds of workers we approach, the advantages for everyone, and the way we operate in a very decentralized way."

Cottage industries of the past existed as puny alternatives to the dominant factories spawned by the industrial revolution. The electronic cottage, on the other hand, is a major, powerful outgrowth of the computer revolution—and will dominate a large part of the economic fall-out of that revolution.

The emergence of organizations like AEC will signal a new era in working from home. The most significant benefits of AEC's contribution to this growing movement will include increased respectability, clout in the political and governmental arenas, sharing of resources and expertise and needs, plus the simple camaraderie of being able to be certain one is not alone "out there."

Extendable Encyclopedia on the Horizon?

Peter Black's idea for a new Encyclopedia Electronica blends several emerging technologies with what the eclectic graphics guru sees as an important new trend in American life: an increasing dissatisfaction with the educational establishment, an establishment that he argues is composed of the formal schooling system and television. He characterizes television as "the remedial school" we all attend when we finish our formal schooling. "Almost everything we learn after we leave school comes from television," he points out. "In that sense, television broadcasting is an ongoing educational process, whether it means to be or not."

Encyclopedia Electronica, which Black hopes to have in some form of introductory position within the next few years, will be built around something he calls, for lack of a more communicative name, an "operating system." He is quick to point out though that he doesn't mean an operating system in the conventional sense of a controlling program that manages the operation of the computer system. "The operating system here," he says, "is an aggregate of conventions for how we display and organize information, experience, and impressions."

Put all of these conventions together with an optical or disk player married to a personal computer and you have the central core of the new encyclopedia, with speedy access to both words and images—and especially to knowledge.

Graphic in Nature

For Black, whose family has been in television and films for many years, the analogies are easy to slip into. "Presenting information graphically is different from presenting it in writing, not just in the medium but in the whole approach," he says. "It's the difference between packaging a piece of news for the six o'clock report on TV and packaging the same story for the morning newspaper. In the process of repackaging, some things are lost, but some other things are gained."

His operating system will include capabilities like those incorporated into MacDraw and MacPaint, two early graphic utility programs on the Apple Macintosh computer. But the core of the works will be the searching mechanism.

"We'll include a key word search capability so that the user can interrogate the encyclopedia and ask it to provide him with everything it knows about some subject by using key words." To do this, Black realizes, requires another step—the categorization of all human knowledge into areas that can be approached on a key word basis. "While my emphasis is of necessity on the information itself," he points out, "there is implicit in it an analysis of human knowledge and ways of displaying that knowledge."

'Perishable' Information

The software that makes up the encyclopedia Black intends to build will consist of two major components: a collection of optical or video disks, probably topically organized, which will contain graphics and information about various subjects; and a telecommunications link to a data bank of "perishable" information: newly discovered data, current events, political activities, and the like.

"The user will combine searches in both areas to trace the broad outlines of human knowledge regarding a given subject," Black offers.

But how does Black intend to have the graphic content in the data base of perishable information transmitted to the user's home computer? "The main knowledge bank on video disk at the home computer," he points out, "will incorporate type fonts, faces, clip art, and the tools for manipulating those items. The knowledge in the remote data bank is then downloaded to the system directly. Once it is in the user's system, it 'calls' on the graphic and typesetting capabilities of the Encyclopedia Electronica, which in turn controls the display of that knowledge on the user's screen.

"By buying more and more video disks covering topics of interest and by use of the remote data bank of perishable information, the user can have a completely up-to-date, easy to use, graphically oriented encyclopedia of knowledge available any time he wants."

That's the essence of Peter Black's dream product.

SAM Brings New Meaning to Answering the Phone

You're stuck in a meeting at a client's office and you can see you're going to be late for dinner. You'd like to call your wife and tell her, but she's not home from work yet herself. This is the only break you're liable to get for a while. How do you get her a message?

You need to call a meeting of a church finance committee but the other members of the committee are often hard to reach. You don't have time to keep tracking them down just to let them know the time and place of the meeting. Who can you get to help you?

A sudden meeting at a colleague's office has come up but you're expecting a very important call on your home phone. You don't want all of your calls being forwarded to your friend's office, but there's one that you *need* to get.

Countless difficult communication situations in business and personal life could be addressed by an emerging generation of intelligent phone-management systems like Dialectron's Smart Answering Machine—SAM for short. Before SAM came along, if you wanted such a device for your home computer, you'd have had to settle for features not much better than a conventional answering machine *or* pay upwards of $1,000 for enough power to be useful. Now, thanks to the software insights and engineering of a physical chemist turned inventor and entrepreneur, you can buy an amazing amount of telephone power for your IBM PC for less than $300.

The Things It Can Do!

Without a tape recorder (the SAM system uses voice compression and digitizing techniques that we'll discuss in a few moments), a home computer owner who has a SAM in his IBM PC could do all of the following and more:

1. Record and change the greeting message callers will get when the phone is answered by SAM.
2. Leave personal messages for individual callers who can only access them if they have a special personal ID number given them by the owner of the system.

3. Have messages forwarded to another number, including being summoned to the phone by a pre-recorded digitized message of the user's choosing.
4. Have one or more messages telephoned to a specific individual or group at predetermined times, with the system continuing to attempt to deliver messages until told to stop or successful.
5. Store and automatically dial hundreds of telephone numbers, including accessing long-distance providers' trunk lines where appropriate.
6. Manage most of the system—including retrieving messages, leaving personal messages, changing the greeting message, redirecting forwarded messages, and storing and ordering distribution of delayed messages.

Each of the above scenarios can be dealt with quickly and efficiently by the SAM system. In the first situation, simply call your home office number (or home telephone) where SAM is connected and leave your wife a personal message. Then when she checks home to insure that you are there, she can retrieve the personal message and respond accordingly.

In the second situation, SAM's ability to send a single message to a selected distribution list on a timed basis and continue trying until it reaches all of the people or is told to stop, can be put to great use. In the last situation, you can simply use your colleague's phone to order SAM to forward your calls. As each call comes in, and a message is left (hang-ups are not forwarded), the computer will automatically dial your friend's office and play a pre-recorded message asking the answerer to summon you to the phone. When you get to the phone, punch in your personal access code and hear the message. When the one you're waiting for comes in, you can remotely order SAM to stop forwarding messages. Since it's a computer on the other end of the phone and not a person, if the forwarded call comes at a bad time, simply wait until it's more convenient to call SAM and retrieve the message.

SAM is the brainchild of a tinkerer named Allan Barker who turned a personal curiosity about whether people called him when he was away from home or not into a small but thriving company. Dialectron is about two years old and began shipping its SAM product early in 1985. By the time you read this, the company will probably have shipped close to 5,000 of the plug-in circuit boards for the IBM PC.

But the real brains of SAM aren't on on the board, they're on the accompanying disk. "The fundamental difference between SAM and other products that try to do similar things," Barker says as he curls up in an old office chair in his apartment cum corporate headquarters, "is that we use software engineering to handle speech compression." Most competitive products use a voice compression chip on their boards; such chips are relatively expensive, accounting for the substantial price difference between SAM and other products of a similar type. "We are doing real-time speech compression on the IBM PC with no specialized hardware," Barker points out.

Dialectron believes there is another significant difference between SAM and its competitors: SAM is easy to use when compared with other similar products. Again, credit goes to software engineering . . . as well as to a particularly open attitude on Barker's part toward other peoples' ideas. "As we designed the product," he recalls, "more than a dozen different people came into the company at various times to help. In each case, the person would find features he or she felt would be useful or important to the product. I synthesized all of these ideas and suggestions together while striving for an immensely simple product."

Disk as Tape Recorder

SAM uses the computer's disk—floppy or hard—as the medium for storing both the user's greeting and forwarding messages and the incoming calls. The user can control the maximum length of a message and therefore disk utilization. In addition, the user can select between two different qualities of voice compression, one of which takes up far less disk space per minute of message. Since the user can delete messages selectively even while he's away from his phone, managing the disk space turns out to be relatively straightforward.

As the voice comes in over the telephone line—SAM uses the phone to which it is connected as the microphone for the user to do recordings—the program at the heart of SAM takes a "snapshot" every few microseconds and stores the waveform (or picture) of the sound wave in the IBM PC's memory. It then compresses these waveforms into far more condensed storage sizes by means of the proprietary algorithm that's at the heart of the SAM design. It records this compressed digital signal on the disk and the user then plays it back later much as he would a tape recording.

What, No Modem?!

SAM is not like a modem in any way except that it happens to connect a computer and a telephone line. Many users, even experienced engineers, don't understand that a modem and a voice-handling system like SAM are totally different. A modem can answer your telephone, but can only respond to the caller with a high-pitched tone that enables his computer to talk to your computer. SAM deals with human voice input and would not know what to do with a computer on the other end.

Where From Here?

Barker speculates that in the next five years, we will see products like SAM that can actually *handle* our communications for us instead of just *assisting* us with them as SAM does. Barker says, "The objective ought to be to design a program that we can just provide the information we want sent and the addressee and the program figures out how to get it there best, fastest, cheapest, and makes sure the communication process happens."

In the nearer term, he sees Dialectron developing adjuncts to SAM. Specifically, he envisions a soon-to-be-released tool kit for programmers who want to make software modifications to SAM for specific products or applications. In addition, he and his partner, Richard Herrold, plan to develop and introduce a SAM-based telemarketing product that would make calls for sales purposes. They hope to bring the product in at a retail price of $50–$95, as opposed to the more than $300 such an IBM PC product costs today.

A Home Away from the World

Telluride is a small (1,100 residents) town in remote southwestern Colorado that boasts some of the best skiing in the ski-rich Rockies. In another 10 years, if John Lifton (see p. 113) has his way, it will also be known as a haven for information society recluses.

The Mesa-Z project is built on the edges of one of the country's best-kept secrets—the ski resorts at Telluride. As presently envisioned, the project will see every home and business in its environs equipped with a local area network (LAN) that will connect residents and workers to each other and to the outside world via satellite uplinks and downlinks (an uplink is when you send something up to the satellite; a downlink is when the satellite retransmits something down to the earth and a receiving station), microwave communications if needed, and a substantial mainframe computer to which all Mesa-Z dwellers will have access. The mainframe will permit residents to handle everything from monitoring home security and energy usage to electronic banking and message transmission.

The selection of Telluride was not made deliberately. The location, however, has an interesting historical "coincidence" associated with it. Telluride was the first town in the world to be electrified. In 1889, Thomas Edison and George Westinghouse were engaged in a bitter debate over whether AC or DC offered the best opportunity for distributed electrical power in this country. Edison was on the DC side of the fight and Westinghouse on the AC side. Westinghouse got a contract to electrify a mine a few miles away—and over a mountain ridge—from Telluride. The miners were so excited by what the light did for them that they extended power lines over the rugged peaks into Telluride.

It seems only fitting, if somewhat ironic, that the first American town to be electrified by distribution of AC power should be poised to become the first outfitted for the emerging information society.

Besides an information utility, Mesa-Z residents will also benefit from centralized passive solar energy that will be the primary source of electrical energy for the community. "It turns out that the southwest exposure that all of the homes here will have is ideal for solar energy efficiency," Lifton says with some delight. "The fact that it is also the best view is a very nice added feature."

The Mesa-Z project that architect and computer artist Lifton is designing will afford people and small businesses the ability to live and base themselves where they want (thanks to the electronic link-ups of the telecommunications world with a unique environment in which to live, work, and play.)

Building on a long, thin piece of land at the south end of an 8,740 foot high valley, Lifton hopes to provide space for as many as 2,200 people to live in a new community specifically built for the information society. All of the homes and businesses will be solar-powered, information-linked, and earth-sheltered. And all will face the southwest with unobstructed views of what Lifton says even veteran Colorado Rocky Mountain travelers agree is "a very special and spectacular place."

"The ground slopes toward the southwest in a series of well-spaced terraces, each of which is 50 to 60 feet below the one to its northeast," Lifton explains. "We plan to tuck the buildings into the sides of these steps, put sod roofs over them and let them become virtually invisible architecture in a place that is far too beautiful to spoil with lots of buildings." Each person can look down on his or her neighbor's roof and see the tops of the next row of houses, but will have a completely unobstructed view of the Wilson Mountains, a series of peaks in the 14,000-foot range.

"Every room in every home in the Mesa-Z project will be required to be equipped with the appropriate links for the LAN when the homes are built," Lifton says. "This connection to the information utility provided as part of the life style here will be the key link for all sorts of activity in which one might wish to engage."

The plan currently is to use fiber optics as the transmission link. "We'll need broad bandwidths and the material has to be able to withstand extremely cold temperatures for long periods. The ground here freezes down several feet during the peak of winter and may stay that way for weeks at a time."

Besides self-employed work-at-homers who can move their bases of operations to a remote place like Telluride (which Lifton describes as located "not very close to much of anything you'd recognize"), Lifton hopes to attract small software companies to an area of low housing cost, spectacular views of the 14,000-foot Wilson Mountain peaks, and superb recreational facilities.

"These companies, which are able to exist without the need for constant physical interaction with their customers or others and who have earned the right to be able to base themselves wherever they want, are going to be prime candidates for our recruiting drive in a couple of years," Lifton promises.

The new development, which is on 1,100 acres of land outside the town of Telluride, also incorporates an extensive wildlife corridor that will separate the new town from a swanky luxury estate area at the southwest rim of the valley, adjacent to a precipitous glacial valley.

"We really have a two-fold objective here," Lifton says. "First, we want to develop and provide a totally self-contained information community that will permit its residents and workers to live in beautiful isolation while maintaining informational contact with the world in which it functions. Second, we want to furnish support services to the rest of the region so that shops, restaurants, and other similar businesses will flourish and the surrounding community can derive some permanent, year-round benefit from its placement here."

Lifton says he and his colleagues, including computer artist Richard Lowenberg of Petaluma, California, (profiled in Richard Lowenberg's *Ape Story* in Chapter 3, Enhancing Our Life Style) "don't want to do more lodging for the resorts but are rather looking to provide a meaningful, permanent environment for people and small businesses freed by their involvement in the information society to live where they want."

When it is completed, the Mesa-Z project's new town will have a population of some 2,200, which is twice that of Telluride's permanent population and near the tourist-season peak of 2,500.

"All we need are something like 500 families out there who are able to and interested in locating in a place like this," Lifton concludes. "I know those families are out there today. The only question is how long it will take us to find them and convince them to come here for a look. They won't want to live anywhere else once they do that."

Lifton expects to see the first of a hoped-for 500 families move into the area this year.

Who Knows? Anybody Who Wants To

Could you easily find answers to these questions?

1. What flights are available from Chicago to New York on Sept. 7, between 1:00 and 1:15 p.m.? For what prices, with what stopovers en route?
2. What patents were granted in the last five years for applications of MIM (metal-insulator-metal) technology to varistor arrays?
3. Who are the board members of Gould Corporation, and when do their terms expire?
4. How many Datsun dealerships are there in San Francisco?
5. What has happened to the selling price of EXXON shares in the past five years?
6. What articles have appeared concerning ExperTelligence's new AI Logo program in the country's major newspapers within the past three days?

These questions can be answered within minutes without leaving the boardroom or bedroom by using telecommunications technology to access information.

Let the Computers do the Talking

Instant access to information takes place via *telecommunications*—computers talking with each other, usually over phone lines. The communication "chain" in the telecommunications technology has seven "links": two computers, two software programs, two modems, and a telephone line.

The software programs control the flow of information between the computers and the modems.

The word modem is short for modulator/demodulator. Modems link the telephone line to the computers by modulating (in other words, changing the characteristics) of the signals at the sending end and demodulating (returning to their original state) those at the receiving end. Baud rate is a measure of the speed at which modems carry on their I/O (input/output) activities. Every

10 baud is equal to one character per second (cps). The most common, least expensive modems operate at 300 baud (or 30 cps).

Flocking With Other Birds of Your Feather

Information is becoming more readily available through BBS's (bulletin board systems). These provide for sharing information among a growing number of people with common interests or concerns. BBS's disseminate information much more efficiently than do the more traditional classified ads or letters to the editor sections of newspapers or journals. Messages on BBS's can be updated every hour (or every five minutes!) and can be responded to at once.

For real immediacy in information sharing on an electronic bulletin board, though, users go into a real-time interactive setting referred to as "CB mode" (after the once-popular personal CB radio) or "chat mode." In these special modes, which are not available on most smaller BBS's because of more complex software and expensive hardware, users interact with each other in groups of two or more. One user types a message and signals the other user that he's done. The second user types a response. Each person sees the other's messages appear on his screen as soon as the other user presses his Return key.

Information for Sale

Information is also being made widely available on *subscriber services*. These typically have a "connect time" charge for every minute the user is on the system. The charges vary widely according to such things as the particular service being used, the time of day, the operation being carried out. Charges range from $6 to more than $200 per hour. Subscriber services may also carry a monthly charge and may charge for the user password and other information required for getting onto the system. A few subscriber services also require subscribers to purchase or lease special software and/or hardware.

Most subscriber services provide access to *data bases*—electronic compendia of information. Data bases, as the name implies, hold data (information) that may be accessed by people through computers. Most data bases are private, belonging to businesses or individuals. A growing number of data bases are available to the public, however. One published index lists 25 public-accessible data bases just on the subject of agriculture.

Finding Which Shell the Pea is Under

A big change will occur in subscriber services in the next five years—streamlining and standardization of access. Subscriber systems at present are relatively difficult to learn and use. DIALOG Information Services, for example, sponsors many workshops around the country every month to help new users learn their way around the system and to help the long-time users learn to use the system more thoroughly. Learning the DIALOG system is a process that never ends. Knowing how to use DIALOG doesn't help a lot in learning how to use the other systems. DIALOG itself offers a less expensive evening service called Knowledge Index, which accesses some of the same files DIALOG uses—but does so with an entirely different set of search commands and procedures!

New users on CompuServe, for another example, often feel like guests at an enormous banquet who do not know how to get silverware and plates, and don't know how to get the lids off the serving dishes. Adding to the confusion, CompuServe doesn't tell in its documentation many of the things new users need to know about "getting the lids off the serving dishes." And to compound the matter, unlike the situation at DIALOG, CompuServe personnel can't be asked about its services directly, since people in the central office almost never answer the telephone, although they do respond to messages users leave on the system.

The problems with CompuServe, DIALOG, and other subscriber services are attributable to the fact that they are participants in a genuine revolution. As in all revolutions, things happen too quickly to go together as neatly as we might wish they could.

The next generation of data base systems and information utilities will incorporate ideas from the world of artificial intelligence so that systems begin to "learn," for example, how individuals expect to find certain data and how they ask their questions.

Even today, though, telecommunications puts the world at our fingertips in ways almost nobody could have imagined five years ago. And, amazingly, the information revolution has only just begun.

Video Teleconferencing

Put the technology of the telephone together with television and you have a mental picture of what video teleconferencing is all about.

The biggest single technical problem retarding the growth of the video teleconferencing industry is one of size. Far more information needs to be transmitted in a video environment than in either a radio broadcast or a telephone conversation. In fact, a single color TV transmission requires as much space as 12 commercial radio signals or 1,200 telephone conversations. This single fact has meant that video teleconferencing has been prohibitively expensive.

But recent improvements in the technology are beginning to provide for less expensive and more efficient communication than was formerly possible. The key lies in reducing the amount of essential information transmitted.

Companies such as NEC and Action/Honeywell have devised methods for reducing to relatively miserly proportions the amount of necessary information. NEC, for example, uses *codecs* (coder-decoders) to store pictures in a digital form and then (on the other end) restore them to their original analog forms. In between coding and decoding the system applies *interframe coding* to record and transmit only those parts of the picture that have changed since the previous frame. The system does not, therefore, repeatedly (30 times every second) transmit, for example, the calendar on the wall behind the speaker's head.

Action/Honeywell, on the other hand, uses codecs to apply a type of "frame elimination" that ingeniously *transmits only every other frame*. When displaying the image, each frame not eliminated is repeated twice. Both solutions work well for situations not involving fast action—in other words, typical teleconferencing situations.

An extreme measure for compressing the signal while still preserving the ability to see the speaker involves *slow scan* television signals, in which a narrow channel bandwidth is used to transmit the picture line-by-line to a receiver where it is collected in a buffer and then reassembled as a complete picture. The method is particularly effective in cases where a page of writing or a graphic of some kind is being transmitted. A variation of this, *freeze-frame*, works better on scenes involving motion of some kind. A systems manager or editor observes the action on a monitor and, at appropriate times, "freezes" the picture that is then transmitted via slow-scan techniques.

Getting the Picture from Here to There

The transmission of digital information is carried out over one of three pre-defined media, named (curiously) T1, 2T, and T2. The three media transmit information respectively at 1.5 million, three million, and six million bits per second, which translates (if you have a modem, or know the language that modem-users speak) into 1.5 million baud, 3 million baud, and 6 million baud.

Intra-urban video teleconferences are often transmitted via coaxial cables, which are either dedicated to the particular transmission use or leased from the local cable company. Intermediate range transmissions—up to 200 miles—will typically be transmitted via microwave relay systems.

An Out-of-this-World Solution to Down-to-Earth Problems

Video teleconferencing across distances greater than 200 miles will involve the wonder of communications satellites. Communications satellites have been available for public and private use since 1972. Most communication satellites are in a 22,300 miles high orbit. Any satellite in earth-orbit at that altitude will complete a circuit of the earth once every 24 hours. The plane of the orbits of communication satellites is the plane of earth's equator, so the satellites maintain an apparently fixed position in the sky with respect to sending and receiving stations on earth. A satellite in this orbit is called *geosynchronous*.

The British science writer Arthur C. Clarke first identified the possibility of communication satellites in geosynchronous orbits in a 1945 science paper entitled "The Space Station: Its Radio Applications." He showed how three satellites spaced evenly above the equator in geosynchronous orbits could cover the entire planet. Intelsat, the international company operating communications satellites, currently has more than 20 satellites in geosynchronous orbits—so the planet's communication needs are thoroughly well taken care of, at least in one respect.

Communication between satellites and earth are carried out by uplinks and downlinks—antennas that either transmit signals *up* to satellites or receive signals *down* from satellites. Of course, two-way conferencing exactly doubles the necessary equipment; antennas are needed at both ends to carry out both functions simultaneously.

Transponders do the real work in a communications satellite. They receive signals from earth transmitters, amplify them, change their frequencies, and retransmit them to an earth receiving station. The most advanced satellites have 41 transponders, each capable of handling three simultaneous TV transmissions. These satellites, therefore, are capable of carrying on 123 simultaneous video teleconferencing events. By 1995 it is estimated that 200 satellite transponders will be needed just for video teleconferencing purposes. This will represent a 1000 percent increase in ten years.

Problems and Promises

Full application of video teleconferencing awaits further refinement of the technologies involved. One problem currently challenging scientists and engineers is lack of space in the proper geosynchronous orbits at points that provide for transmission to the entire North American continent. The problem is one of density—getting enough transponders packed into orbit at those critical points to handle the continent's growing communication needs. Communication satellites will become more effective and efficient in carrying out their tasks, or the shortage of appropriate space (get it?) would become acute.

Another problem that will be resolved in the next several years involves widespread incompatibility of the various parts of the entire communication system among themselves. Different kinds of codecs, for example, do not communicate with each other; power supplies and TV screen display standards vary from one country to another. Eventually these problems will be resolved.

As the technology becomes much more sophisticated and the costs much less expensive, video teleconferencing will grow from a multimillion dollar industry to a multibillion dollar industry. It will then be a mass-media form of communication.

The day will come when almost any of us will be able to "put our heads together" in full color and sound, regardless of where we individually might happen to be on the planet (or off).

What it's Like to Ask a Data Base Something

If you have never used a data base before, here's what the experience is like.

Imagine you are writing a book on what is going to happen in technology in the next five years. You have already talked with many people and have most of your ideas. You want published sources, however, to reinforce the writing a little. How long will it take to locate a couple of books or articles to provide some additional background?

You have a computer, a modem, and a subscription to an on-line data base service. You can, therefore, ask for information on-line. (Any resemblance between the illustration and this book is purely coincidental.)

An appropriate data base would be MAGAZINE INDEX, which contains articles from 435 magazine and journals covering November 1959 through current publication dates. You can search that for articles. Some details in the following description might vary from one system to another, depending upon the kind of hardware, software, and subscriber service being used.

Hooking up the modem. The modem is the "magic box" for translating between the telephone line and the computer. First you plug in your modem to the telephone line and to your computer, then turn it on.

Loading the modem communications software program into the computer. The communications software is the program that makes the modem work.

Dialing the subscriber service. Depending upon how "smart" your modem and software are, the computer may take care of this task for you. When connected, your computer (or terminal) will be in communication with the computer used by the subscriber service; in this case you use DIALOG Information Service.

Logging on and entering the data base. Once connected with the service, it will be necessary to type in your password. Passwords accomplish two things: They tell the subscriber service who is using the service for billing; they also prevent unauthorized use of the service. Once "logged on," it will be necessary to tell the service what data base you are going to use, in this case MAGAZINE INDEX.

Typing in the "Search Terms." Searching is done in most data bases, including MAGAZINE INDEX, by looking for occurrences of terms that will pick up the data you are seeking—in this case for current information on what is going to happen in technology in the next five years.

Terms appropriate to your search include COMPUTERS and TECHNOLOGY. You are also interested in other forms of the terms—COMPUTER in the singular form, for example, or the adjective TECHNOLOGICAL. You can tell the computer to search for all these forms by 'truncating' the terms. Dialog does this by including question marks at appropriate points. COMPUTER? and TECH? will find all occurrences of any word beginning with those letters no matter how the words end.

Keep the search focused upon the topic. You realize you don't want to find *all* the articles that mention the two terms. An article on political campaigns, for example, might contain the sentence, "Senator Snodgrass was noted for his mistrust of *tech*nically sophisticated bulk mailing services." In order to prevent this you type a /TI,DE after the terms. This tells the computer, "Find terms that occur only in a *TI*tle, or that are identified by the data base as important *DE*scriptors of the article's content."

You don't really want all the articles on these two topics, you want only those that have to do with the future. You can search for any articles that mentioned the word FUTURE in either the title or in the list of descriptors, so you search for FUTURE/TI,DE. Just as a hunch, you decide to also throw in any mention of the 1990's, by searching for 199?/TI,DE.

Running the search. You run the search itself by typing in the line,

```
S (COMPUTER?/TI,DE OR TECH?/TI,DE) AND
  (199?/TI,DE OR FUTURE/TI,DE).
```

The line means "Search for articles in which occur any terms that begin with the letters COMPUTER or TECH and 199 or FUTURE, either in the title or in the list of article descriptors."

When the line is run, the computer displays search terms and number of "hits" made with the terms. The search terms are displayed on the right and the numbers of "hits" on the left.

```
3403 COMPUTER?/TI,DE
3447 TECH?/TI,DE
  18 199?/TI,DE
 173 FUTURE/TI,DE
```

The computer then displays:

```
82 (COMPUTER?/TI,DE OR TECH?/TI,DE) AND
   (199?/TI,DE OR FUTURE/TI,DE)
```

This means that the search netted 82 articles that included at least one of the first pair of terms and one of the second pair. You examine the titles and descriptors of the articles.

You instruct the computer to print the abstracts and bibliographic data on these 82 articles so you can examine them more thoroughly off-line. One of them looks like this:

```
1699364  DATABASE: MI File 47  *Use Format 9 for FULL TEXT*
Winners and losers in the fifth generation; the race is
on in four technologies that will be crucial to information
processing in the 1990s.
Withington,  Frederic G.
Datamation    v29  p193(8)   Dec 1983
CODEN: DTMNA
illustration;  graph; chart
AVAILABILITY:    FULL TEXT Online
LINE COUNT: 00372
```

You log off and the service tells you the charges assessed for the search:

```
$33.85  0.403 Hrs File647 4 Descriptors
 $8.20  82 Types
$42.05  Estimated Total Cost
```

You look at a description of all 82 articles. You then log back on and print the full text of the article displayed above (which was the fifty-second article on the list).

It is a *great* article! And finding and printing it has taken less than an hour of your time. In addition to the $42.05 for the search, the service charged you $39.65 for printing it out. Some people would consider a cost of $81.70 prohibitively high, and for most of us it would be—if information is being sought for personal or recreational purposes. If, however, information is needed to enable professionals to accomplish their purposes, the service is a bargain. Consider for a moment the alternative method.

- Drive to library and back (30 minutes).
- Consult the reference materials to discover the 82 possibly appropriate articles (at five minutes per article) (6 hrs., 50 minutes).
- Check the articles carefully enough to have at least a one-sentence idea of what each article contains (at five minutes per article) (6 hrs., 50 minutes).
- Pull the magazine to check the desired article (15 minutes).
- Copy the article (10 minutes).

That's a total of 14 hours and 31 minutes. Subtract the hour required for running the search and printing the article, and you find a net savings of 13 hours and 31 minutes.

Not only was the on-line research more efficient, it was far more effective. By hand, your great article might never have been found. How many years would it take in print media to search for all articles in up to 25 years of back issues of 435 magazines that use any form of the words "technical" and "computer" and that contain any references to the 1990's or to the word "future"? Years!! How much would your electronic search cost per hour when compared to doing the same thing by hand? Far less than a single penny!!

3
Enhancing Our Life Style

Our exploration of the future of microcomputing will now focus on ways in which computers will enhance our enjoyment of culture. "Culture," in this sense, refers to aspects of life that give pattern, meaning, and value to our day-to-day activities as human beings.

In a sense, the whole book is about culture. For example, the discussion about telecommunications contained a great deal that will impact on the style and quality of our lives by affecting communications. Interpersonal relationships, built as they are on communications, are an integral part of the culture in which we live. As another example, the degree to which computers extend our minds and become appliances, assisting us in thinking and making decisions will also significantly influence our daily living, both together and separately.

Some aspects of the microcomputer revolution, however, apply the computer directly to specific phases of our daily lives. These must be addressed if our assessment of the future of microcomputing is not to be hopelessly barren.

This chapter, then, will turn its attention to three aspects of culture that the microcomputer will dramatically impact in the remaining years of the 1980's. The three areas are: the arts, education, and daily living. Daily living encompasses published information like newspapers, books, and magazines; our work; and the role played by environments and robots in our mid-term future. These three areas are the most important manifestations of culture that will be altered by the microcomputer.

Computers and the Arts

The microcomputer will enjoy increased popularity in the next several years as both collaborator and medium in music, the visual arts, and the world of creative writing.

As a collaborator, the computer will assist musicians, artists, dramatists, filmmakers, and other creative people in their explorations of art and its forms.

The computer already plays this role in the lives of many artists. Others, overestimating the intelligence of the machine, fear that the computer will become, as one musician put it, ". . . a juggernaut rolling over their creative contributions." But, as we will see in the discussion that follows, microcomputers are simply too limited to play the role of serious *creator* of art and music. They can only suggest direction and play "what if" with designs and concepts. They "create" art or music of their own, however, only in a shallow sense.

Computers can *appear* creative by using randomness, one of their cleverest intelligence-imitators. But they will not take over for human artists. Creativity, when it comes from a computer, is always as an extension of the creative powers of the person who wrote the program.

The computer is not a creating entity but is only a creative instrument or tool, much like a piano, palette, or typewriter. It is, to be sure, different from all of these in the sense that it is capable of being "told" to perform certain tasks and then of performing them flawlessly and endlessly. But it is still a tool, at best an obedient assistant. Its contribution to the human experience will be substantial, if the technology is placed into the hands of talented people.

With those caveats and preliminaries in mind, we will explore the possibilities of the microcomputer in the arts, beginning with music, then moving to the visual arts, and concluding with thoughts about the microcomputer and the creative writing profession.

Computer Music

The most sophisticated home and personal microcomputers on the market have limited sound capabilities when judged by the standards of musical instruments and symphony orchestras. The early microcomputers, for example, the Apple II and Radio Shack's TRS-80 Model I, had only one voice, or sound, the user could control. With programming skills, the owner of one of these early computers could create raspy, buzzy melody lines. Harmony, however, was beyond the grasp of these early machines. The early seventies' computers produced sound by putting signals through a built-in, decidedly low fidelity speaker.

In the mid-1970's, Atari and Commodore introduced computers that could produce four-channel sound through the speaker of the television set or display terminal to which they were attached. This enabled harmonizing of the four voices and, for the first time, something sounding like "real" music began to come out of computers. Soon, Texas Instruments, Timex, and Coleco, among others, followed suit with even newer and more sophisticated sound production.

By the early 1980's, some products on the market, using the sound controllers in these computers and clever programming, permitted microcomputers to "speak" words typed in at the keyboard or stored on the disk or in memory by a program. In a few years inexpensive microcomputers had gone from hoarse beepings and clickings to a semblance of human speech.

Sound on computers has not, however, made a great deal of progress since that time. There are now a few somewhat more sophisticated computers, notably Apple's Macintosh, Atari's 130ST and Commodore's highly touted Amiga, which can perhaps simulate human speech a bit more efficiently and effectively than earlier computers. A few microcomputer-based music editors and programs produce music with an interesting sound. But most advances in this aspect of the industry have taken place in the development of peripherals—synthesizers, keyboards, and recording apparatus. These attach to computers and produce sounds that are close to genuine music.

In the last year, some exciting developments have taken place in the world of computers and music. The emergence of the MIDI (Musical Instrument Digital Interface) standard has made it possible to connect music synthesizers directly to personal computers. And personal computers have begun including MIDI hardware and software capability to accommodate this creative connection.

The emergence of low-cost (translation: under $500) full-power synthesizers capable of being coupled to home computers has brought us one giant step closer to the reality of the one-person recording studio. Major instrument manufacturers like Wurlitzer and Yamaha have begun including MIDI interfaces in their organs and Casio, which has made a small fortune in intelligent portable musical keyboards in the past two or three years, promises a full line of low-cost synthesizers. Yamaha has also begun marketing a line of such products, which are not typically available in computer stores but rather in music shops.

That will continue to be the case for the foreseeable future. Major advances in computer sound production design will not take place. One reason for this is that the issue falls into a kind of crack in the market. Music professionals will probably not find acceptable anything computer makers do to make music sound as if it had more quality. Trained ears will always demand real instruments connected to the computer. Non-professionals are already incapable of discriminating between sounds and sound quality well enough to pay extra for a computer with higher quality sound. So there is no incentive for the computer manufacturers to make major changes in the sound now being used in home and personal computers.

Yet musicians will continue to stretch the musical limits of the computer. There seems, indeed, to be an almost uncanny link between musicians and computer professionals. In researching this book, we talked with dozens of people who are doing exciting things with computers and found that a disproportionately high number of them were interested in music well beyond the listening stage. For example, Pierre Bierre is an artificial intelligence researcher who plays synthesizer in a new wave rock band in his spare time; Dr. Robert Lindamood, founder of a computerized family and psychological counseling service, has played music since his teen years and remains a devotee of Thelonius Monk.

The link is not surprising. In its theoretical base, music is a very mathematical, regular, symmetrical, orderly, and predictable phenomenon. The patterns that create the sound of notes—the waveforms generated, for example, by the plucking of a guitar string or the vibration of a reed in a saxophone—have interesting mathematical properties that lend themselves very well to the world of electronics. It is not surprising, then, that much of the early work in computers that took place in engineering laboratories on college campuses across the country in the 1960's and 1970's focused on music. Musicians and engineers tend to have more in common than those who belong to one group but not the other would probably want to admit.

Two men interested in the connection between music and computers from different perspectives will provide some insight into the potential for the relationship between these two seemingly unrelated art forms.

The Musical Mosquito and Robb Murray

By day, Robb Murray, age 31, is a systems analyst for the Chicago headquarters of Beatrice Foods. By night, he is a music composer who " . . . never heard my music played accurately or up to speed by anyone, including myself, during 12 years of composing" until a friend introduced him to the Radio Shack TRS-80 and a software-hardware add-on called Orchestra 80 (Orch 80 for short). Now he has released the first record of originally composed music written for the instrument that is the microcomputer.

His 45 r.p.m. record "Classical Mosquito" has eight original compositions. The record sold only a few hundred copies in its first year on the market, but was well-received by local radio and TV stations. Its introduction got Murray notice in the national press.

"Classical Mosquito" earned Murray plaudits from such diverse publications as *Polyphony* magazine and a newsletter called *Small Computers in the Arts News*. The record's eight original compositions have a definite Baroque organ sound—in a higher pitched tone. This is not surprising, considering Murray does most of his original composition work on a fifteenth century virginal, or harpsichord.

"Going the independent route in music distribution is really difficult," Murray admits. "I learned the hard way about packaging, merchandising, competition, and the other non-musical aspects of this business in bringing 'Classical Mosquito' to the market."

Murray was able to convince a number of Chicago area record stores to handle the record, but says he'll do things differently the next time around. "For one thing, the 45 r.p.m. format was wrong," he says candidly. "I guess it was a throwback to my younger days when my parents had me in a record-of-the-month club at the age of two and taking serious music lessons at age five. At that time we had 45 r.p.m. records. Next time, I'll use one of the new 33-1/3 r.p.m. single record formats."

Another change Murray expects to make is the kind of music he produces. " 'Classical Mosquito' was fine for my intended audience," he says. "But I realize that if I want to get more attention from the buying public, I'm going to have to compose in some other musical style." His next effort will probably be on an Apple IIe with playback through the external speaker connector. And it will be in the pop/rock/folk genre rather than the classical Baroque vein.

As to the technology, Murray is an enthusiastic supporter and an avid fan. "I can hardly bring myself to leave the computer alone," he says. "The technology is a major advance in the democratization of composing." The computer enables budding composers who can't afford the expense of studios and musicians opportunities to try out musical ideas, hear their compositions played as they expected to hear them, modify, and produce them. Murray expects the microcomputer to awaken a resurgence in original American music composition.

Orch 80 permits users to program music in four simultaneous voices over a six-octave range. At the time Murray began his musical exploration on the micro, this was the most advanced and capable peripheral for music on the market. Today, there are a few that are far better, but they work with the Apple II family rather than the Radio Shack line of computers.

"When I compose," Murray says, "I use the computer as a collaborator and a sounding board. I can program a phrase, a few measures, or a whole composition, listen to it played back, pick up nuances I'd like to change, make the changes, and listen to it again."

Like most composers, regardless of the final instruments they intend their compositions to be performed on, Murray first works out the basic idea and melody line on a musical keyboard. He then takes the melodic line to the microcomputer, types in the appropriate codes to produce the desired note values and durations, and listens to the composition play back through the synthesizer at the heart of Orch 80.

Though he's not at all ready to give up his full-time job, Murray clearly is fascinated by computer composition. The quality of the music he composes and produces goes well beyond most of what passes for computer music and has an organ-like quality that is vaguely familiar to the untrained ear.

He believes in the next few years, as more and more composers, professional and amateur alike, discover the microcomputer and what it can do for them as musicians, there will be a dramatic increase in the business of selling computer music.

Making Composition Easier

If Murray provides an example of music *performance* on a micro, then Dan Sevush provides a corresponding example of music-composing *techniques* for the little computers. Sevush is the designer of a product that he hopes to have on the market in the next year or year and a half called Music Productivity Tool, or MPT for short (see Musical Virtuosos on a Disk?). Sevush is one of several people we uncovered who are working on programs to make the process of composing music on a micro easier and more creative.

Sevush has some interesting ideas to combine with his new product. "For the composer," Sevush believes, "the computer should be an assistant, helping to complete ideas. It should do things like suggest harmonies, melodic completion ideas, and even arrangements of original pieces." The ideas propounded by Sevush go well beyond the music editors in use today.

Current music editors are tools that enable a composer like Murray to put his composition into terms the computer can use to reproduce his music. But they cannot, for example, provide automatic harmonization. By programming such a tool to know about harmonies and to suggest alternative harmonies to a composer, Sevush believes he can free the composer to concentrate on the more artistic elements of the work. At the same time, the human composer remains in charge; he can override the computer's suggestions, modify, or accept them.

Sevush even sees the possibility for a music composition computer program to help the composer bring a good, strong melodic line design to a logical and musically sound conclusion. "Sometimes," the accomplished musician says, "the progression of notes we have created for the bulk of a piece cries out for some logical conclusion. A computer can help us to find that conclusion by analyzing the movement of the piece up to a certain point and then pointing the way to the next steps."

Addressing Murray's observations about hearing one's own composition played as one intended it to be played, Sevush plans to incorporate personality modules in his MPT product that will enable the musician to pick a famous performer on a particular instrument and hear how that musician would perform the piece. One of the performers the program "knows" about might even be the composer himself.

Music Made Easier: Mac Style

Most musical composition programs require a great deal of understanding of music theory to be usable. This is true even of those programs described by their users as "easy to use."

To create musical compositions using these programs, the would-be Mozart must understand harmonics, pitch, timing, measure definition, and a host of other difficult parts of musical theory.

Apple's Macintosh computer is beginning to solve this problem. Two programs currently on the market make it possible for *relatively* uninitiated music lovers to program their own music into the Mac. One of these, MusicWorks, was created by the well-known and well-heeled Hayden Software. The other product is ConcertWare, from a start-up company called Great Wave Software of Menlo Park, California.

ConcertWare is perhaps the most exciting product we ever saw on a microcomputer. We demonstrated the program to friends who were themselves computer programmers, and they observed that the program performed in ways they didn't know were possible on a computer. When asked to guess the price of the software, guesses ran between $300 and $500. The initial retail price, however, was under $50.

ConcertWare will be a precursor of creativity-enhancing programs to come; as such, it is worth spending a few moments describing.

ConcertWare is described by musicians as bringing the power and scope of a $30,000 synthesizer to a $2,000 computer. With it, would-be composers can create whole new sounds (which can then be given instruments' names and even icons—small pictures—by which they can be called into use). Users can also change the instrumentation in an arrangement or composition.

ConcertWare provides users with limited knowledge of musical theory a great deal of benefit and enjoyment. On one level, entering existing music into the Mac to be replayed later is as easy a process as we've seen anywhere. Users select which of four voices they wish to enter music for. Using the Mac's ubiquitous mouse, users simply click on a note value (whole note, dotted quarter note, etc.) and then place it on the desired staff line. ConcertWare takes care of the rest. It simply adds the note to the already existing score or, if in editing mode, it inserts the note in the position selected. The program is smart enough to know when to insert measure lines, even when human users are not.

Users even less sophisticated musically than that can simply enjoy hearing the nearly three dozen pieces of music thoughtfully provided by Great Wave Software. The selections range from Bach and Bartok to Scott Joplin and well-known folk songs. Adventuresome users can easily change the instrument(s) used to perform each piece. For example, you might want to hear how Scott Joplin's "Entertainer" would sound with saxophones instead of the piano. Go ahead and try it! Or try a saxophone on one voice and pianos on the other three. This brings a level of "what if" experimentation to music that has been difficult or cumbersome to obtain using earlier microcomputer software. Exactly as electronic spreadsheets made the way computers dealt with numbers more human, so programs like ConcertWare (and its follow-up, ConcertWare +) and Hayden's MusicWorks will bring a measure of humanity to the way computers handle music as input and output.

ConcertWare and other music composition programs on the market and soon to come for the Mac require no external hardware. You may, however, wish to plug a speaker or (as one friend did) a pre-amp and a stereo system into the Mac's external speaker jack to hear the sound played more fully and loudly.

ConcertWare is just a beginning. More and more programs like ConcertWare will appear on the market in the near future to assist artists, authors, musicians, and other creative people to do their jobs more enjoyably and easily—and to provide possibilities for hours of creative fun for all of us.

Since the Mac appeals broadly to people who have not previously been computer owners or users, many new artists will emerge from this new medium.

The Interest is Serious

There is a layer of very serious interest in the computer as composer or instrument. A very serious think tank in Stanford, California, known affectionately as "karma" (from its acronym CCRMA, which stands for Center for Computer Research in Music and Acoustics), has spent several years researching the use of computers as music synthesizers and instruments.

Armed with grants from the National Endowment for the Arts, National Science Foundation, and nearby Stanford University, CCRMA has undertaken leading-edge work in the field of computer music. The center has a composer in residence, Fred Malouf, and a whole gaggle of computer gear based on the obscure Foonly F4 processor.

In a recent newspaper interview, Malouf pointed out that "Acoustical instruments have not evolved as fast as contemporary music has." The last acoustical instrument invented was the saxophone, more than 100 years ago!

Although CCRMA scientists and musicians are not working on a microcomputer, the work they are doing will undoubtedly influence the next wave of music composition software for the micro world.

The Computer as Composer

Before we leave the subject of music and computers, we should pause for a few moments' reflection on the question of whether a computer program, given some built-in artificial intelligence capability, could in fact compose a musical piece that human listeners would find satisfying. Recognizing the subjective nature of that judgment, it is still possible to answer with a qualified yes.

For example, the computer could be programmed to generate quasi-random groups of sounds fitting within certain parameters and meeting certain rules. It could then play those notes for a composer-user who is looking for an idea or a theme. If the computer found something the composer thought was intriguing, he could then save that combination of notes on the disk and begin using them as the kernel of a new composition.

A purist might argue that a computer producing random combinations of sound in accordance with certain rules and parameters can hardly be thought of as composing, at least not in the same sense as Mozart or Bach or even Robb Murray. But we understand almost nothing about the human creative process, for all we know, randomness *is* creativity. Ask a professional composer how he comes up with ideas for new pieces, and the chances are he will not be able to explain the process either.

Whatever we call it, however we characterize it, there will be an increasingly close connection between computers and the world of music in the next five years. The "boom" in that industry may not come in that time; in fact, it almost certainly won't. But rapid growth of new compositions, new tools, and new ideas is all but inevitable.

Someday, we may all stand in line to pay for the right to listen to a little black box on a stage play original compositions for us. It's only a question of time. More and more talented humans are adopting and adapting to this technology.

Computer Images as a New Art Form

The quality of pictures generated by the personal computers that are the focus of this book are a far cry from the quality of those generated by a television from broadcast signals. Anyone who has ever seen a television show and then looked at a computer display on the same screen generally needs no convincing. Diagonal and curved lines are irregular, stair-stepped, and funny-looking.

Graphics expert Peter Black believes that graphics on microcomputers will improve until the computer can produce television-quality images, which he refers to from a graphics standpoint as "medium resolution." They would clearly be very high resolution by today's standards in micros.

"A TV screen," Black says, "is capable of handling 483 vertical lines and horizontally about 600-800 color pixels, or dots. A good quality monitor not meant for TV reception, like those used with some computer systems, could get many more pixels, both horizontally and vertically."

Microcomputer graphics will not get better than TV resolution. "There is," Black says, "no market demand to go higher than TV quality in resolution in the foreseeable future; TV is what people's expectations of computers are coming to, if they haven't indeed already reached that point."

The major advances in the next five years in computer graphics will, Black believes, result in more and more color "bandwidth" in the color graphics business. "Basically, that means we can put more and more colors on a screen at once." He believes that achieving realistic flesh tones with computer-generated video is "definitely attainable in the five-year time frame between now and 1990."

The biggest constraint on better quality video graphics on microcomputers right now, Black points out, is the cost of the memory chips in which the image must be stored before it can be displayed on the video screen. "As the cost of RAM memory comes down," he believes, "the sophistication level will go way up."

Color limitations mean that the display can be bright and vivid but often not very realistic. Selection is limited to the colors that may be viewed on the screen, what colors may be used together, and at what level of resolution various colors and color combinations may be used (see Computers Get the Picture). But that doesn't make them acceptable, particularly to artists.

Yet computer art is one of the most visible and rapidly growing areas of the use of microcomputers in the world. Strong, meaningful graphic displays have long been viewed as being essential elements in video games, educational programs, and elsewhere. A great deal of experimentation in the field of computer art has been undertaken. Some of the results are quite good.

Richard Lowenberg: A Serious Techno-Artist

One of the people who has played a leading role in what has happened in computer art is well-known video artist Richard Lowenberg (see Richard Lowenberg's *Ape Story*). Lowenberg describes the area of technologically aided art as one fraught with problems. "There has been—and I have done—very little that could be called art, but a great deal of technical demonstration and exhibits." Believing it will require 10 to 15 years of work with this new medium before something "artful" can be produced, Lowenberg is, by his timetable, just reaching that point.

For someone who has been involved with high technology art since his early days as a videotape experimenter and guru in New York, Lowenberg has a strangely iconoclastic attitude about the role of microcomputers in the life of the artist. "These tools, still in their infancy, are nonetheless tremendous educational aids that enable and even force us to think more broadly and differently about problem-solving."

Not confining his interest in art to microcomputers, Lowenberg has experimented with satellites, multi-spectral imaging devices, bio-telemetry/sensing, and many other technical tools and tricks. He gets support for such work from the National Aeronautics and Space Administration at NASA's Ames Research Facility in Mountain View, California. "NASA has a mandate to share technology with the private sector," he says. "But most of the requests they get are from people who want to use the technology in commercial applications, which is quite different from my interests. I discovered that they were required to be helpful to the private sector and began to build relationships there which have been helpful in a number of projects." He has, for example, been taken along on free-fall flight tests where he and a small troupe of dancers were choreographed while rigged with biofeedback devices. The digital image resulting from this exercise could then be converted to music—or to numerous other forms—and examined for artistic potential.

On one occasion, Lowenberg found a way to do something particularly satisfying to his sense of social responsibility for the technology. "NASA had given me access to a wireless biofeedback mechanism, called an EMG device, which they had developed to help keep track of astronauts' muscular movements and functions in space. We were doing some interesting experiments with it as a possible art medium. Meanwhile, they were using the same device with children in Stanford Children's Hospital who were suffering from degenerative muscle diseases, monitoring their muscle movements and trying to determine where problems were."

Lowenberg got the idea to hook these children's EMG units to a digitizer that would in turn create sounds from their movements in such a way that coordinated muscle action resulted in pleasant musical sounds and muscle action not being well controlled by the patient resulted in noise and sound effects. "Instead of just monitoring them, we found we could often make some progress in helping them recover some control of muscles and limbs by this feedback technique," he says. The obvious satisfaction of having had a role in such an event is evident in his voice.

Lowenberg sees art as one subset of information being communicated and moved around in the information society. A few years ago, he got interested in gorillas as possible communicators. He helped design the habitat in which the world-famous gorilla Koko, who communicates with her human friends in American Sign Language, lives in the San Francisco Bay-area. As he explored gorillas further, he found that re-creating believable gorillas on the stage required ". . . a great deal of work and technology."

His currently in-production play, *Ape Story*, has a gorilla as the main character. "We use a new skin membrane, advanced prosthetics (limbs and other artificial body parts), robotics (particularly to make facial movements accurate), and underneath it all a liquid-cooled suit from NASA without which the human actor inside the realistic gorilla system couldn't last for very long."

Parts of the play were slated to be performed in late 1985, with the full production set, hopefully, in mid-1986.

Lowenberg's current favorite art form for the microcomputer is the theater. "It is," he says firmly, "a form ripe for dealing with the computer both as a contributor and as a danger to society." His play is intended for live presentation but strikes a balance between live performance and the use of film as a backdrop against which the action takes place.

On a deeper level, Lowenberg is concerned about "the role the arts have to play in the proposed information society that is largely commercial in its interests." As a result of that concern, he is seeking innovative strategies that can be explored to involve the companies who are creating this new society in supporting the arts. "I hope to get a lot of small amounts of technical and financial support from lots of companies rather than having a single sponsor for the production of a piece like *Ape Story*. Getting sponsorship at all will be particularly difficult since the play doesn't always present technology in a favorable light."

He is, however, opposed to negating technology "merely out of ignorance." Instead, he insists, "the more we learn about the technology—how it works, its real potential—the more sound reasons we have for being cautious about its application to our daily lives."

Lowenberg and a dozen or so other artists interested in high technology as a medium regularly display their works at such industry-wide events as the annual SIGGRAPH graphics conferences. The subject of the arts in the forthcoming information society is always widely and heatedly discussed during these conferences.

Artist in Control of Machine

Another computer artist encountered in researching this book was John Lifton, who will be known in the next few years for his contribution in city-building rather than in the visual arts. Lifton (see John Lifton's Parallel Worlds) is working on an opera that marries that classic art form with high technology.

"As a result of years of work in the field, I am very interested in the issue of delegating high-level creative judgment to machines and maintaining human control in the process," he says. "The opera on which I am currently working involves strong interaction between the performers and a synthesizer. The machinery will be under the musicians' control; the music will be created by the performance itself."

This interactive live music environment offers, he says, "a good specific container within which to focus my work and interest in the area of creativity and computers." His goal: "We have to find ways of making the machines understand our ways of thinking and then forcing them to be compassionate with us."

A San Francisco Bay area artist who has become widely known for his experimentation in interactive and artificially intelligent *objets d'art*, Stephen Wilson, an art professor at San Francisco State University, has set up interactive works of art in such unlikely places as a department store window on a busy urban street and the escalator wells at the University of Illinois at Chicago campus.

Professor Wilson offers a warning: "Artists have historically stood watch at the cultural frontier. But now they are in danger of failing as interpreters and forecasters of culture as the frontier becomes increasingly technological. The traditional materials they use will lack the creative punch of the technological developments to which they respond."

Wilson is a countering influence to that trend. He has focused his work almost exclusively on the computer, more specifically on the micro. Professor Wilson engaged in a variety of innovative art creation:

- interactive performances—decisions about how a story line should proceed are made on the basis of audience desires as expressed through microcomputers,
- interactive environments—including computerized street events, the department store display, and
- works like "Time Poet" that connect and respond to changes in their environment.

"Time Poet" capitalizes on the fact that micros keep track of time. The computer creates visual images and sounds that vary from time to time during a day and from day to day as seasons progress. The program also keeps track of how long it's been running—its age, if you will—and comments on the number of passings of suns, moon, and seasons it has "lived" through.

Speech, memory-dependence, and multi-user environments have also been working media for Wilson's state-of-the-art art, but it is perhaps in his application of the ideas of AI to creation of art that Wilson is most advanced.

One AI art experiment, where audience participation determined plot direction, was entitled "Interactive Computer Theater." Wilson had four audience groups of human observers in plain view of one another. A fifth voting group was hidden behind a curtain so that in any given situation five votes were being cast. The fifth group, which appeared to be merely separated physically from the other groups, was actually a computer program. "I tried to design a voting 'intelligence' that would purposely antagonize other groups. At the end of the evening the computer asked all groups to individually applaud each of the other groups who had participated. When the computer screen asked for applause for Group 5, I opened the curtain to reveal no one was there."

Wilson sees this as a variation on the Turing test theme (see p. 54). He indicated it was quite successful.

These artists who make technology their canvas and their brush are examples of how advances in microcomputer technology will indelibly change art in the next few years.

Another aspect of culture that is in for some (potentially) rude awakenings is the field of creative writing.

Tales of the Policeman's Beard

In late 1984, a book called *The Policeman's Beard is Half-Constructed* appeared on the nation's bookshelves. It was billed as the first book ever written by a computer. The book was the product of a computer program called Racter, which was designed by William Chamberlain and Thomas Etter. The program is commercially available for the IBM PC.

Essentially, Racter chooses words and phrases semi-randomly from files of words and word patterns. Earlier computer programs had been designed that did the same thing, but their literary products made little or no sense most of the time. Racter, on the other hand, has been programmed to understand some connections between certain classes of objects and events in real life.

Racter's products *sound* somewhat intelligent—some of the time. Most of what Racter generates is gibberish and nonsense, but occasionally the program turns out a paragraph that seems to make sense and almost all of what it produces has some kind of logic to it, even though the connections may not be all that clear to a rational human being.

A reading of samples from the book and from subsequent program runs published elsewhere (see Racter) reveals a kind of illogical logic, a connection between things that is not part of reality but that nonetheless makes some kind of sense.

Although the appearance of Racter's literary effort has focused attention on the subject, the issue of computers as tools and collaborators for writers has been around nearly as long as the use of computers in music. Hobbyists spent time in the late 1970's and early 1980's experimenting with artificial intelligence on home computers. They often used a program that generated Haiku poetry (a highly structured, expressive, and concentrated form of verse native to Japan). Some of the poems could be read with understanding and even something akin to appreciation.

Many of the productivity tools on the market are aimed at the vast number of people in this country who write. They may write professionally, as authors of books, articles and newsletters; vocationally, as managers who write memos, reports, and correspondence; or recreationally, as people who write letters, notes, and meeting minutes for local clubs and their own families. Word processing packages, spelling checkers, typesetting programs, and a host of other pieces of computer software are designed to make writers more productive, efficient, and artistically fulfilled. Whether they have had that effect or not remains to be seen, but the fact is that a great many professional writers—including myself—would no more think of turning on their old electric typewriters than they would return to pencil and paper. There will always be some writers who will buck such a trend, of course, but on the whole writers either already have such support tools or wish they could have them.

Beyond such tools, which may make a writer more productive but have little or no impact on his literary style, there are tools aimed at improving the quality of what we write. Two recent ones include a grammar and word usage checking program and a thesaurus. There are several examples of the former. Their role is to check for consistency between nouns and pronouns, spot trite, overworked phrases and suggest alternative wording, and look for other common grammatical and syntactical errors the writer may want to correct before sending his material to his publisher. Some of these programs allow the writer to add a list of hackneyed expressions the computer will attempt to help the writer correct.

Another helpful tool for writers is the electronic thesaurus. The best one we know of is Synonym Finder, marketed by Mike Weiner of Writing Consultants. Weiner's story is told elsewhere in this section.

Synonym Finder, based on the linguistic work of Chuck Woolford, has a 90,000-word dictionary: 9,000 words you can find synonyms for, each of which produces an average of 10 synonyms. To use it, one simply positions the cursor over the word for which a synonym is desired and presses two keys. Part of the screen display is replaced by the word (if it's in the thesaurus) or the one closest to it in spelling. All the synonyms for that word appear in the window with the word itself. The writer can then choose any of the synonyms merely by positioning a cursor on the word to be substituted and pressing the Carriage Return key. Synonym Finder automatically replaces the word in the text, adjusting the spacing if necessary and retaining upper and lower case in equivalent positions in the new word.

Writing Consultants has followed another trend outlined in this book. As we were going to press, the company lowered the price from the original $125 to $80, acknowledging the movement toward lower priced, fully functional software.

Another class of programs designed to aid writers and others with the creative process are the idea processors, sometimes referred to as computer-assisted thinking. These range from outline generators to real decision-making aids like ods/CONSULTANT. More information on this class of software products can be found in Software Advances, Chapter 5 of this book.

Beyond Tools

If the microcomputer did no more than has already been out-lined to help writers to be more efficient and perhaps express themselves better, it would have become entrenched as a highly desirable tool for writers to possess. But experimenters in artificial intelligence have gone even further in their explorations of the relationship between computers and writing. They have designed programs that write stories with beginnings, middles, and ends. The stories are primitive and not very interesting, but research is still being carried out in this area. With Racter trailblazing the path, the last half of this decade will see a collection of stories created by an artificially intelligent computer program appear on the bookshelves—perhaps even a novel or a novella.

If that happens, we may have Dr. Roger Schank and his Yale colleagues to thank. This group has done much of the pioneering work in the area of Natural Language Processing (NLP), the branch of AI research that is interested in the ability of a computer to be trained to understand and communicate with human beings in their natural languages instead of in its languages.

James Meehan of Yale, a colleague of Dr. Schank's, has been an early leader in this field. He did his Ph.D. dissertation on the subject of "The Meta-novel: Writing Stories by Computer" and is the author of a program called TALE-SPIN. This program, which runs on a very large, mainframe computer, "simulates a small world of characters who are motivated to act by having problems to solve," Meehan says in describing the software. From a limited choice of characters, settings, props, and events, TALE-SPIN generates a story that has a beginning (the occurrence of a problem), a middle (the characters' discovery of the problem and their attempts to solve it), and an end (successful resolution, in most cases).

This kind of approach to programming and the use of programs could conceivably lead to a situation in the next few years in which a writer can obtain a program that will help to overcome one of a writer's greatest fears, writer's block.

Writer's block occurs when we can't come up with an idea or a concept we need to begin or continue our work on a writing assignment. If we had a variation on the TALE-SPIN theme, we could say, in effect, "OK, computer. I've got a situation where my characters are thus and so and my situation is like this and I'm stuck. Any ideas?" The computer would spin out a small tale, or part of one, which, even if it isn't terribly good or salable in its own right may trigger some thinking on the part of the writer.

We do not, we should point out in conclusion, subscribe to the theory that a computer will ever replace artists, musicians, or writers. The concept of creating involves the concept of purpose and, while we certainly can't deny that monkeys, apes, gorillas, and other animals have definite senses of purpose in many situations, their purposes are not the kinds that can be satisfied by writing a book or a story.

Nonetheless, it is unarguably true that one of the characteristics that sets man apart from other animals is his ability—and motivation—to create. As computers approach this lofty goal and ambition via improved software and hardware described here and belsewhere in this book, they cannot help but be perceived as more human and humane. After all, who could get mad at a computer that could make up—and tell—a clever bedtime story?

Education: The Unfulfilled Promise

When television burst on the American scene in the 1950's, many commentators thought they saw in it a limitless potential for educating the masses of America. Now, some 30 years after its arrival, this promise has been largely unfulfilled.

In the 1970's and early 1980's when microcomputers exploded into American consciousness and became a part of our TV advertising-supported way of life, many other commentators thought they saw in the new technology a limitless potential for educating the masses of America. The parallel with TV is, so far, intact: Computers currently appear to be failing in reaching their potential as educational tools. The next few years, however, will see a big advancement as computers become major educational tools. Education is one aspect of culture where the computer will have an *irresistible potential* for great enhancement.

The next five years will see home and personal computers begin to realize some of their potential unleashed by new developments as aids to learning. Whether American buyers broadly take advantage of this new potential remains to be seen. These developments will be manifested in three significant ways: making education more accessible, making education more enjoyable, and making the creation of computer-aided education easier, so more subjects can be taught well using microcomputers than might appear possible today.

The accessibility issue is dealt with in Chapter 2, Broadening Our Community. The most significant development that will make greater access to educational programs a reality in the years just ahead is telecommunications. This technology allows a computer in a home or office to communicate with large computer systems in other places—even in other countries—by the use of telephone lines, microwave transmission, or satellite. On-line universities offering full degree programs are already a reality.

Making education more enjoyable is really only one aspect of the whole issue of computer-assisted learning. A great amount of research firmly indicates people who learn subjects using computers learn better, retain what they learn longer, and can use what they know more effectively than people who learn using more conventional methods. This is not a secret. Nor, for the most part, is it any longer subject to the wrenching debates that wracked the educational establishment in the late 1960's and 1970's when this research was being done.

So far, the microcomputer industry has developed learning programs aimed primarily at the younger portion of the student audience: pre-school, early elementary, and early secondary school students. There has been very little work on commercially available material for adults or even college-level education. Much of what has been done in those areas has been done on college campuses for specific courses and instructors and would generally not find broad applicability outside that setting.

Computer-assisted learning generally falls into one of two broad categories: computer-aided instruction (CAI) (see Computer Aided Instruction) and simulation. CAI is a method of teaching objective facts and conveying information. Simulation provides the user with an opportunity to learn by doing something in a way that resembles the application of the skill or information involved as it would be applied in a real-life setting.

A simple example of this is a program available on Apple computers called Lemonade Stand. Users run a lemonade stand and make choices about such things as how much advertising to order and how much lemonade to prepare for the next day's sales. The choices are made on the basis of a daily weather forecast, which is sometimes not very accurate. The program then tells how much lemonade was sold that day, what the expenses were, and what the current profit/loss situation looks like. Users are then given a new forecast and a new opportunity to buy advertising and prepare more lemonade.

Another variation on that theme goes by various names, the best-known of which is Hammurabi. The program permits users to govern a mythical kingdom, trying to maintain a balance between the amount of grain planted for harvest, the amount sold (and for what prices), the sale and repurchase of land, and other variables.

At the end of each year, or turn, the computer performs some calculations and informs the player of the degree of success or failure. After a 10-year reign, the player is rated with some very humorous comments, for example: "Because of your stupidity, your reign of terror has come to abrupt end in open rebellion. You are far below average, Hammurabi."

Programs like Lemonade Stand and Hammurabi were pioneers. They served as models for a number of simulations that followed. Some of the best-selling software currently on the market include stock market, commodity trading, and business management simulations. An AI program, Truckin', discussed in Extending Our Minds, is the most advanced example of such a product.

Simulations have looked like games and so had been shunned by the educational establishment until recently. Some of the best-known simulations involved re-staging famous battles in American history where the student becomes a field general and positions troops under his or her command as desired. Sometimes multiple players compete against each other to see who can alter the actual outcome of the battle.

In the process of engaging in the simulation, the students learn a lot of material about the subject: who the original participants were, where the battle was fought, the strategies involved, the problems to be overcome, the consequences of defeat or victory, the difficulty of real time life-or-death decisions, and perhaps even the reason the battle was fought in the first place.

Other simulations provide the user with the opportunity to test a skill that would otherwise be difficult, impossible, or dangerous for him to test in a real-life situation.

Two prime examples of testing difficult or dangerous skills are programs that simulate a nuclear reactor in operation and a flight simulator.

The nuclear reactor programs involve highly complex, realistic representations of a nuclear reactor control room during an emergency situation. Users help construct the reactor and in the process learn a great deal about pressures, flows, temperatures, reactions, valves, and controls. They must then make accurate split-second decisions to avoid having the simulated reactor blow up or melt down.

There are several flight simulator programs on the market. These permit student pilots to take off, fly, and land various kinds of aircraft at various real-life and fictional airports, under all sorts of simulated weather and emergency conditions. Obviously, simulation provides the student with opportunities to develop skills which, if improperly used in real life, would not offer very forgiving learning situations.

Such simulations have about them an aura of reality, but it is an aura only. Efforts to make both CAI and simulations more enjoyable and valuable are being made by people involved in research in AI. Programs that incorporate AI concepts into them will be able to learn from the student where he or she is having particular difficulty and provide reinforcement of the learning process. Similarly, such programs will be able to detect areas where the student's skill level has already reached a plateau and offer greater challenge and stimulation in those areas. In other words, the programs will be able to adapt to the user's needs, interests, and even learning goals and objectives.

These programs will be friendly in their interactions with their student-users. They will keep track of students' previous answers and problems, and tailor feedback to the student to a degree far beyond today's simple-minded, "That's right, Jenny. Good answer!" which is how most computerized educational programs limit their feedback to the student.

Another current trend in educational software is the appearance on the market of logic games. These products, discussed in more depth in Software Advances require the user-student to solve logic problems. Some of these products are quite well suited to adult audiences.

A big flaw in a great deal of the educational software on the market is that it does not tie into school curricula very well. Some of it does, but on the whole the computer has been viewed as an enrichment learning tool that amplifies mainstream learning rather than directly supporting it. This is partly because the best person to create educational software that will be relevant in the classroom is the classroom teacher.

Unfortunately, tools for developing useful, entertaining, and relevant educational programs have not been particularly helpful or accessible to classroom teachers. The present tools have tended either to create boring, straightforward learning materials, which were characterized by their users as "mere page-turners," or they were complex to use. In other words, either they took the place of a book without adding anything to the learning process or they required the teacher to learn programming or at least grasp how the computer could work to handle a particular subject or situation.

Useful tools have now begun to appear, and many more will become available between now and 1990.

One such tool will be marketed by a start-up company, Microlytics, of Fairport, New York. This company (see Mike Weiner: A Boost from Xerox and He's Off!) has a unique deal with Xerox enabling it to bring to market software products that the giant company can't figure out what to do with.

The first product, Tutorial Generator, will teach skills like repair, maintenance, operation, and use of equipment. (It will probably not be particularly well suited to teaching the fine points of Aristotle's world view, however.)

The product is a breakthrough in terms of its ability to permit non-computer people to develop sophisticated, educationally valid programs to teach other people. There will almost certainly be other breakthroughs and more competitive products of this nature in the late 1980's.

Micros in Daily Life

This section looks at the impact of the microcomputer on publishing and working. It will conclude with a brief discussion about the future of robots in the near-term future.

Your Morning Paper on TV?

The microcomputer during the rest of the decade will alter the way we get information and the way we work, even the work we do. Personal robots will *not*, however, be a part of our lives before the mid-1990's. Robots remain an attractive idea but are far removed from practical implementation.

If you live on the West Coast and get up before your morning newspaper arrives in the morning, you can go to your personal computer, turn it on, hook up via phone lines to a computer in Ohio, and peruse this morning's *Washington Post*, or any other of a dozen or so newspapers available on-line through CompuServe and other information utilities.

Before the decade is over, the morning paper won't have to be delivered physically to your doorstep if you'd rather have it brought to your home electronically. This is perhaps the most evident and visible way the phenomenon of electronic publishing will affect our lives in the rest of the 1980's.

Electronic publishing is also known as "soft publishing" or "demand publishing." It refers to the electronic publishing of information when the user or buyer wants or needs it rather than at some pre-defined point in time.

The implications of electronic publishing are enormous. We are a nation using more paper than any other resource. We use huge amounts of paper in the United States for conveying information and moving data from one place to another. Some futurists in the 1970's predicted that microcomputers would provide for the advent of the paperless society. Far from that happening, we have created a demand for more paper of more kinds than we needed before. And yet paper is a long-term renewable resource; it is theoretically possible to use it all up and then have to wait while the supply of trees from which it is made is regenerated.

Another problem with paper as a vehicle for information is that it adds a step—and therefore a time delay—to the process of moving information around. The information society we are creating cannot afford or forgive unnecessary time delays; it has an immediacy about it. Stock quotations that are even an hour old can provide misinformation in making decisions. Morning newspaper readers are often infuriated to find that the paper contains very little that wasn't covered on last night's 11 o'clock TV news. That shouldn't surprise us. The newspaper was being printed about the time the nighttime news was going on the air. Information, far more than goods and services, has a very limited shelf life. Its electronic delivery is an important part of its usefulness.

Because of these facts, electronic publishing will unfold as a major trend in the last half of this decade. By 1990, it will be an accepted part of our way of life and by the end of the century, it will have totally supplanted conventional, or "batch" publishing on paper.

The near-term future will ease us into a world of newsscreens rather than newspapers, and magadisks rather than magazines.

Today, we can subscribe to some magazines that are delivered to us in electronic or computer readable form. Several, like *Symphony. . .Conducting Your Business* and the pioneering *CLOAD*, cater to users of a particular program (Lotus' Symphony) or computer (in the case of *CLOAD*, the TRS-80).

Dozens of such magazines, which are delivered on diskette, have been born in the past year or so. Delivered by mail, they lack the immediacy of other fully electronic publications discussed below, but they have the advantage of containing information in a form that we can put to immediate use in our computers. The *Symphony* magazine's premiere issue, for example, contained a telecommunications program enabling users to log on to a subscriber service automatically. At a late-night hour while users are asleep, the program automatically extracts stock information and disconnects from the phone link. When users come down for their morning toast, they hit a few buttons on the IBM PC and examine the performance of key stocks and economic indicators from the previous day. The program even generates graphs of the performance so if users are too bleary-eyed from late-night hours of work to read the reports, they can "get the big picture" at a glance.

Scholastic, the company that puts out the *Junior Scholastic* and related publications for schools, has a product called *Microzine* that is effectively a children's activity magazine combining learning and fun ideas on a disk. Unlike others of its genre, the Scholastic product was not initially available on a subscription basis but was sold through stores.

There will be more and more of these magazines on disk. They provide an excellent way to distribute software to users who are known owners of a particular type of computer or program because they have subscribed to the publication.

But magazines on disk are only the tip of the electronic publishing iceberg. Another example of electronic publishing is one that has some of the immediacy discussed earlier. It is a magazine called *On-Line Today* (OLT), published by CompuServe for its subscribers. *OLT* is printed monthly and mailed to the 200,000 or so people who use CompuServe. But in between publication dates, CompuServe subscribers can read articles on-line by logging into the area where the magazine publishes its electronic edition. Some of the material that appears in the electronic issue will also appear in the printed copy, but not all of it.

When researching this book, we left messages on several CompuServe bulletin boards for people with products or ideas to contact us. (If the idea of electronic bulletin boards is foreign to you, read the chapter Broadening Our Community for more background.) An *OLT* editor picked up one of our notes, got an editor's approval, did an on-line interview, and, within hours, published a brief article outlining what we were doing with this unusual use of their medium. The whole process took only two or three days instead of the months that would be required to get such a piece into a printed publication.

The next five years will bring a great deal of demand publishing of works that might otherwise be found in obscure places or not at all. You will be able to walk into some bookstores and ask for a relatively unusual or out-of-print title and be told to come back in 30 minutes to get a copy. The bookstore will hook its computer up with a central computer at the publishing house and "order" a copy, which will print, complete with illustrations, on a high-speed laser printer, right in the bookstore. There will be no inventory for anyone to keep, no need to try to anticipate accurately every buyer's potential interest in a particular book, and no drastic markdowns and lost profits from books nobody wants. (See Tabletop Libraries.)

Ultimately, beyond the end of the decade, there will be bookstores that will only deliver books electronically. Finally, all bookstores will handle all of their sales this way. The advantages are simply too great for this technology not to penetrate the huge book industry.

Electronic Advertising, Too?

When we move from printed publications to the electronic delivery of publications, we'll find new ways to inject advertising into the product mix. Advertisers pay the freight for all magazines; subscription revenues rarely pay even the costs of printing and mailing the magazine, let alone the editorial, promotional, management, and overhead cost of operating the publishing organization. Granting that the costs of publication will probably drop substantially as we move to electronic publication and distribution, these costs won't disappear. Advertisers will inevitably have to find new ways to get their message in front of readers who can control their access to the contents of the magazine with great precision.

One innovative solution to this problem has been the invention by the *On-Line Today* people of something called Electronic Bounce-Back, or EBB. Using EBB, a reader of *OLT* can spot a product about which he would like more information and place an immediate request for it electronically. Usually within a few days, the material he asked for reaches him. This compares with several weeks to as long as four months from the time you check a box or circle a number on a printed magazine's reader response card and the time you get the information requested. By that time, you've probably forgotten why you asked for it in the first place.

Several people we talked with during the preparation of this book were in the advertising business. Predictions are that within five years specialty ad agencies will assist customers in selling products via electronic media. One group, which failed to get funded and is now on hold, was made up of New York ad agency executives who had the vision of establishing an on-line service where users could use free electronic mail, banking, and job-hunting services in exchange for their patience in reading and watching graphic advertising for products of interest to that market.

"There is clearly a real marketing vacuum here," one of the founders of that group said. "Conventional advertising agencies don't take this means of communication very seriously and a lot of good ideas are floating around out there crying out for this kind of innovative marketing approach."

It is not yet clear *how* the advertisers who make the publications successful will get their message in front of users who can, with the simple flick of a button, turn their ad off or skip it entirely. It is certain that as electronic publishing emerges as an important field in the next few years ways will be found to accomplish that goal.

Advertising won't go away; it will, however, change its form and approach.

Work and Home

The small home computer systems will drastically alter the way we work in ways that would have been unpredictable five years ago. In this section we will answer the question: "What kinds of jobs will benefit from and which will be damaged by the continuing introduction of high technology into American life?"

We would be unwise to list the jobs for the rest of this decade that will be good to keep and those in which the impact of technology will be negative even if we could. But we can point some direction and offer some guidelines.

Conventional wisdom has been that blue-collar jobs—production, assembly line, secretarial, and support positions—would be the first to be negatively impacted by high technology. White collar positions—administrators, managers, decision-makers, planners, professionals—were felt to be safe from the intrusion of technology.

That has not turned out to be as true as people predicted. Studies by the U.S. Department of Labor for its *Occupational Outlook Quarterly* consistently indicate that the growth in white-collar jobs—projected at about 26% by 1990—will barely exceed that of blue-collar jobs, which will grow by some 25% during the same time. The demand for service workers will rise by some 30% during the same period. White-collar jobs became the dominant segment of the labor force, accounting for more than 50% of all employees in 1980. While demand for laborers shows steady decline over the next few years, the need for craft workers, operators, and technicians remains steady or grows slightly, depending on the method selected for classifying workers.

Clearly, use of expert systems (see Extending Our Minds) will become important as the 1980's draw to a close. Expert systems will impact more white-collar workers than any other class. Such systems are designed to help people make decisions, an activity traditionally reserved for white-collar managers and supervisors. Meanwhile, technicians who operate, maintain, and support such systems will be in greater demand.

Programming will probably not be a high-demand job in the rest of this decade. James Martin, considered by many to be the world's foremost authority on information management, has indicated that he believes that "the concepts in programming will change dramatically."

Graphics interfaces, which permit users to program their own applications and customize their work environments without the aid of a programmer (see Software Advances), will reduce the need for applications programmers, though the demand for systems programmers to create these tools may show a sharp, albeit temporary, spurt.

Robots? Not Yet

The idea that personal robots will have a significant effect on our daily lives and culture in the rest of the 1980's is an attractive one. Robots have been written about, dreamed about, and designed for decades. They have been in real-life use in factories and plants where their speed, accuracy, and ability to withstand hostile environments have been major assets.

The early 1980's saw the first companies introduce small, microprocessor-driven robots that *seemed* suitable for home use. But, for a number of reasons, robotics will be insignificant in homes and small businesses in the next few years.

One of the biggest obstacles to robots becoming useful, particularly in the home, is their relative lack of mobility. They cannot yet negotiate stairs, even relatively small one- or two-step affairs. Robot vision is not yet sufficiently well developed that a robot maneuvering in an environment with lots of changes going on would be able to function at all.

Another reason home and small business robots will wait in the wings for a few years yet is because tremendous research advances in the field of AI are needed before robots can become really useful. Problems of communication (natural language processing) programming (goal-setting) and fuzzy thinking (cognitive analysis) loom large on the horizon of robotics.

Humans communicate in ambiguities; a computer (which, robots are, after all) insists on precision and rule-following. One can picture the friendly family robot responding to the unfinished instruction, "Get Uncle Robert" when the next words would have been "a drink." Uncle Robert might be slightly miffed at being dumped unceremoniously at our feet by our efficient and obedient mechanical friend.

Humans are likely to resist the introduction of robots and their more-human descendants, androids, with far more strength than they resisted the development of the microcomputer. A robot is, after all, capable of being in a place where it's not wanted, of destructive behavior that extends beyond its own physical limits, and of injuring, at least theoretically, its owner. If they are built with the ability to "learn" from their environment, the unfounded but real fear that these mobile devices could become smarter and somehow take over may become yet another psychological barrier.

But there are two overriding reasons why robots will not be significant factors in the microcomputer world in the next five years. First, research is barely under way on robots that could be used with practical value in the home. Work on all aspects of robotics must be completed before a functional, useful, and usable robot can expect to be introduced to the home market.

Second, the issue of functionality is of overriding significance in the near term. One industry analyst has asked, "Who (besides the Pentagon, perhaps) would spend $3,000 on a robot that makes coffee when a $30 percolator will do? Even if robots learn how to cut a lawn, it might be easier to pay a kid $20 for the same task. At least he won't short-circuit when it rains." In other words, the real bottom-line question is, "Will a home robot be able to do anything useful?" For now, the answer must be no.

If we revise this book in five years, the answer could be different.

Opportunities, Strategies, and Decisions

This chapter may *seem* to have less to do with the practical, decision-making kinds of effects on which we have been focusing in this book than the other chapters. But there are indeed important signposts here for people who must make key decisions about their lives in the last half of the 1980's.

Careers   Those with career decisions lying just ahead who are inclined toward the arts should certainly consider following the example of several of the people mentioned earlier and interviewed in the profiles following this chapter. Marrying technology and the arts may lead to more lucrative jobs and more rewarding assignments—and ultimately to a chance to make a significant and high-visibility contribution about how technology will be used in society. Once again, the theme of a multiple-career appears on the ever-approaching horizon.

Investment   Investors have a unique opportunity in this realm to combine support of the arts with investment in scientific achievement and a touch of philanthropy. Artists like Lowenberg will be establishing new rules about art and what it is; those who are intrigued by the idea of being a part of a major change in the way our lives are enriched and affected by science and technology may make sound investments in such enterprises as *Ape Story* and AI-based artworks.

Management   Most business managers will find that the trends outlined in this chapter may speak less specifically to their needs than do the contents of other chapters. However, there is a message of great import here: As creative employees gain access to tools that will make them better producers and contributors to the company's efforts, openings must be made in the corporate armor for unusual tools to aid them in their thinking. In other words, open-mindedness about how a particular program or type of program could help the company's people be more creative, will be essential to managerial success in the next few years.

Successful managers will be characterized by a willingness to experiment with things that may seem outlandish at first but that may enhance creativity on the part of employees, an area traditionally viewed as not being subject to automation on any level.

Richard Lowenberg's *Ape Story*

Richard Lowenberg, an artist in his late 30's, has earned a reputation as a leader of the avant-garde electronic art movement afoot in this country. His works have been displayed in a number of museums and his short art films have been shown all over the world. For an artist who spends most of his time coping with technology, Lowenberg has a strangely irreverent attitude about the gadgets of modern life. "All of this stuff," he says, and by "stuff" he means microcomputers, satellites, and other electronic wizardry, "is really still in its infancy. Today, the tools limit the creativity of the artist at least as much as they open up new areas of creativity."

Born in Israel, Lowenberg and his family migrated to the United States when he was five years old. He spent four years in full-time study at Pratt Institute in New York, but never bothered finishing the requirements for a degree. His focus, however, was on environmental design with a minor in filmmaking. "I'd known from the time I was four that I was going to be an artist," he says. "I didn't want to be an architect, but a grounding in environmental design seemed like an excellent way to get a well-rounded art education. Film adds movement to any art form, and so it seemed like a natural medium to want to explore."

Lowenberg was an early innovator in the field of video tape. He quickly built a reputation as someone who knew how to manipulate the tools of that art form in subtle ways that led to startlingly imaginative results.

Lowenberg has also worked in the area of thermal imaging—taking "pictures" of the various heat patterns generated by body movement or settings using analog-digital techniques. He has also worked with biofeedback as a source of art.

His acclaim, though confined to the relatively narrow field of computer art, is genuine.

Yet Lowenberg says he has not really begun to do anything meaningful with these new art forms. "Almost everything I've done until now has been a byproduct of performance works. We're in rehearsal on something and I'm taping it for later study and it works artistically to some degree so it gets displayed."

But far from being an iconoclastic recluse concerned only with what he is creating, Lowenberg professes and exhibits " . . . a profound sense of concern about the role the arts will play in the emerging information society." And he has done a lot of thinking about that subject.

His current major work, *Ape Story*, is a theater piece involving a continuously running film background and a communicating ape who, by actions and reactions, comments on the pluses and the minuses of the information society. A highly ambitious work, it has been more than two years in the making.

The story is loosely based on a little-known play by Franz Kafka called *Report to an Academy*, which was a commentary on the theory of evolution. Lowenberg's production " . . . updates that a bit. The ape comments on society rather than on origins," the artist says after one of his frequent thoughtful pauses. The main focus of his work, he says, is on the *values* associated with the technology and the driving force of the information society.

"It's not all positive, and it's not all good news," Lowenberg says pensively. "The 'information society' has different meanings in different parts of the world, and its impact on people varies a lot from place to place and from time to time. I want to express broader dimensions of information and technology based value systems."

In at least one respect, Lowenberg is highly unusual, if not unique. "There have been," he points out, "many artists who have ventured into this territory and left it disillusioned. They were unwilling to cope with the obstacles and problems inherent in working with technology that is owned by others and access to which is not within one's own control. I have been willing to stay, to work with the system, even though that's been highly frustrating at times, and to work my way into a position where the quality of my work determines access to the tools I need."

Lowenberg is a pioneer in techno-artistry who will blaze a path in applying technique and technology to human communication and social cooperation. It will be a path that many artists who follow in years to come will benefit from being able to trace.

Mike Weiner: A Boost from Xerox and He's Off!

Microlytics, Inc., the brainchild of Mike Weiner of Fairport, New York, is not a typical start-up. Launched in February 1985, the company started life with a mid-six-figures nest egg from Xerox, marketing rights to a couple of exciting products, and access to Xerox's extensive research facilities and the products of the thinking of the scientists in those facilities.

Quite an interesting beginning for a company. But then Weiner is quite an interesting person to be starting a company.

In some ways Microlytics parallels an experience Weiner had in the early 1970's. He spearheaded a difficult and dangerous attempt to organize hundreds of independent fishermen in Florida into a cooperative to fight price gouging by middlemen fish buyers. Weiner, then in his mid-twenties, had ventured to Florida because life in New York City got to be too stifling for him. He'd had very little fishing experience and was a maverick in the industry from the beginning, he recalls.

"Getting 100 or so fishermen who didn't trust themselves, let alone each other, to form a cooperative was much harder than getting Xerox to see the potential in the Microlytics idea," Weiner says.

It is easy to see the tools that helped him win both battles: tenacity and intensity, added to a probing, listening, analytical mind that seems never to miss even a tidbit of a sentence it might find useful someday.

Weiner carried the day with hundreds of hours of hard work, whipping up local media attention to the problem, investigating government resources that might be available, convincing fishermen one at a time that they were being taken advantage of, and putting himself more than once in danger of being physically harmed. The result was the Treasure Coast Fisheries Cooperative, a group that provided fishermen members with an alternative outlet to the arbitrary and tough fish buyers. Until the co-op's formation, these buyers were the only means of income for the fishermen, who lived in fear of reprisal for anything they might do contrary to the buyers' selfish interests.

During the first year the co-op operated, it was able to obtain prices that were 60 percent higher than those previously paid to its members without the wholesale price going up at all. The co-op sold the fish directly to outlets in the Northeast, eliminating the middleman buyer.

Weiner eventually tired of the fishing life—getting up at 4:30 A.M. every day, battling the weather and the buyers, and expending an excessive amount of manual labor. He began looking for a more "conventional" job.

He settled on a sales position with Xerox in Florida. "I put on a suit, brushed my hair, and marched into the local Xerox office," he says cheerfully. "They asked me how I could succeed in sales when I had never done any of that kind of work. I asked them what time I had to start work and they told me 7:30. 'I've been getting up at 4:30 every morning and selling people the fish I catch for the last few years,' I told them. 'I don't see why I can't get up at 6:30 in the morning and sell people something they need.' I got the job."

Once again, Weiner's indomitable spirit and his Brooklyn-bred drive to succeed surfaced. Two years after joining the company, Weiner designed a dual cassette method of storing paper in trays of Xerox copiers. This approach, used on almost all copiers today, makes continually available the two most commonly used sizes of paper, enabling them to select one or the other with a simple switch. In 1978, it was innovative. Four years later Weiner became one of just 18 people in the mammoth company to receive a President's Award in recognition of the value of that achievement.

In late 1983, Weiner started a company in his home, with Xerox's approval, called Writing Consultants. The company was built around Weiner's wildly successful book, *Proportional Spacing on WordStar*, of which he sold thousands of copies by direct mail. He later designed a program that automatically makes the changes in WordStar's program described in the book. That software product, called ProportionalStar, has also been quite successful. With his wife handling the management responsibilities, the newly formed operation achieved more than $100,000 in sales of these two products by the Fall of 1984.

Software Bug Bites

By then, the software bug had bitten Weiner. He defined a new position inside Xerox called Manager of Software Market Expansion. "I went around the country to the skunk works Xerox was operating and saw some mind-blowing products just sitting around. They didn't have a place in Xerox' marketing plans because, even though they had incredible potential, they were too small in the overall Xerox picture to get attention. And they lacked a champion to bring them high enough up in the organization to be noticed," Weiner explains.

Meanwhile, Writing Consultants became involved in marketing other people's products for them using the successful direct selling techniques Weiner had been employing with his own titles. By early 1985, he was handling Synonym Finder, the first commercially available on-line thesaurus—originally marketed for the PC. Another product is LePrint, a product that permits dot-matrix printers to produce output that is at least letter quality and often appears as good as typeset; and MathStar, a package that enables WordStar users to carry out math operations inside their text documents.

But Weiner's idea stretched beyond Writing Consultants. "It was a good proving ground," he says. "I was able to parlay that into a proposal to Xerox in the Fall of 1984." Basically, Weiner suggested the unprecedented move of creating a spin-off from Xerox in which the copier-computer-communications giant would have a minority interest. This company was started partly with Xerox money, partly with another source of funds, partly with Xerox properties in search of markets, and partly with Weiner's income from Writing Consultants. It was designed to be a satellite company to Xerox.

After months of meetings, discussions, plans, reviews, analyses, and presentations, Weiner got the word in early 1985: his idea, called Microlytics, had been approved. February 11, 1985, would be his last day as a full-time Xerox employee. Later that month, the funding would be issued and the company would be launched.

The Tutorial Generator, a product of some of the AI minds at

Xerox's PARC facility in California, is the first product Microlytics will take to market with Xerox's approval. If the launch goes well, Xerox has promised Weiner an inside track at many other products languishing on laboratory shelves. Weiner already knows what his next acquisitions are likely to be.

But we can't help wondering about Weiner and where he's headed next. "All big companies have lots of products they can't develop to marketing readiness," he says. Microlytics, he believes, may set the pattern for other entrepreneurs inside big companies to find ways of leaving that will be mutually beneficial to their former employers and to themselves.

Pretty grandiose thinking, but then what would you expect from a guy who believed, as a Yankee, that he could organize the ragtag fishermen of Florida's Space Coast . . . and did it?

A New Tool for Teaching: A Tutorial Generator

You're a technical trainer at a major aircraft manufacturing plant. Your boss has just given you an IBM PC, a pile of drawings of a new jet engine, a manual written to (shudder) military specifications, and instructions. Your job is to prepare a hands-on, computer-aided tutorial on how to troubleshoot and repair that engine.

What's your next step?

Well, after reading this section, you'll *know* what the next step should be: call Mike Weiner of Microlytics, Inc. Weiner, thanks to an unusual relationship he has worked to establish with Xerox Corporation, will soon market a Tutorial Generator that can only be described as definitely "state of the art."

For openers, the tutorial creator is diagram-driven; it works from layers and sub-sets of pictures prepared using its artwork generation capability. For your jet engine repair training assignment, you'd simply begin by drawing a picture of the engine's externals. Then you'd pick a sub-assembly of the engine, use a windowing technique to explode it out of the main drawing, and draw the sub-assembly. In the process, you'd describe, in English terms, the connections and relationships among the various levels of sub-assemblies and their function in the overall engine performance.

The program generates high-quality, high-resolution artwork. Thanks to a compression technique developed at Xerox, the program occupies only about 55K bytes of storage on the disk and in the computer, which means you can have several screens resident in the PC's memory at one time, considerably speeding up the processing of the tutorial when it is being used.

The Tutorial Generator defines relationships graphically. It also permits chaining from one lesson or lesson segment to another and branching inside a lesson or lesson segment based on user actions. The program is designed to respond to voice input as well.

Weiner sees a potential application area for the product in the process control and factory floor automation industries. "Here, the Tutorial Generator would be used to create an overall description of the flow of work in the factory environment," he explains, "and yet enable managers to examine in detail any phase of the operation where a problem might arise or a change might be needed to see what relationships with other pieces would be most seriously affected."

The product would have another major use in the factory environment. The program would give factory managers the power equivalent to a financial spreadsheet. They could play "what if" simulation games without having to move or buy expensive and heavy equipment. Supervisors could plan and distribute work hypothetically, examine the impact on various parts of the process, and then redesign until a particular floor layout or process was optimized for the desired results.

"The product also has built-in artificial intelligence capabilities," Weiner says. That's only fitting for an idea that comes out of Xerox's Palo Alto Research Center, where some of the foremost thinking about AI's applications to industry and manufacturing has been taking place in the past few years. In the case of the Tutorial Generator, the AI capability enables designers of complex system descriptions to avoid clashes between various phases of the design and description.

For example, if you've said that Widget #23 is a three-inlet hydraulic gizmo and then you define four different aspects of the system as being inputs to it, the Tutorial Generator will spot the error and point it out to you so you can fix it.

On a more complex level, you might define certain outputs to be routed to certain places in the system and ultimately some feedback process creates a closed loop: Tutorial Generator will notice the problem and inform you. As it works with you in a specific design, it incorporates what it learns so that it becomes more and more expert at assisting you with the design process.

The Tutorial Generator grew out of a project dubbed Trillium at Xerox PARC. In that project, a team of researchers watched design engineers lay out the designs for control panels of copying machines, logically enough. As they watched the process, they gained an "understanding of their understanding," explains PARC research staff member Austin Henderson. They translated that understanding into a set of tools that permits a designer to sit down at a terminal in a Xerox facility, define buttons, controls, output display formats, responses, and the other parts of a copier's user interface and then test the result to see if it performs as desired. It is no longer necessary to write huge tomes called specifications, to take reams and reams of paper to try to explain to an engineer in one plant how the design engineer wants the user interface to look and work. Instead, the designer can send the engineering staff a working demonstration of the user interface on the company computer and the two can modify, fiddle, and redesign to their hearts' content.

That's an ambitious undertaking, but it is one that Xerox has all but perfected. We saw a demonstration of Trillium during our research for this book and were greatly impressed with its ability to handle the complexities of the design process.

Now Microlytics intends to bring that power to the world of IBM PC's. The results will be wide-ranging.

Musical Virtuosos on a Disk?

You've just composed a haunting, lilting little tune. You've listened to it play on your home computer and an inexpensive synthesizer. It's nice, but not yet good enough. You want to see what it would would like if Itzhak Perlman played the violin part and Oscar Peterson played the keyboard.

With a product to be marketed in a couple of years—Music Productivity Tool, or MPT for short—you'd be able to do just that. Plus, you could play "what if" with music composition. "What if I took the violins up an octave? What if I had the tympany come in here? What if I substituted an oboe for the French horn in this phrase?" You'd be able to hear them played, in virtuoso style, on your home computer.

MPT is the idea of Dan Sevush, a Lotus Development employee with a background in music and filmmaking who "got into software by mistake." As yet, MPT is only an idea. Sevush has been unable to interest Lotus in the product and is pursuing its design as a hobbyist for the time being. He hopes to fund the development of MPT himself from profits made selling a new telecommunications program he's been working on in his spare time.

As Sevush sees it, MPT would be a collection of programs that would run on most popular home systems. It would incorporate the ability to edit, compose, arrange, harmonize, conduct, perform, and record music. Interfaces to synthesizers, musical keyboards as input devices, graphic printers, high-resolution display screens and standard typewriter keyboards would be incorporated.

"The experienced musician, interested in composition, would be able to do something as simple as sit down at the musical keyboard and lay down a few tracks, which the MPT programs would digitize and store for him," Sevush says. "Then he could edit the sound, play with the quality, add harmonizing voices, adjust the timing, and generally tweak the composition until it was exactly the way he wanted it. Then he could route the output to a multitrack tape recorder and have a master from which to produce a recording for sale or performance."

Sevush realizes that a great deal of work must yet be done to bring the idea to execution. "But," he says warmly, "the technology is already there. We don't have to invent anything new; we just have to get existing pieces to work together." Part of the secret to that is the MIDI bus, a new standard for sending musical notes and signals over a standard serial communications link between computers and peripheral devices.

"The bus is kind of like the ASCII of music," Sevush points out. (ASCII is a standard that enables computers and printers and modems to "understand" characters they send back and forth to each other. MIDI is a similar standard for the transmission of musical data.)

Although Sevush is reluctant to talk in detail about MPT until it's closer to reality, he indicates that he anticipates the user interface will have to be usable by both accomplished musicians and relative novices. "For the professional, we need the ability to show him a score sheet with the notation in place and let him manipulate the notes using a pointer of some sort. But the beginner needs to be able to type his notes into the system using more conventional notation like G2 (for G on the second octave), F2# (F-sharp on the second octave) and so forth." The ideal, Sevush says, would be to be able to see both the text input and the score sheet on the screen at once, using windows. But that won't work on many of the older-technology home systems, so he indicated he will wind up making some trade-offs there.

The inclusion of a personality module in the programs is another unique idea of Sevush's. Not only will the program come equipped with data describing the playing styles of major instrumentalists, Sevush says, but it will also be capable of "listening" to users play, interpreting portions of their style, and storing them. This would enable the program later to replay pieces in the composer's own style, even with multiple-voice harmony and unusual timing that he may not be able to execute directly.

Racter

The world of computers and artificial intelligence has spawned its first artificial lunatic.

It is common knowledge that computers are high-speed idiots. For example, if you ask a computer, "Do you have a brain?" the computer will typically respond by going immediately into some error condition.

Now a program called Racter will turn a computer from an idiot into a lunatic. At least that's what one of Racter's creators, Thomas Etter, admitted in a recent interview.

Certainly Racter *sounds* like an artificial lunatic when he speaks. Racter's first sentence was, "Hot wines are wounding our cold expatriate." The suitableness and comprehensibility of Racter's comments have continued at that general level ever since that first pronouncement.

Of course, like any lunatic, Racter doesn't know what he's talking about. If he asks the question in an interview (as he will) "Where are you from?" he will assume the answer to be the name of a place. If, for example, he asks, "Where are you from?" and you answer "San Jose, California" he might respond, "You say you're from San Jose, California?" If, however, you answer, "Why do you want to know?" Racter will respond, "You say you're from Why do you want to know?" instead of saying something like, "I was just curious."

Now think a moment, if you met a human person and the person asked you, "Where are you from?" and you answered, "Why do you want to know?" and he said, "You say you're from Why do you want to know?" you would probably say (or at least think) "Man! You're crazy!" See? Racter isn't an idiot, he's a madman.

The engaging thing about Racter (and about human lunatics, as well) is that in his mad ravings he sometimes stumbles upon the imitation of brilliance. When somebody asked Racter, "Where did you learn to write?" he responded,

```
I learned how to write in the ocean. If a sleeper had
fled to the town dump, fat city would be horrified!
```

> When one lives in a blue funk, the ocean is very
> attractive. . . .

Racter "speaks" by randomly stringing words together. The randomness is qualified by three things, which makes Racter's "talking" work: The program follows rules of grammar, knows the meanings of words, and has a stock of pet phrases, quotes and aphorisms that make their appearance from time to time.

Lunatic or not, Racter is a published author. His is the first book to be authored by a computer (certainly not the first one authored by a lunatic). Racter also named his book—it's title being one of Racter's pronouncements—*The Policeman's Beard is Half Constructed*. The book is published by Warner books. For people who would like to have the engaging lunatic live at their house, Racter may be purchased from John D. Owens Associates, Staten Island, New York. It runs on the IBM PC.

By the way, when asked, "Do you have a brain?" Racter responded, "Of course not . . . Did you hear about Byron? Byron was an indifferent feeler but an inspired feeler . . . Byron's ox threw up on John McEnroe, then ate himself. Poor Byron! But that's how feelers are. If 'I do have a brain' occurred to a pugilist, he would be a simple pugilist . . . AAAH-choo!! sniffle."

Man! He's crazy!

Computers Get the Picture

It's easy to look at a computer graphics display—of a race car driving along an obstacle-strewn road, for example—but it may not be so easy to understand how the effect is created. It's even hard to understand what graphics programmers are talking about; like most disciplines, graphics programming has developed a language all its own.

Where They Come From; How They are Shown

Information for generating graphics on computers resides in two places in a computer system. One place is in the circuits of the computer, in which case the information forms part of the computer *hardware*. The information also resides in the programs being run, called *software*. The initial screen on the Apple Macintosh, for example, displays menus that can be "pulled down" and a "desktop" that can be moved around and sized to suit the user's needs and tastes. The routines to create these are hardware parts of the system. MacPaint is a Macintosh graphics generating program and is, of course, software. The capabilities of the Macintosh hardware are used by MacPaint and the various other Macintosh software programs.

Computers display everything they produce, including graphics, on a VDT (Video Display Terminal), which in the case of some home computers is simply a TV. VDT's display images by *raster-scan* methods, which are also used in normal television display techniques. Raster-scan uses a standard television signal to create images by rapidly modulating the strength of an electron beam passing over the 262 lines on the surface of the display tube. The lines contain graduated areas of light, dark, and (in some systems) color. As the lines are displayed one above the other, they create the image on the screen.

Two common ways of creating the images with computers that will be scanned-in on a VDT include character graphics and pixel graphics.

What a Bunch of Characters!

Character graphics are available on all microcomputers. The simplest of these are the letters and symbols available on the keyboard itself. Repeatedly pressing the underline key, for example, will create a straight line; X's can be used together to simulate shading; the percent key, the two parenthesis keys, and the ampersand key can be used in various combinations to create graphic images.

Some programs for computers with limited graphics capabilities use standard keys in ingenious ways. Video game programs designed for stodgy business machines, for example, may create little characters represented by a "q" when running left or a "p" when running right.

Most computer systems permit creation of much more sophisticated character graphics images by providing keys that when pressed produce various "pieces" of graphics shapes. The pieces can then be put together to create larger pictures. For example, four corner pieces, vertical line pieces, and horizontal line pieces may be put together in many different combinations to create all kinds and sizes of boxes. A set of special character graphics might include all kinds of filled and unfilled shapes, left and right diagonal lines, a smiling face, the four symbols on playing cards, chess pieces, circles, parts of curving lines, etc. If these pre-packaged character sets prove insufficient, graphics programs for creating one's own character set are available for many computers.

The Pixel in the Middle

Still more flexibility is provided through the use of "individual picture elements," called *pixels*. A pixel is simply a dot on the computer screen—the smallest resolution point that the computer program will permit. The size of the dot is quite small in hi-res *(high-resolution)* mode, much larger in lo-res *(low-resolution)*. Lo-res modes will typically produce 1,920 resolution points (48 across by 40 down) on a screen, while a typical hi-res mode will produce 44,800 resolution points (280 across by 160 down). The computer *bit maps* the entire screen—a single bit in the computer's memory corresponding to each pixel on the screen.

Computer images are freely produced by putting the dots together in various combinations. In lo-res mode, diagonal lines assume a familiar "stair-step" quality, since the pixels are large enough for each to be clearly distinguished. Even in hi-res modes, however, a diagonal line will not be perfectly straight; under magnification the presence of the individual pixels, offset slightly from one another down the length of the line, will be clearly revealed.

A trade-off is often required for graphics on computers offering color capabilities. Lo-res modes provide the greatest number of colors; the highest resolution mode (in other words, the mode with the smallest pixels) is often available only in monochromatic (one color).

Speaking of monochrome . . . a few video games, of the sort that you pay quarters to play, achieve marvelous graphics effects by using a *vector image* (or vector-stroke graphics) display process rather than the raster scan used on our small systems. Vector image display systems do not draw lines; they electronically "paint" the image directly on the tube. The Battle Zone video game uses this technology. Vector image display technology completely eliminates the stair-step effect; they are limited, however, to monochromatic images.

Some of the newer computers, for example the celebrated Macintosh, do everything in a hi-res, monochrome mode using pixel graphics.

There are a few drawbacks to pixel graphics. Some computers do not provide pixel graphics unless an extra printed circuit board is installed. A second disadvantage is that pixel graphics, particularly in hi-res modes, consume relatively large amounts of memory. Slower running programs and memory limitations are two results of the larger memory problem. A third disadvantage is that pixel graphics may not generally be easily used on the same screen with text; it is necessary to create text as graphics or, alternatively, to create "windows" in which text may appear. A distinct advantage of character graphics, on the contrary, is that they may be combined easily with text.

Shortcuts to Computer Images

Graphics programs, and especially new graphics systems, permit many sophisticated graphics-generating opportunities. Some systems permit creating graphics with a "mouse." Once again, Apple's Macintosh provides the best-known example. The mouse is a small control that is moved around on a flat surface causing corresponding action to take place on the screen. For example, a line may be drawn with the same proportions, curves, and angles as the motion of the mouse. The motion of the mouse is noted by the computer and is "digitized"—translated into a form the computer can understand, process, and respond to.

Another device, the *light pen*, resembles a regular pen but connects to the computer with a wire. The user "writes" with it directly on the screen of the VDT. The movement of the light pen on the screen provides information to the computer about where to draw lines and put marks.

A feature of most new graphics programs and systems is a "telescoping" facility. When this feature is used, the section of the graphic image being worked on is enlarged to the size of the entire screen work area. Under this magnification, pixels are large and easily turned on/off. This permits the user to refine graphic images to a more precise level of detail.

Among the new graphics peripherals are digitizing cameras, which transfer pictures directly to the computer's memory. The opposite application is also on the market—systems that transfer computer generated graphics directly to slides.

Giving Programs a Spritely Motion

Most sophisticated animation for microcomputers is done with *sprites*. These provide shortcuts to computer animation by allowing the programmer to create, for example, a little man, which then can be moved around on the screen under the program's direction. Individual sprites may contain a sequence of shapes. Overlaying "series" assigned to a single sprite make it possible, for example, that when the little man moves across the screen his arms swing and his legs move back and forth in a walking motion.

Sprites represent a significant improvement over the former approach to computer graphics animation. The older computers produced animation by successively showing an image, erasing it, relocating it a small amount (perhaps only a pixel or two), and then redrawing it. The process required time-consuming programming, and results did not run smoothly or well.

Graphics on computers provide a dimension to computing that makes the technology effective and even exciting. From the user's point of view they are the "friendliest" parts of the computer.

Computer Aided Instruction

Computers are changing the experience of learning for millions of people. The revolution is occurring through the impact of three kinds of educational programs.

Drill and Practice Tutorials

The type of learning closest to the center of public education is rote learning—multiplication tables, ABC's, states, and capitals. Drill and practice tutorials on computers are more fun than with pencil and paper, even when the programs merely give questions and check answers, and they usually do much more than that!

The program will typically contain many "bells and whistles." A simple one would be asking for the user's name, which the program then uses in "talking to" the user. A more complicated augmentation would, for example, draw a picture of a track with a race car. The race car then will move faster or slower depending upon whether or not correct answers are being given.

Programmed Instruction

Programmed Instruction provides for a somewhat more powerful learning experience than drill and practice. The method carries out learning tasks by providing blocks of instructional text, each presenting a single concept, followed by questions testing whether the learner grasped the concepts covered in that particular block. Educational research has indicated, insofar as any topic can be broken down into a list of concepts, that topic can be taught more efficiently through the use of programmed instruction than any other kind of learning method.

Simulations

Higher levels of learning are attained through simulations. Simulations cause a computer to "simulate," or model, some behavior or action. Simulations are the environment of video games. Learning purposes take simulation far beyond the game-playing mode. Flight simulators, for example, provide a realistic milieu in which pilots can learn basic flying skills with much more safety than actual flight, at a fraction of the cost. Simulators have been built that accurately model battlefield situations, providing military officers with opportunities to learn the realities of wartime command with none of the risks, losses, and expense of actual battle.

Other kinds of learning simulation do not involve graphics. Programs have been written, for example, which model patients' responses to questions in a diagnostic interview. Questions may be asked of the "patient," for example, "Are you taking any medicine for the pain in your arm?" The computer will then respond with a statement of whether medicine is being taken and, if so, (and if the medical student thinks to ask for it) what medicine it is. These programs, in a realistic way, drill medical students on diagnostic skills—teaching them what questions are important to ask and what diseases and ailments some complaints indicate.

AI and Computer Aided Instruction

The advent of genuine, inexpensive AI learning systems will permit the development of CAI programs that will accomplish learning purposes with astonishing ease. Future learning programs will be able to "learn" about the user. In five years drill-and-practice and programmed learning programs will accommodate themselves to the progress and abilities of the individual user. The programs will automatically increase or decrease the difficulty and/or pace of the instruction to a level appropriate to the user and thus maximize the efficiency and effectiveness of learning.

Simulations will also have the ability to learn from experience—so if something is encountered in one session, for example, that the program does not recognize, it will learn what the response should be and will therefore not make the same mistake or experience the same problem during subsequent sessions. The value of such programs increases as they become more "intelligent" and, therefore, able to model more realistically the conditions being simulated.

Tabletop Libraries

The age of electronic publishing is arriving. The idea of electronic publishing has been around for a long time. Facsimile technology emerged in the 1930's and some thought at that time that electronic delivery of newspapers was imminent. Now the old promise is being realized in ways the people of that time could not have imagined. Electronic publishing is available in *teletext* and *videotext* systems.

Teletext is the technology of one-way electronic publishing. It is limited to certain specific applications; the continuous display of news and weather on some cable systems being one of the most elementary and familiar. Videotext, on the other hand, is the technology of two-way, interactive, electronic publication. Users control what pages of what publications they will receive.

A third kind of technology involves a hybrid merger of electronics with traditional print materials. Books or articles are saved on magnetic tape and printed as orders come in. This eliminates the need to warehouse materials.

The hybrid technique of electronic publishing provides for an effective information delivery system. Modern printing techniques make possible extremely fast creation of the printed materials, so the response time between receiving and filling an order can be minimal. Of course, a further advantage is that the production time between when a book or article is available for publication and when it can actually be obtained becomes identical to the response time between receiving and filling an order.

A variation of this type of application of the technology is currently in widespread use in electronic transmission of facsimile mail such as that offered by, for example, Federal Express' Zap Mail service.

Application of the technology in its pure videotext form reduces delivery time to the time required for downloading, transmission, and uploading. Transmission is the real bottleneck in the operation, because transmission over telephone lines is limited to the speed of the modem being used. It would take about four hours to transfer a full-length book at 300 baud. Some modems are much faster than this, but even at 300 baud the time required is minimal compared with waiting three weeks or a month for your local bookstore to try to get the book you want from some distributor.

Transmission times become much faster than is possible over a modem if carried out over coaxial cable lines.

Electronic publishing has been used in hybrid systems of two-way communication; communication by the user to the system over the telephone and by the system to the user over a cable.

What's the Latest?

Electronic publishing technology is naturally being applied to the publication of news, weather, and other dated information. Business information like stock market reports is obviously a place where current, up-to-the-minute, on-demand information can be very valuable. Add to these advantages the fact that print journalism in particular is wasteful of resources, and this application becomes very attractive indeed.

The pure videotext application of electronic publishing eliminates the need for manufacturing paper, buying and operating printing presses, and physically delivering or mailing the print products. Ted Turner, cable TV station owner and executive, made the following comment in a public speech: "There's nothing more inefficient than chopping down trees and making them into paper and printing the paper every day. And then driving them all over town and sticking those bulky things in everybody's mailbox. And then we have to send garbage trucks to pick them up."

The same technology that provides for electronic publishing via videotext systems makes possible electronic mail, also referred to as E-mail. More and more videotext publishing services are adding E-mail options, providing for user-to-user mail between subscribers on the system.

Electronic publishing stands at the point of becoming an important technology. Longstanding barriers are falling. The technology is becoming more sophisticated at the same time costs are being greatly reduced; resistance to computers is being broken down; thorny issues of copyright and ownership are being addressed.

Someday we will have enormous libraries on our tabletops— electronic access to the stored information, literature, and art of the entire planet!

2

BACKGROUND

The Nature of the
Coming Changes

Introduction

Our gaze will now shift from the impact of microcomputer technology. We will look at the specific changes in high technology that will take place between now and the dawn of the decade of the 1990's.

The following pages emphasize the changes themselves rather than how the changes will affect us. The two emphases are, of course, inextricably linked, and we should not be surprised to find in the pages ahead a more specific discussion of ideas that were indirectly introduced in the first part of the discussion.

This following segment of the book is divided into two sections: hardware, which also includes systems and interfaces, and software. The astute reader will recognize that the boundaries separating hardware, systems, and interfaces have become less and less distinct in the past few years. We expect that blurring process to continue. Within a few years it will be inappropriate to divide any discussion along these lines.

We will review some exciting products that will have impacts like the products discussed in the first part of the book. We will also meet some of the people behind those products.

In the pages that follow, we will learn diverse things: from how the integrated circuits, which are at the heart of this revolution, are designed and made, to alterations in how the things we create on our personal computers will look when they are printed.

The changes in the hardware and software industries are taking place at great speed. And, what's more, the pace of change will accelerate in the next five years.

Some of the things you will discover in the following pages include:

- a voice-activated workstation that doesn't even *have* a keyboard;
- a word processor that tries to help us type by suggesting words from its ever-expanding vocabulary;
- an artificial intelligence program that enables us to learn about AI

while we try to outmaneuver each other in a trucking contest; and
- a graphic language interpreter that allows us to program and control our computers in pictures instead of words.

These are but a few of the products on the following pages.
Let us continue to wonder.

4
Hardware Advances

The microprocessor revolution is over.—Phil Kaufman, president, Silicon Compilers, Inc.

In a few years, the keyboard will be history, a thing of the past.—Denny Bollay, president, ExperTelligence

Dozens of new computer systems will hit the microcomputer market during the rest of the decade. None of these new products, however, will be so revolutionary in nature as to change the way we use computers.

Changes in computer hardware will be *incremental* and evolutionary rather than revolutionary. There will, however, be major advances in hardware technology inside the computer—in the microprocessors and memory chips that are at the heart of a system. Major changes will also take place outside the computer—in peripherals devices like laser printers, optical disks, modems, and interfaces.

There is an inevitable cycle in the microcomputer business already even though the industry is scarcely 10 years old. First comes a major hardware advance of some sort—the very first widely available micros, the introduction of 16-bit machines, or the presentation of a revolutionary product like the Macintosh. Then, for a few years, the software industry races like mad to catch up to the capabilities contained in the hardware change. Finally, the hardware part of the industry, having spent several years in research and development, launches another new product and the cycle begins anew. In 1984, the industry experienced a major hardware leap with Apple's Macintosh introduction. Several other companies—notably Atari and Commodore—have introduced Macintosh look-alikes. The software must now catch up (how it will do that is detailed in Software Advances).

It is reasonable to predict that much of the new microcomputer hardware, as with a great deal of the software, introduced in the next few years will look very much like the Macintosh. Atari's so-called "Jackintosh" ST Series (named for Jack Tramiel, who purchased the troubled computer maker), is in some ways a less-capable Macintosh that sells for considerably less and incorporates some features missing from the Macintosh (notably color display). A software company, Digital Research of Monterey, California, has introduced the GEM Operating System. GEM is used by Atari in its new Mac look-alike and permits computers to look as if their interface is similar to that of the Macintosh. Other companies will follow suit in the next few years. Commodore's Amiga system is in some ways a response to the Macintosh. (See The Colorful Amiga.)

The following trends will take place in the next five or so years.

Inside the machine—at the level of the chips that make up the hardware—established technologies will gain in importance, those like CMOS (a manufacturing process described below) and gallium arsenide (a high-speed replacement for the silicon of which most chips are made today). Memory densities will increase in the very near term so that one million-bit memory chips will be widely available and rapidly declining in price by the end of 1986. The growth of very large scale integration (VLSI) and associated design techniques will make very sophisticated hardware relatively easy to design and build.

Computers themselves will be characterized by one major trend—portability. Fueled by CMOS technology advances and increased capability of liquid crystal display (LCD) devices, these new portable computers will further increase the demand for compatibility of programs and files.

Outside the computer, the next few years will see the advent of peripherals such as optical disks with huge amounts of storage, laser printers with increasing print densities and lower prices, graphics devices that make significant improvements in visual display, modems with built-in intelligence capable of a great deal more than today's modems, and voice/speech interfaces.

The following pages will explore each of these trends to see where the next steps in the computer revolution will take us.

Chip Technology Changes

By now, it's likely that everyone in America has heard of the integrated circuit or "microchip" ("chip" for short) on which the microelectronics revolution has been built. (See Those Revolutionary Chips.) We tend to think in terms of these chips being in computers and electronic appliances like television sets and microwave ovens. The fact is that these tiny slivers of silicon pervade our daily lives.

A powerful trend in microcomputers in recent years has been a push to CMOS. This direction has been fueled by the explosion of interest in portability of computer systems. (See What's Happening With These Chips? for a description of CMOS and other parts of hardware development.) We discuss the trend toward portability in the next major section of this chapter. CMOS is clearly the technology preferred by people designing portable computer systems. The low power requirement means the devices can be battery-operated and users who hold the small computers on their laps or set them on desktops aren't made uncomfortable by the heat generated by the systems.

But microcomputers seem to have an insatiable desire for speed, spurred on by users. It is typical, for example, for a new computer owner to buy his first home computer and use cassette tape for a storage medium. Cassette tapes are relatively slow by computer standards, but are so much faster than the manual methods formerly used that the user is delighted over the remarkable speed of his system.

In a few weeks or months, however, he begins to long for a disk drive for his computer. Disk drives store and retrieve data hundreds of times faster than cassette tapes. With the disk drive firmly attached to the computer and ensconced on his desk, our user seems to be content. But in a few months, he begins begrudging his friendly computer the 30 seconds it sometimes takes to store a document and starts yearning for a "hard disk," a higher capacity, higher speed version of the floppy disks with which he is now working. And so it goes.

Higher speed of processing is one of the forces driving the rapid conversion of the microcomputer market from the older 8-bit microprocessors to the new 16- and even 32-bit central processing units (or CPU's, a term for the microprocessor that is the brain of the microcomputer). System designers have recently begun to decry the relatively slow operating speeds of MOS-type devices and have begun looking elsewhere for their designs. They have found a new chemical base to be used as the substrate on which the semiconductor can be built.

Gallium arsenide (chemical symbol: $GaAs$) conducts electrons about five times as fast as silicon and yet permits the chips to be designed in the same ways as chips that use silicon as the substrate. In very high-speed demand situations—for example, high-frequency communications—GaAs devices are already de rigeur. As the trend in portability continues and accelerates during the last half of this decade, GaAs devices will find their way more and more often into products all of us use. (An interesting sidelight: The first major worldwide producer of such chips may turn out to be, not one of the major semiconductor companies, but *Ford Motor Company*. The big automaker announced plans to go into the GaAs semiconductor business the spring of 1985.)

Besides speed and power, one other factor by which semiconductors are often measured and discussed is capacity. This is especially true in the area of memory chips, which is where most of the experimenting with new technologies and designs takes place. This is because mistakes are far easier to find in a chip with one purpose— storage of information—than in a multifunction chip like a CPU.

It is already quite clear that the next major change in microcomputer memory capacity will be the emergence of a single chip capable of storing more than one *million* bits of information. In early 1986, several companies were reported to be preparing to make small quantities of these huge-capacity chips available for their customers. Production-quantity shipments can be expected in 1987. Putting just eight of these chips into a computer system enables that system to store a full me*gabyte* of information—more than a million characters!

Prior to the introduction of the one-megabit chips, the largest memory devices available were 256K devices. These chips are capable of storing just one-quarter of what the new one-megabit chips can handle. When *they* were introduced, however, some people believed the limits of semiconductor technology were stretched about as far as would be possible without some major breakthrough in processing or manufacturing techniques.

The "K," by the way, in 256K stands for 1,024—the closest number to 1,000 we can get by raising the number two to higher and higher exponential powers; 1,024 is, in fact, the value of two raised to the tenth power. K is the standard measurement of memory capacity. A 64K computer is often spoken of as having a 64,000 bytes capacity, when in actual fact it has room for 65,536 bytes. A one-megabit chip holds 1000K, or 1,048,576 bits of information.

The implications of the availability of a one-megabit chip are staggering. It means we can store information in less than 1/16 the space we needed for the same information just two years or so ago when 16K chips were the standard in the industry. Portable computers capable of storing significant amounts of information and manipulating huge amounts of data are now possible. And the lower capacity chips will now drop in price as the new, high capacity chips take over the high-priced end of the market.

Where will this end? There is, literally, no end in sight. The issue is how thinly a line can be etched in the materials of which semiconductors are made without adjoining lines touching each other. At some point, those lines will touch, but before they do, someone will come up with a way to etch the lines differently so they don't or so that it doesn't matter if they do!

The relevant question for us is whether there are likely to be any more significant breakthroughs in memory density in the next four or five years. There will not be another quadrupling of memory capacity before 1990.

For one thing, market demand is absent. A 16-bit microprocessor, like those used in the IBM PC and look-alikes, can typically address a maximum of only one megabyte of memory at a time. (The eight-bit chips can handle only 64K bytes of information at once.) The 32-bit microprocessor is already with us, though in fairly limited quantities and applications. The 16-bit processor will dominate the microcomputer industry for at least half as long as its 8-bit predecessor (about ten years) and, in the absence of a demand for a huge number of chips with more than one megabit of capacity, semiconductor manufacturers will probably take this opportunity to regroup their research and development efforts and begin to look at other refinements in processing and design.

Besides, single-purpose chips may be going the way of the dinosaur if advocates of very large scale integration (VLSI) are right. And they are!

VLSI and Systems-on-a-Chip

Today's microchips are described as LSI devices, the LSI standing for large-scale integration. This differentiates them from their predecessors, SSI (small scale integration) and MSI (medium scale integration). These designations are arbitrary; no precise dividing line marks the point at which everyone would agree that a chip leaves the SSI world and becomes MSI or moves from MSI to the vaunted heights of LSI. But in the past couple years a great deal of attention has been focused on a new level of integration—very large scale integration, or VLSI. VLSI permits designers to implement entire computer *systems* on a single chip.

Research in VLSI began in the late 1970's and by the early 1980's had resulted in the formation of a small handful of companies attempting to bring the ideas of VLSI to reality in a product. By 1984, some VLSI products were beginning to appear, and the market for these superchips appears poised for a major movement in the next few years.

To understand the implications of this technology, we talked with Phillip A. Kaufman, president of Silicon Compilers Incorporated, of San Jose. Silicon Compilers is doing some of the most advanced work in VLSI design, as is only befitting the company formed by the acknowledged original master of the art, Dr. Carver Mead of California Institute of Technology. Dr. Mead wrote the pioneering work in the field and has been a super-consultant to many of the companies that entered the field.

Kaufman explained the significant differences between designing a traditional integrated circuit and designing a VLSI circuit. In fact, he believes that the advent of VLSI circuitry has resulted in the passing of the age of the microprocessor. "The microprocessor revolution," he says matter-of-factly, "is over."

Before we can fully appreciate what Kaufman means by that startling statement, which he admits is made somewhat for its shock value, we must take a slight step backward and delve into the design of integrated circuits.

When integrated circuit designers begin to work, they have in front of them two basic tools: a design objective (i.e., a statement of what the chip is to accomplish), which was probably written by a system designer, and a figurative pile of transistors. Their task is to assemble these tens of thousands —or hundreds of thousands— of transistors into a configuration that will accomplish the goals in the design document. They work with individual transistors or, in some cases, with very small groups of transistors that make up what designers call "logic blocks" or "gates."

To be sure, some standard methodologies that permit these designers to think slightly, but only slightly, above these very microscopic levels, have been built in the first 15 years of the semiconductor's life.

LSI chips are designed by people who are called, logically enough, integrated circuit designers, or IC designers for short. There are, at best, 20,000 people in the world trained to do this meticulous and demanding work. In fact, Intel Corporation, the company that started the microprocessor revolution, for most of its early history had a great deal of its IC design work done by a small special team in Israel. On the other hand, hundreds of thousands of people qualify for the title system engineer and are capable of designing entire systems and sub-systems using integrated circuits as building blocks without understanding what goes on in the circuit itself.

The wall between system designers and IC designers was a thick one. There was little communication, and quite often the chip designed by the IC specialists was far different from what the system designers wanted. The latter accommodated themselves to the less-than-ideal reality because it was simply too costly and time-consuming to go back for a redesign of the chips.

VLSI devices have as many as 400,000 gates on one chip. The chip itself is now a system. A prescription for failure obviously lies in a product development program creating these superchips with system designers separated from IC designers. Resources are wasted as system design people attempt to work their expertise on a VLSI prototype that has been given to them by the IC designers as a kind of *fait accompli*. The company is liable to enter a series of frustrating rounds of redesign-reevaluation-redesign, with people on each side of the fence trying to work their will on the other side. A multi-million-dollar product development program operating under these circumstances will likely founder in a storm of hard feelings and mutual recrimination.

Silicon Compilers has discovered a solution to the problem. Their product (see Silicon Compilers' Workstation) places a tool for designing chips into the hands of system designers. The expertise of the IC specialists, in other words, gets built into a computer program that efficiently and effectively allows system design engineers to carry out IC design without specific training or experience in that area.

The program allows system designers to specify the functionality and architecture of the proposed chip and then have the computer synthesize an implementation to meet this specification. They can specify the heart of a microprocessor, known as the Arithmetic and Logic Unit (ALU), as a function, bring in memory circuits of just the right size and configuration, add input/output control logic, all as generic architectural building blocks that they can further control and specify to be exactly the version needed. They can do all of this by defining rather large blocks of functions which the computer system then turns into a mask design to be used in building the chip.

The program permits designers to move components around, optimize their locations relative to one another, alter relationships, and add or delete portions until they have achieved the right balance between their often conflicting goals for low power, high speed, higher functionality, and low cost.

"We asked ourselves, 'Where can the system engineer's brainpower be best used?' Then we went and built a system that would enable that to happen," Kaufman explains. Silicon Compilers is clearly the leading company in the VLSI design tool business today, only two years after it hired Kaufman and only three years after it started business with four people, a vague idea about helping system designers to design chips, and about $500,000 in funding from the venture capital firm Kleiner-Perkins. Kaufman (see Phil Kaufman's Combination Just Right for SCI) described it as "the most confusing and unusual start-up company I'd looked at," which he claims to be the reason why he took on the job of president of the new firm.

The company shipped its first products to test sites in the fall of 1984. By the spring of 1985, it had installed five systems in the field.

Among the company's early successes was a contract with giant minicomputer manufacturer Digital Equipment Corporation (DEC). "The DEC people came to us and asked if we could put their big minicomputer, the VAX, onto a VLSI chip and do the whole job in six months. We were the only ones they found who were crazy enough to say we could. We did." The result is DEC's MicroVAX 1™, completed in just five months by a design team at Silicon Compilers using Silicon Compilers products and methods.

"We believe the only way we can do the job of staying in touch with the usefulness and quality of our product is to use it in real-life design situations ourselves," Kaufman explains, "so we take on difficult and challenging design assignments for potential buyers of the system. They get the results, we learn more about how to improve our product and they often become buyers of the system. Everybody wins."

VLSI design is clearly the wave of the future, just as microprocessors were the wave of the future ten years ago. There are now less than a dozen companies involved in doing VLSI design or selling development tools to others to do so. That number will reach more than 100 by the end of the 1980's.

But all of these chips—LSI or VLSI, NMOS or CMOS—ultimately end up having an impact in terms of the products they are used to build—and one major place where microprocessors and systems are used is in computers.

We now turn our attention from the fascinating internals of the computer to the computer itself.

Computers on the Go

When computer industry pioneer Adam Osborne first introduced his portable Osborne 1 computer in 1982, the industry didn't quite know what to make of it. Nobody had tried to make a full computer portable before, including display and disk drives, and the idea seemed novel enough. But would it sell?

The meteoric rise of Osborne Computers, Inc., as of the rush-to-market imitators and emulators, eloquently answered that question. (Osborne's later collapse had nothing to do with the market's readiness.)

Several major companies are still making millions from the take-your-computer-with-you set. One can often tell how successful a particular segment of an industry is by seeing how fast that segment, in turn, segments. Portable computers now fall into two categories: suitcase-sized portables (also called "luggables" by some now-more-muscular owners) and lap-sized. The former are portable in the same sense as early portable TV sets—they have handles. Luggable portable computers tend to be in the 30-pound range, and typically lack independent battery power.

A computer weighing that much and that must be plugged in is not really portable, but *transportable*.

The lap-sized units, on the other hand, use batteries for operation and typically weigh 10 pounds or less. This makes them usable in terminals, cars, conference rooms, on airplanes, (which initially banned the little systems but now largely permit their use), and in other places where electrical outlets are not conveniently available. Lap-size, battery-operated computers are true portables.

Until recently, true portables were hampered by a lack of memory capacity, absence of disks or other mass storage media, and small displays that didn't function well under frequently encountered lighting conditions.

Manufacturers have recently dealt with these limitations and have introduced small, powerful, lightweight, large-screen, battery-operated computers.

The movement from trendy but bulky transportable computers to lap-sized portables was initiated by Tandy Corporation with the introduction of the TRS-80 Model 100 in 1983. The original basic unit had 8K of memory, some limited-use built-in software, and an 8-line by 40-character screen made with liquid crystal displays (LCD's—the same display technology used in most digital watches). It sold for about $700; a unit with 24K was $1,000.

Today, you can buy the fully-loaded Model 100 for less than $500 and the souped-up Model 200—with more memory and a resident spreadsheet in addition to a larger display—for the $1,000 you would have spent on the Model 100 not many years ago.

Several companies have entered the portable computers with disk drives market. In the next several years, dozens of companies—some established and some start-ups—will cash in on Americans' well-documented penchant for being on the move. IBM introduced a lap-size product in spring, 1986. Zenith Data Systems stunned the micro world in early 1986 by winning a huge government contract with the IRS for portable, lap-top computers with built-in disk drives.

The lap-sized portable market is large. Knowledgeable industry analysts project continued explosive growth for the next couple years.

The portables are made possible by CMOS technology (see What's Happening With These Chips?). Some of these portable units even have CMOS microprocessors (like Tandy's units, which have an 80C85, a CMOS version of Intel's industry workhorse 8085 microprocessor).

Other key players in the lap-sized portable market include Epson, Sharp, Data General, and Texas Instruments. Zenith will shortly introduce a low-end product. Kaypro, maker of one of the most popular and best-selling luggables in the CP/M world of microcomputers, introduced an IBM-compatible lap-sized portable in mid-1985 that seems to set another trend with lots of features and 16-bit power.

Epson's entered the market with a Radio Shack look-alike with 64K of memory and built-in CP/M operating system; it is the only lap-sized machine sporting the 8-bit operating system.

Sharp, with the PC-5000, makes the tactical mistake of using high-priced bubble memory as its storage medium, resulting in a computer priced near the high end where built-in disk drives are becoming available, but that is not substantially better than the lower priced Tandy and Epson units.

Data General and TI made big splashes in the lap-size market in 1985. The former's DG/One unit was launched with great fanfare and a multi-million dollar TV blitz featuring the DG/One emerging, space-launch style, from the innards of a PC. The DG/One features built-in disk drive and IBM PC compatibility. Its screen allows 25 lines of 80 characters each, the standard size for full-sized CRT displays.

TI began shipping Pro-Lite in the spring of 1985. It is similar to the DG/One, with the same built-in drive and 256K of memory, along with a 25x80 LCD display. Both are priced in the $3,000 range.

One or more Japanese companies will introduce a truly low-priced portable with built-in disk drives, PC-compatibility, and a full-size display in the immediate future. When that happens, if the computer sells in the $1,000 price range, the war in the lap-sized market will be over before some companies have the opportunity to fire an opening shot.

Besides CMOS and the unexpectedly high demand for mobility by computer users, one other technology has driven the portable computer market: LCD displays. When Tandy introduced the Model 100, the 8x40 display was the best anyone could produce in quantities. The size is a limitation—though people who use them regularly, the author included, find the limitation to be one to which it is not difficult to adjust. On the other hand, visibility of the screen under less than optimum lighting conditions tended to be poor. In fact, the LCD screen is impossible to see under certain circumstances. Glare was a problem.

In late 1984, a Sunnyvale, California company, CrystalVision, solved the problems associated with LCD displays of large size. The company ran out of money before it moved into manufacturing on a large scale, but its solutions were sold to other companies. Therefore, lap-sized portables will soon appear with greatly improved displays.

The CrystalVision solution permits viewing the display from a 50-80-degree angle (vs. 15 degrees for most LCDs) with an unaided contrast ratio (light-to-dark ratio for readability) of 6:1 or even 8:1 as compared with 3:1 for most LCDs and only about 10:1 for the light-dark contrast of the words on this page.

Manufacturers of lap-sized portable computers will quickly take advantage of this technology to turn out products with very highly readable screens, plenty of built-in memory, inherent 3-1/2-inch floppy disk drives, and light weight.

A battle will shape up in this market, with a shakeout in late 1986 and a settled-in marketplace by early 1987.

Some of the portable makers will also experiment with plasma gas and other less traditional display methodologies, but it seems unlikely that any of these alternatives will catch on enough to become the standard to replace the inexpensive LCD's now that some of the technological problems in that design approach have been addressed.

One final point about portable computers. Color displays on lap-sized systems will not be available at a reasonable price before 1990. Manufacturers of LCDs are just getting to the point where they can build LCDs in color in very small sizes; the large size LCD required for a 25x80—or even an 8x40—display for computer use is, by LCD standards, huge. It will be a number of years before LCD units that size can be built economically with color technology.

As portables become the watchword of the personal computer business, large numbers of executives, journalists, sales representatives, consultants, and other similarly mobile workers will end up owning two systems. The lap-sized one will travel with them wherever they go to meet with clients or customers. They will use modems and phone lines to dial up their larger, desktop units at the home office (or at home), which will become more powerful and incorporate more and more mass storage. Users will then transfer any data between the home system and its traveling companion with a simple phone call and a command or two.

The two-system approach to dealing with conflicting needs for lots of mass storage capacity and true portability will catch on in the next couple years.

The trend will have an important fallout effect—an increasing demand on the part of users for standardization of software and compatibility of equipment. This movement, which puts smart terminals into the hands of relatively sophisticated users, will do more for software compatibility than anyone imagines today.

It's a safe bet, too, that the system at home or at the home office will be equipped, during the last part of this decade, with sophisticated and helpful peripheral devices. Let us shift our attention to that area for the last part of our discussion of hardware advances in the last half of the 1980's.

Outside: Massive Changes

As we move outside the computer itself, we find ourselves in a world where everything seems to be happening at once. Companies who want to cash in on the microcomputer revolution but who are too late or too small to build a new micro themselves delight in building devices to hook up to those computers.

The next few years will see major advances in mass storage of computer data, the quality of graphics printed and displayed, telecommunications equipment, and the human interface. We will take a brief look at each of these areas in turn.

Mass Storage

No one doubts that the coming rage in mass storage in microcomputers is optical disks, particularly for small-business and high-end home computers. Low-priced card readers capable of handling small to moderate amounts of program or data at a time at very low cost and high transportability will also have a market presence (see Software Advances and the discussion about Cardettes, page 265). But the big news at the high end of micros will definitely be optical disks.

Optical disks (see Optical Disks) will permit storage of unheard-of amounts of information in relatively small spaces. Billions of bits of information—enough to contain whole libraries of data—will be stored on these devices that appear to be a cross between a video disk and an audio recording, with something of a floppy disk thrown in for good measure.

Atari Corporation was working on a low-cost video disk interface for its home computer line before ex-Commodore chief Jack Tramiel bought the company in mid-1984. The status of this development, like everything else at Atari, is no longer easy to ascertain, but rumors persist that before long an Atari optical disk unit will appear that will sell for less than $500. Such a product would be quite a coup for Atari. Commodore, however, may beat Atari.

A company that is known to be spending many resources on video and optical disk technology is IBM. "Big Blue" will announce a video disk controller system in the near future. Another company to watch in this respect is DEC. Expect news about a disk product from them in the next several months. Digital Research, of Monterey, California, who produced CP/M, the first standard operating system, had a video disk project under way, but has since discontinued it.

The coming movement of IBM into the technology of marrying computers and video disks for real-life applications will not shock anyone watching the industry or IBM. Regardless of who produces it first, such a product will appear within two years.

It will not be possible, initially, to store any of your own information on an optical disk; the science of writing information on such a medium requires expensive and precise equipment, and the writing, once recorded, is permanent.

Several Japanese companies are reported to be at or near a solution to the problem of writing data on optical disks, erasing it, and writing new data on the same disk. Some companies are reportedly poised to introduce a "write-on" optical disk in the late 1980's. These disks will be able to serve as storage devices but not as places to store continually changing information. Commercial availability of affordable personal units may be more than five years away.

Optical disks will one day offer an excellent way of providing large data bases to personal computer owners or of selling huge libraries of software or pre-designed graphics for use in other programs, but they won't do away with floppy disks for the foreseeable future.

There is one remaining unanswered question: What will consumers *do* with all of that storage capacity? Many industry observers believe the answer will be a resounding, "Nothing," which will result in optical disk becoming yet another microcomputer industry version of a solution in search of a problem. Many people who own 10-megabyte hard disks—only 1/30 the storage of even the smallest optical disks being widely discussed—report

they never fill them up at all. While we can store an entire encyclopedia or small library on such disks, of what use will they be
that can't be served as well or better by on-line information services? And even though the price per megabyte of memory will be
incredibly small at the point these devices become commercially
available, the readers will boast a price tag in the $500–$1,000
range, a range that already keeps many owners of personal computers from adding a second floppy disk drive.

Not everyone, however, is so unsure of the potential market.
Peter Black, president of Xiphias of Southern California and a
recognized graphics expert, sees the emergence of video disks as a
computer-related medium as particularly significant.

"This step will force us all to redefine what business we're in,"
he says. "All of us are really in the communications business, just
like (filmmakers) Steven Spielberg and George Lucas. We use the
technological media available to us to convey our perspectives,
thoughts, and ideas."

Black goes one step further and predicts that video disk technology, when mated successfully with microcomputers, will result
in "production value" being added to software and data used in
homes and small businesses.

"Video quality will improve markedly when we can store
video information on a disk and display it directly on the
screen, perhaps overlaying it with graphics or text generated
by the computer directly," he says. "Production values like appropriate color, good lighting, editing, cinematographic technique, and other approaches will finally be brought to bear on
the home computer."

What You See Is What You Get

In the world of computers, what you see is almost never what
you get. The advent of display screens of very high quality and the
emergence of the laser printer promise to change all that in the
near future.

The correspondence between what we see displayed on a screen
in front of us and what prints on our printers, particularly when it
comes to graphics (including special typefaces and fonts that

appear to be words to us but are graphics to the computer), is simply not present in today's systems.

We envision a layout for an advertisement in a newsletter we are publishing. We see it with typefaces and fonts, variable sizes, and a drawing or two. Then we try to put that same layout into our personal computers to produce a finished product, and the process breaks down in frustration. We find that what we see on paper and what we can get a computer to display are two different things.

There is usually an even bigger gap between what we can get the computer's display to show us and what the printers we have will produce for us. The end result is very little resemblance between the original idea and the finished product.

Computer displays that can produce graphics in the colors and shapes we expect are available today—at prohibitively high prices. The problem is that before we can display an object on a screen, we have to place a representation of that object into the computer's memory. Until very recently, memory devices have been too expensive to allow us the flexibility we'd like for graphic displays at reasonable prices. A few simple calculations reveal the reason for the problem.

Let's look at the Macintosh, Apple's prize product of 1984. It has a screen resolution of approximately 640 lines by 480 horizontal dots, or pixels. Each of these places on the screen must have a value stored in memory that indicates whether it is to be "on" (i.e., dark) or "off" (i.e., light). Multiplying 640 by 480, we find that we need 307,200 *bits*, or 38,400 *bytes* of computer storage just to hold the contents of the screen.

In an 8-bit microcomputer with 64K of available memory, this would have meant devoting over half of the memory to the screen display alone. If we decide to add color to this display, the numbers get even bigger. For example, let's say we want to have four colors on the screen at any one time. We will need two bits to represent these four colors (a bit value of 00 means the first color, 01 the second, 10 the third and 11 the fourth), plus a bit to indicate whether to display the dot or not (i.e, an on-off bit), unless we make one of our colors black, in which case it could be argued we have only three colors. In any event, instead of the 38,400 bytes we used to need, it will now take 76,800 to 115,200 bytes to store a screen representation of four colors.

The problem, as we said, has been of memory cost. With the introduction of one-megabit chips and the corresponding expected price reduction in lower capacity devices, the ability to display enough colors and enough screen locations to produce smoothly rounded and diagonal lines should become widely available on the new microcomputers introduced in the rest of the 1980's.

In fact, the Amiga, Commodore's new machine, has a screen resolution of 640x200 and is capable of displaying 32 colors on the screen at once, which is the most of any product on the market in a reasonable price range. We have, however, seen a plug-in printed circuit board for the IBM PC that will be available in the immediate future, which permits the display of up to 512 colors on the screen at one time!

All of this increased display quality will be nice to look at, but unless we can translate it into printed output, its use will be limited to situations where we can show someone our computer screens. That's where printers, specifically, *laser* printers come in.

Laser printers made their initial appearance on the personal computer market in late 1984 with the advent of a product from H-P (Hewlett-Packard Company of Palo Alto, California). The H-P LaserJet printer was initially designed and released for H-P computers, but interfaces to the IBM PC, and other popular micros were soon introduced by other companies.

At a price tag of about $3,500, the LaserJet turns out typeset-quality printed pages of hard copy at the rate of 15–20 pages per minute. By contrast, a high-speed dot matrix printer will generate about two pages per minute. In addition, laser printers do not look or sound much like the bulky, noisy devices we have come to know and love. They look more like copiers—and sound like them, only quieter. They are virtually noiseless, an important factor in business and professional offices where early acceptance of the LaserJet was very high. (The operation of these machines is explained in Laser Printing—Writing with (Coherent) Light, page 251.)

In early 1985, Apple Computer introduced its own laser printer, the LaserWriter, to match up with its Macintosh and Lisa computer lines. The printer was introduced at nearly $7,000.

Apple's LaserWriter has drawn a great deal of attention because of the way Apple chose to control it. Apple contracted with a Palo Alto-based company, Adobe Systems, to design a software interface to the LaserWriter printer that would enable users to do very sophisticated printing via the complex graphic structure of the Mac and the now-discontinued Lisa. The result was a printer that comes equipped with an Adobe Systems program called PostScript. "Post-Script basically puts all of the smarts about typesetting, graphics, and printing into the printer," explains Rob Auster, former director of product support for Adobe.

The LaserWriter printer has its own processor, two megabytes of its own memory, and built-in interfaces to the outside world. It is, in effect, a printing computer.

"Basically, this product combines three diverse technologies," Auster explains as he ticks them off on his fingers. "There is image processing, which is basically analysis of what an image is and of what it consists; graphics, which are shapes and structures rather than pixels as we've been accustomed to thinking about them; and typesetting. I could do a whole sales pitch about type as art and there's a lot of 'magic' in how typesetting is done."

By combining these three technologies into one software-hardware product, Adobe Systems came up with a product that Apple founder Steve Jobs (then still the kingpin in new product development for the computer maker) liked the first time he saw it. The resulting LaserWriter printer produces copy very quickly, almost silently and with 300x300 dot-per-square-inch resolution. This compares to a resolution of 72 dots per inch on the best dot matrix printers and "only" 140x160 resolution on Apple's ImageWriter printer.

The printer mechanism itself is purchased by Apple, which also manufactures the controller board designed by Adobe Systems. Adobe sells Apple the software that drives the printer.

"From MacDraw (an Apple-produced graphic drawing package), we can set up all kinds of graphic and typesetting combinations and route them to the printer with instructions to enlarge, reduce, rotate (even at unusual angles), or flip them," Auster explains. "One of the things the software handles, for example, is the gray tone quality problem."

Gray tones are made up of patterns of dots packed closely together: the closer the density, the darker the gray until we reach black where the dots are immediately adjacent to one another. If we take a square, say, three inches on a side and put a gray pattern into it so that the gray dots are packed 30 to the inch and then enlarge that square to a square nine inches on a side, we lose a lot of the gray tone. The dots are enlarged along with the square and the spaces between them are also enlarged. But PostScript "understands" graphics and shapes and tones and automatically adjusts the gray tone as we increase or decrease the size of the objects we send to it.

Adobe's founder is John Warwick, formerly of the Utah-based Evans and Sutherland Company, a computer graphics pioneering organization. Warwick designed the product to be independent of the computer or of the resolution desired on the printed output.

"There are," Auster says confidently, "no page formats that will 'break' the printer, in other words, no formats it could simply not print."

Adobe is in the process of licensing the "engine" at the heart of PostScript to other companies, some in the computer business but some in the typesetting business.

One of the key selling points of the PostScript software— implemented on the Apple LaserWriter or elsewhere—is the fact that Adobe was able to convince Mergenthaler, a world-famous company in the typesetting business, to license all of its fonts to Adobe for inclusion in PostScript software.

"There has never been anything this good in the computer industry just in terms of the artistic quality of the type," Auster claims.

As good a product as the LaserWriter and the LaserJet might be, the price range is still out of the reach of most users of home and personal computers. But laser printers with less capability than the LaserWriter, and perhaps a bit slower or otherwise less capable, will be available for home computer users within a year. Several companies are reportedly already at work on Macintosh-compatible laser printers that will also interface smoothly with Apple's graphic standard.

At the upper end of the laser printer business, expect to see, within the very near future, a product (possibly from Xerox) with

1200x1200 dot per inch resolution—the quality equivalent to or better than phototypesetting.

"Give a person a small computer, a good idea, and a laser printer and he can turn out quality printed messages conveying his opinion about any subject you can think of," Auster says. "The laser printer is the modern and improved equivalent of a printing press and has the potential for having as great an impact on society as the printing press had. The ideas of the common man will be indistinguishable, graphically, from those of professional publishers."

A lofty thought for a printing technique that more closely resembles Xerography than pen-and-paper, but one that is turning out to be quite accurate. Literally hundreds of companies, schools, universities, and printing plants have flocked to laser printing in combination with Apple's Macintosh computer and Aldus' Page Maker newsletter layout program or similar products. Their aim: to become in-house publishers of their own newsletters, customer reports, proposals, and other publications. They expect to reap great rewards in greater control over the quality and timing of the finished product as well as in cash savings.

Next Up: SuperModem!

You may never hear the name SICOM, but chances are excellent that if you buy a modem in the next year or two it will incorporate technology developed by that Santa Cruz, California, company and its chief scientist, Lee Hearn (see Lee Hearn Knows Modems).

"Modem" is a shortened form of the term modulator/demodulator. It is a device for connecting computers to one another over telephone lines. (The importance and use of modems are discussed more thoroughly in Chapter 2, Broadening Our Community, page 66.)

SICOM is about to release what Hearn calls a "Universal Modem Module" that the company plans to sell as a component to be added to printed circuit boards made by microcomputer manufacturers and modem companies.

"Basically, this product combines nine modems into one device," Hearn explains. The nine modems provide variations of baud rates and communications "protocols." Protocols are the standards by which various countries and companies agree to transmit data. Protocols govern the format in which data is sent, how sending and receiving units will know when the other is done transmitting or has successfully received the data, and a host of other technical details that are transparent to modem users but of great concern to modem designers like Hearn.

The Universal Modem Module incorporates three baud rates: the now-standard 300, the 2400 baud, and the 1200, which will be a standard in a few years if all goes as expected. Each of these baud rates is offered in both European and American standard protocols, for a total of six modems. Then add three other modems that are 1200- and 2400-baud with the ability to have communication take place at high speed in one direction and at very slow (150 baud) rates in the other.

This last combination is particularly useful. Data being transmitted from a remote computer to your terminal at 300 baud is being displayed on our screens far more slowly than we can read. We would like to speed that process up since we generally pay for time used on such systems. On the other hand, our typing back to the main computer is far *slower* than 300 baud as a rule, so we'd like not to have to pay the higher hourly rate for 1200 or 2400 baud while we plunk away on our keyboards at 100 or 150 baud. The dual-speed modem gives us the best of both worlds.

Hearn's design can be implemented at very low cost, which is one of its main advantages. "A standard 1200-baud modem sells for something like $500 to $800," Hearn says. "If you bought all nine of these modems separately, you'd spend maybe $3,000. We will sell the Universal Modem Module for under $35, including two semi-custom chips that are the brains of the unit."

At this point, the modem is to some degree overkill for home computer users, though not necessarily for small business buyers. Home system owners can usually communicate with the computers they deal with—primarily information utilities like CompuServe or local bulletin board systems—only at 300 or 1200 baud. In fact, most offer only 300 baud communication. Small business owners are in a position, at least potentially, to control the transmission rate at which they can communicate with the mainframe computers they own and thus should be able to make instant use of the SICOM technology.

A problem facing high-speed modem usage is telephone line quality. Users who communicate with remote systems via modem at 1200 baud experience data not being transmitted correctly. The problem is caused by bandwidth limitations of voice-grade telephone lines. Hearn's Universal Modem Module deals with that issue by using a form of artificial intelligence known as "adaptive equalization" that balances the signal levels, voltage levels, and noise content of the transmission line adaptively as the transmission is in process. This modem thus "understands" what the transmission should look like, anticipates problems, and conditions the line to avoid them.

Hearn and his company have been approached by a number of major modem manufacturers about incorporating the Universal Modem Module into future products. Thanks to this technology, the communications bottleneck caused by many people wanting to access the same computer and tying up limited phone capacity for long periods may be sufficiently alleviated to accommodate a major expansion of that business in the next few years.

Now, Listen Here, You Computer!

We speak of "talking" to our computers. Unfortunately, what we *mean* by talking to a computer is almost always typing information into it via a keyboard or sending it information over some sort of cable. "My PC won't talk to my Radio Shack," we say. What we mean is that we are having trouble getting our Radio Shack computer and our IBM computer to communicate with each other.

Soon, we'll have to clean up our language to be more precise, because the day of the computer that listens to our speech is just around the corner. In fact, if you have enough money, it's here already.

Limited use of speech with microcomputers has been around for a year or two on an experimental basis. Two years ago, a company called Auricle demonstrated a product that would permit a person sitting at a terminal with a headset to give the computer terminal verbal instructions related to editing a document and the computer would obey.

"Down," the user would command, and the cursor would move down a line. "Insert," the voice would say, and the computer would set itself up to receive new information to be inserted at that point in the document. The user could then type in the new information and say "Adjust" and the computer would reformat the screen to include the new data within the margin settings.

The device had to be reprogrammed for each voice that was to be used with it. In fact, that is true of all voice recognition systems on the market so far. The problem is simple. The way you say "Down" and the way your aunt says "Down" may bear little or no resemblance to one another. The computer, which only sees a digitized image of the voice pattern anyway (see Voice and Speech Systems) must be *told* that the two voice patterns—so radically different from the computer's viewpoint—are intended to mean the same thing. That is why we can speak in terms of specific voice recognition, but not yet in terms of the more general speech recognition.

A number of products on the market permit computers to respond to the human voice in some limited way. Texas Instruments, before it bowed out of the home computer market, had demonstrated a baseball game that was played by two players who took turns wearing a headset through which they instructed the program where to position players, when to throw the ball, etc.

So far, none of these programs or products has been wildly successful. For one thing, their vocabularies are so limited that their application is of necessity narrowed to the use of one program at a time, and then generally only with a subset of the available commands in that program. For another thing, their error rate tends to be unacceptable. Finally, they have been too expensive to be able to be considered for widespread implementation in home computer systems and will probably remain so for the next couple of years.

But their arrival on the home scene is inevitable. And they have already begun to show up on the business scene with products from IBM, AT&T, Rolm Corporation (now a subsidiary of

IBM), and a small San Jose firm called Sydis, Inc. Sydis is one of the more exciting companies visited while researching this book. Their VoiceStation System (VSS), described in detail in Executive Workstations Without Keyboards, permits the storage, editing, and transmission of voice messages from one user to another.

In the future, Sydis plans to have a workstation that is also *controlled* by voice, permitting the elimination of even the programmable function keys that now border two sides of the screen on the terminal, and the ubiquitous mouse.

As exciting as the Sydis VSS terminal and system are, they are still relatively expensive and well beyond the reach of the very small business or home user. Another product using voice is clearly not intended to be in that rarified price range atmosphere. Rumors persist that we will soon be able to purchase a voice-activated Kurzweil typewriter. These rumors would be hard to believe if it weren't for the fact that this is the very same inventor who gave the world full-page optical character recognition (OCR) a few years ago in the face of huge obstacles of computer "understanding" of character shapes read by means of optical lenses.

Reportedly, this typewriter will have a vocabulary of many thousand words and be able to turn out copy at the rate of 150 words per minute. The technical community has been abuzz with the idea for several months. The reality may be within a year of being achieved.

While voice is the "sexiest" of the alternatives to the keyboard as a way of getting information into the computer, it is by no means the only way. In fact, today it isn't even the most significant. Other devices being used to input information into a computer include the following:

Optical Character Recognition (OCR) Devices OCR devices optically scan printed materials and enter the characters into the memory of the computer. A program then translates the information into words the system can use. Recent months have seen a dramatic decrease in the price of OCR capability, with the most remarkable price being Oberon International's Omni Reader. The Omni Reader works with most popular home microcomputers and costs just about $500. To be sure, it is slow and somewhat unreliable, but for home and small business use it represents a positive step in the right direction. OCR readers with price tags below $300 and capable of reading many different type faces with great accuracy will be commonplace by 1990.

Mice Popularized by the Macintosh from Apple, this method of input has the user roll a small object around on a desktop to manipulate a pointer or cursor on the screen so that it points at things to be done. A click of one or more buttons on the mouse then has the effect of instructing the computer to do whatever the object being pointed at stands for as an instruction.

Graphics Tablets These have not quite caught on as some people thought they would. Apple markets a digitizing tablet for its family of computers. Digitizers have been accepted and used by engineers who wish to enter drawing information into a system, but have not met with widespread acceptance otherwise. The Santa Clara firm, Koala Technologies connects digitizing tablets to home and personal computers as means of getting information in and out and entering drawings and graphics into the system.

Touch Screens Tried with limited success by Hewlett-Packard on its HP150 personal computer, these have been less enthusiastically received than digitizing tablets in all but limited applications.

Light Pens Designer Steve Gibson has created this idea and championed it for years. It has not been widely accepted on home systems, but where it has been implemented in businesses, user response has been generally good. Using this technology is a take-off on the touch-screen. Instead of using one's finger to touch the screen at a point that the computer interprets as an instruction, one points a pen-like object at that point on the screen and clicks a button on the pen.

3-D "Joystick" Replacement In the summer of 1985, a Campbell, California, company called Soniture, Inc., introduced a three-dimensional "Space Pen" that needs no wires to attach to a computer display device. It permits the user to control objects on the computer screen in three dimensions. Software will have to be modified to take advantage of this product, and given the state of that industry the level of interest in doing so may be insufficient to make the Space Pen successful. But there is an attraction to "painting in space" that many people find irresistible. At first, only game and graphic software seems destined to take full advantage of the Space Pen but Soniture president Paul Terrell believes his company's pen can find use in 3-D spreadsheets like Crunch! Version 2.0 as well.

Clearly the keyboard is under a strong attack as the main means of getting data into a computer. Equally clearly, it will still be around as the means of accomplishing that end when the 1980's draw to a close. ExperTelligence president and long-time computer camp counselor Denny Bollay disagrees with that assessment though. "The keyboard will be history within five years," he says firmly.

The keyboard surely has limitations, not the least of which is the fear or unfamiliarity of most people. Beyond that, the keyboard layout itself is cumbersome and was in fact designed to slow down early users of typewriters so they wouldn't be able to type so fast as to jam the mechanical keys into each other. But with all of its faults, it is the least expensive, least error-prone, most universally understood and—perhaps most importantly—the most widely used of all of the input devices. It is going to be difficult to dislodge from that position.

(The future will lie in making the keyboard susceptible to intelligent human usage, a software problem addressed in the next chapter of this book. Some exciting products have emerged to deal with this super-problem.)

Opportunities, Strategies, and Decisions

We've covered a tremendous amount of material in our glimpse at the future of hardware in the microcomputer industry. Out of it all, at least the following ideas emerge.

Careers If you are making a career decision, you'll want to avoid careers that fail to take a systems approach to their areas of specialty. The jobs of the future will be held by people who can generalize, can see the big picture, and are able to design systems to solve problems.

Integrated circuit design will not be a growing field in view of the emergence of VLSI.

If you are artistically inclined, seriously consider not only learning to use computers as tools but perhaps having some influence on how they use and produce graphic designs; your ideas will be more welcome than ever in the next few years.

Investment Investors should be aware of the fact that the emergence of VLSI will probably fundamentally change the way the semiconductor industry does business. To survive, companies may have to make difficult choices between being fabricators, sellers, or designers of ICs. Up to now, the young industry has been dominated by a few major companies who do everything, but the prospect of literally throwing away whole factories and starting over every five years will have to take its toll.

Beyond that, companies with smart peripheral devices or firms who are responding to the growing demand for portable computers will probably do well in the next few years.

Management Making management decisions based on the contents of this chapter won't be so clear-cut. Be ready, for your more mobile employees will begin asking for powerful lap-sized portable computers, if they haven't already done so.

Telecommunications will clearly become more sophisticated and require your host system to deal with a variety of problems. Begin now developing standards and flexible rules about that area of your computer's usage by your employees.

Finally, it's probably not a good idea to permit people to postpone using a desktop system because they want to wait until the keyboard gets replaced. It will be a while. In the meantime they are being less productive than they might otherwise be.

Phil Kaufman's Combination Is Just Right for SCI

"When I first heard about what Carver Mead and Dave Johannsen had started, I figured this silicon compiler stuff was crazy, not for the real world," says Phil Kaufman.

The fact that he is speaking from his spacious office in a prominent corner of Silicon Compilers Incorporated and serves as the firm's first full-time president indicates he changed his mind somewhere along the way.

Kaufman may have been one of very few people in the world whose background and experience suited him to running a company, which in order to be successful, had to combine the skills of integrated circuit designers, systems designers, and software systems engineers into a smooth blend of VLSI development tool designers.

In the mid- and late-1960's, Kaufman, with an MSEE degree from the University of Michigan and a specialty in signal processing and communications theory, moved to California and worked as an engineer and later a product planner. During this time, although his background was primarily in systems design and software, Kaufman managed the design of a set of integrated circuits for use in the first 16-bit LSI minicomputer. By the mid-1970's, it was clear to Kaufman that microprocessors were the wave of the future, so he started listening to job offers from companies involved in that business.

In 1976, he was recruited by Intel Corporation, founders of the microcomputer industry, to run that firm's non-integrated circuit design operations. Later, he was moved to a position on Intel president Andy Grove's staff in strategic planning and then became general manager of the microprocessor operations area, where he spearheaded efforts to develop Intel's hot new processors, the 80186 and the 80286.

"One day, I looked around and decided it was time I tried to do a start-up," Kaufman recalls. So he began letting the word get around that he would be interested in a start-up company if the right fit could be found.

Meanwhile, Kleiner-Perkins, a well-known venture capital firm, had given Dr. Carver Mead of California Institute of Technology a few hundred thousand dollars to try some ideas in VLSI design approaches, an area of activity that was then extremely new.

"Carver had been working as a consultant to Kleiner-Perkins for a few years, helping them do technical evaluations of products," Kaufman says, "and when he suggested this VLSI stuff might be a good idea in a couple of years, they said, 'If you think it's a good idea, let's do it now.' This company didn't start like any other start-up I'd heard about."

In early 1982, Kleiner-Perkins and Mead decided the company, Silicon Compilers Incorporated, needed a president to take it to the next level of growth. The fit seemed right to Mead and his backers, but Kaufman was a little hesitant.

"Here was a company," Kaufman says, "which had eight people, no business plan, and just an idea for how to give system engineers the ability to design integrated circuits. It was the most screwed-up company I'd looked at.

"So naturally, I took the job."

As the company grew, Kaufman's background in both design and system engineering, as well as his grasp of strategic planning and its importance, paid off for Silicon Compilers.

About a year after he took over the helm, the company reached what Kaufman refers to in retrospect as a "jeopardy point."

"No one felt they needed anyone else," he says, shaking his head. "I'd find myself sitting in a conference room with four key software guys who would tell me they could finish the project in six months if they were just left alone. Fifteen minutes later, four IC design people were saying the same thing."

The problem of combining several cultures—IC designers, system engineers, research people, and software designers—had become a major obstacle.

Kaufman's solution? "It was clear to me that none of these groups fully understood the scope and the impact of what we were trying to do," he said. "In the course of expanding the company, we'd forgotten to make sure the message got across."

So Kaufman shepherded the professional staff of the company off to the seaside resort of Pajaro Dunes where they spent several days exploring with one another the relationships among the groups and disciplines, considering the company's mission, and just getting to know one another outside the pressures of daily deadlines.

The result is apparent. The company today has 110 people from all of the original disciplines plus a few more. But the various engineering groups talk to each other. In fact, they talk to each other so well that Kaufman is confident his company will move from $3 million in sales in the first year to $20 million in the second.

As for his future, Kaufman is not looking for anything else to do outside Silicon Compilers. "We're still a long way from our ideal," he says somewhat wistfully. "The ideal is when a guy sits at his desk and says, 'I wish I had a chip that did so and so' and he opens a box and out pops the chip that does so and so."

To move the company closer to that wishful goal, Kaufman says the firm needs to focus on increasing the level at which systems engineers interface with the workstation and with the design. And it needs to explore the world of artificial intelligence to see what it can add to what's being done now, a step that has already started as Silicon Compilers has hired its first AI experts.

"We'd better spend a lot of our time obsoleting our own products," Kaufman says firmly, "or someone else will."

For the moment Silicon Compilers appears to be doing an excellent job of obsoleting themselves—and becoming a memorable success story in the process.

Lee Hearn Knows Modems

Lee Hearn, SICOM owner-founder and designer of the Universal Modem Module, has been involved in telecommunications most of his engineering career.

Hearn was, at age 11, the youngest amateur radio operator in the history of the state of Alabama. Though no longer active in "ham" circles, his interest in communicating over vast distances has stayed with him.

Hearn, now 52 years old, holds a bachelor's degree in electronic engineering from the University of Louisville, two bachelor's degrees in physics and math, and an MSEE from New Mexico State University. He has done post-graduate work at the Universities of Maryland and Santa Clara in computer design, data communication, and related fields.

Hearn can't talk much about his earlier career when he was on contract with the National Security Agency. "I learned modem design there. We were doing some incredibly advanced, but very secretive work there in the years I was with The Company," he says.

Only recently has some of his earlier work become declassified so that he could use his research on the outside.

Hearn later worked for several modem companies, including Prentice, a leader in the industry, where he worked on the first "line driver" devices designed to transmit data without modulation over ordinary twisted-pair wires.

Later, Lee joined Atari Corporation where he served as a senior vice-president of Atari subsidiary Scientific Telecommunications Systems. There, he worked on a number of projects involving data, voice, and graphic communication systems for possible incorporation into future Atari home computer products.

In the financial difficulties and management/ownership shuffles that took place at Atari in the past few years, Hearn has not seen any of his product designs come to fruition, though he expects some will someday.

For the past several years, Hearn, who lives in Santa Cruz, with his wife, Jackie, has been a consultant and president of his own company, SICOM. He has a large, well-equipped laboratory at his home in the mountains where he spends most of his time in research.

Silicon Compilers' Workstation

A system designer sits down at a Silicon Compilers graphics terminal connected to a minicomputer system in the next room and begins to translate his idea for a system on a chip into a design. Using a mouse and a few editing commands, he begins to define the needed functions of the device on a full-color screen. The chip, which a year ago could only have been designed by one of a relative handful of experts, begins to take shape before his eyes. In a matter of weeks, instead of months or even years, he has completed the design, simulated its operation, and determined it will meet the needs he has defined. An integrated circuit is about to be born.

This kind of interactive design of a complex integrated circuit— one combining hundreds of thousands of tiny transistors into a horrendously complex design—has become possible in the last year thanks to the work done by Silicon Compilers Incorporated of San Jose, among others.

Silicon Compilers takes its name from the analogy between automatic generation of VLSI designs to be etched into silicon and generation of machine language software and software compilers (such as FORTRAN and COBOL).

In the past, only computer programs were compiled; now, hardware designs can be compiled from high-level descriptions, displayed graphically on the screen, and then simulated and optimized into a finished chip layout that can be used to manufacture an integrated circuit.

Silicon Compilers' first product, The Genesil Silicon Development System, is a four-user system incorporating four full-color graphic terminals, complete with mice, full keyboards, and a DEC VAX minicomputer. It goes well beyond the traditional functions of CAD and CAE (computer aided design and computer aided engineering, respectively) systems. Using expert systems technology, it enables the system designer to build chips that meet specific system needs without the need for special training as an integrated circuit design specialist. Silicon Compilers prices these four-engineer systems at about $600,000 and says that at that price "market reception has been astronomical."

Besides the ease with which a design can be specified, simulated, and analyzed, the Silicon Compilers system also permits the design engineer to do what is called "exploratory design." This process involves making basic decisions about the possible architectures of the chip and evaluating these alternatives. It is one of the most potentially significant tasks that the engineer performs in the course of a VLSI design.

"Our system," Silicon Compilers' president Phil Kaufman explains, "lets the user put a little information about the design approach into the system and get back information that enables him to make the architectural decision early in the design process." This is vital, Kaufman says, because ". . .' the difference between the right architecture and a poor architectural choice for a given design can be a factor of several times in the size of the finished chip."

The current Silicon Compilers systems fall short of being what could be called artificially intelligent, but they incorporate some of the features of an expert system. "We have the knowledge and the rule-based system in place in the computer now," Kaufman says, "but there's no real learning going on. The system doesn't try to learn from design decisions made by its using engineers."

Kaufman clearly intends some future product development to take the system into the classification of a genuine artificial intelligence.

In the meantime, a major new development for Silicon Compilers will be to enable their systems to develop the highly complex testing programs needed for manufacturers of VLSI chips to check out the finished product to be sure it works as expected.

This process, required on all integrated circuits, becomes vastly complicated as the number of functions and transistors to be analyzed and tested increases. "Because our product has some semantic knowledge about the chip design," Kaufman explains, "it should be able to generate a test program in a fraction of the time it would take a human test programmer to do the same job."

In other words, the system has both functional and contextual understanding of the design and interrelatedness of the parts in the tentative design. The system does not see a chip merely as a collection of transistors and gates as with conventional CAD systems. Kaufman believes this semantic knowledge sets the Silicon Compilers product apart from potential competitors and gives his company a long-term edge in the emerging VLSI development tool marketplace.

The next immediately visible step in the growth of Silicon Compilers will be the availability of its functions on a Daisy System product. Daisy, which is also in the CAD/CAE business, builds multi-functional systems that can be configured for a single user. Daisy and Silicon Compilers have signed a deal that allows Daisy to incorporate into its products the software and knowledge base at the heart of the Silicon Compilers product.

"This will enable us to give users a single-user entry point and will permit users to perform many different tasks on a single workstation," Kaufman explains. He also indicated the company intends to announce its own single-user version.

Development of the Silicon Compilers was far from a straightforward task. "This is easily the largest and most complex software system developed under UNIX," (the popular Bell System-developed operating system) the Silicon Compilers' chief says.

"We broke the operating system many times and spent a lot of money fixing it."

The resulting product, however, is one with no current competition and one that Silicon Compilers believes will set the standard in VLSI design approaches for the foreseeable future.

Executive Workstations Without Keyboards

Sydis Inc. of San Jose, CA, brought the idea of voice processing to commercial reality in late 1984 when it began shipping its VoiceStation System (VSS). By early 1985, some two dozen systems had been installed and the company was on its way to becoming established as a leader in the field of voice-data communications. Cash flow problems coupled with the well-publicized computer industry slump, is currently causing the company serious problems. But it is a safe bet that much of its technology, described here, will show up in many places.

Using a Sydis VSS, an executive can send voice messages to subordinates and superiors, dictation to a secretary, and instructions to his management team, all without touching a conventional keyboard. In fact, many VSS terminals are installed at executives' desks with no keyboard attached. Terminal control is handled by means of 21 buttons arranged on the left side and across the bottom of the terminal unit. The function of these "soft keys" changes as the application changes, with labels being displayed directly on the terminal's screen so that the executive or other user can determine at a glance what to do next.

Talking to a Computer

J. B. Wallingham is a hypothetical business executive who, like many of his colleagues, can't or won't type. On his desk is a futuristic looking VSS terminal, with a telephone handset integrated into the side of the cabinet.

This morning, he comes into his office at 7:30 A.M. and activates his desktop terminal by pushing a button labeled "Desk Top." A message appears at the top of the monochrome high-resolution display (a display that looks reassuringly like a piece of paper to him). "Good morning, J. B." The message used to say "Good morning, Mr. Wallingham," but he's come to like his workstation so much he had the programmer put him on a first-name basis.

As he reaches for a pencil in his desk pen set with his left hand, he punches a button on the bottom of the screen with his right index finger. "You have a message waiting," the screen tells him. Two more quick button pokes and he's looking at a memo from the Manufacturing VP about an urgent quality control problem at the Peoria plant. In the third paragraph, he notes the VP has briefly mentioned that the problem is "just like the one we had two years ago at San Diego." He can't for the life of him remember what that problem was.

Using the buttons along the side of the terminal, J. B. moves the pointer in the message to the place where that comment is located. He then pushes a button marked "open voice," or "voice comment" and the labels on the bottom row of keys suddenly change to read "Stop," "Fast Forward," "Play," "Record," "Rewind/Cue." He pushes the one marked "Record."

"Jim," he begins. "I've forgotten about that incident in San Jose you mentioned here. Could you give me a quick refresher on it, please?" As he talks, a line appears in a window on his screen showing him how long he is talking, where his pauses are and generally giving him the feeling that a piece of recording tape is passing by, picking up his voice.

He pushes the button marked "Rewind," and the pointer moves back to the beginning of the tape-simulation line. He presses the "Play" button and listens. Did he say "San Jose"? He'd *meant* to say San Diego. Using the "Rewind" and "Play" buttons, he repositions the marker to the place where the mistake is, presses a button marked "Edit," moves to the end of the mistake, and presses it again. Then he presses the "Record" button again and says "San Diego."

Satisfied, he sends the memo back to his vice president. A little speaker symbol in the margin of the memo alerts his colleague that there is a voice message at that point, which the subordinate will hear—with all of J. B.'s own voice and inflection, faithfully reproduced—when he activates his own "tape recorder" function.

Mixing Voice and Data

The above scenario closely represents how one would use the Sydis VoiceStation. Some button sequences might vary depending on which version of the product you were using and how it was configured for your particular office. The workstation of the future may already have arrived.

Sydis' product is among the most advanced and newest on the market at this writing. The underlying *idea* of digitizing a voice and recording the resulting digital image on a disk for later editing, transmission, use, and storage is most important.

Digitizing sound isn't a particularly difficult task by today's computer science standards, though the very idea was at one time mind-boggling. The problem is that to reproduce voice accurately, its input into the system must be "sampled" extremely frequently so that storing one second of digitized voice data on a disk can require as much as 8,000 bytes of storage. At that rate, a five-minute memo would take about 2.5 megabytes of disk capacity, which is more than any floppy disk available for most microcomputers can hold. A 10-megabyte hard disk would hold only a 10-minute letter with no room left over for the word processing program to print it!

Compression is a key idea in voice/data integration. Technical experts at companies like Bell Labs, IBM's Rolm Division, and Sydis spend a great deal of time and creative energy finding ways of compressing this huge amount of incoming data into manageable amounts so that computer-based systems with reasonable disk sizes can be used to implement voice/data integration in executive systems. The greater the compression—without sacrificing any of the quality of the message—the more usable the system will be to the final buyer.

It Plugs Into the PBX

The Sydis system and others like it plug directly into a company's existing telephone system, even a complex PBX (Private Branch Exchange). It is interesting to note that, in Sydis' case, the "guts" of a PBX could be easily added to the system but Sydis, seeing private telephone companies as buyers of its products and partners in their installation at other firms, chose to stay out of competition with one of their biggest markets.

Each Sydis unit occupies the space of a two-drawer file cabinet as its central processing unit and is capable of handling up to 200 users. The units can be daisy-chained together to handle as many as 600 users in one company on one PBX system. Each desktop unit occupies about as much desk space—what designers refer to as the "footprint" of the terminal—as an ordinary five-button telephone sitting on a pedestal of that size. It is triangular in shape so it can be pushed to a corner of the desk against the wall and be out of the way when the workstation owner wants to work on other tasks.

Although the executive workstation described above does not incorporate a keyboard, each station can be customized to each user's interests and needs. A keyboard, a mouse, or both can be attached directly to the terminal, which then responds to commands entered at these input devices as if they had been entered at the terminal's built-in soft keys.

Extensive windowing is used in the Sydis system. It comes with word and voice processing, electronic mail, telephone control, a spreadsheet, and a data base manager—all of which work together to permit automatic dialing of people or companies by finding their name in the built-in phone directory, for example. The soft keys are also programmable to some extent. In fact, in its early installations, Sydis found that secretaries were able to define one of their keys to be a "Call Home" function which, when pressed, looked up the phone number, dialed through the PBX and let the user talk, hands-free, over the built-in speaker phone that doubles as the system's microphone. When the managers saw that feature, they wanted it, too.

The push button, voice-activated world of the future is just around the corner.

The Colorful Amiga

Commodore has boldly attempted to set a new standard in color graphics with its Amiga computer. Like the Macintosh, the Amiga uses "friendly" graphics to help users operate the system. Unlike the Mac, of course, it has colors—lots of them. The Amiga can display up to 4,096 separate colors and shades—up to 32 of them on the screen at one time. This is no record-breaker, but the Amiga handles those colors and shades with unprecedented ease. Impressive pictures and graphics have been produced, demonstrating remarkable capabilities for shading and detail. Maximum resolution (640 x 400) is higher than on the Macintosh (512 x 342). By "interlacing" pixels, the resolution appears to the untrained eye to be higher than on the IBM PC even with the most expensive graphics card.

As part of its character as a graphics machine, the Amiga employs windowing more extensively than any comparable system. The use of windows makes computer operation flexible and easy. Up to 50 windows may be displayed on the screen at a time—though most of them will be covered by other windows, of course. (Only the window[s] currently placed "on the top of the stack"—or to one side of the top window—will be visible.)

Other advantages growing out of the Amiga's large-capacity memory, include:

1. Blinding Speed—At 7.8 MHz, the machine is faster than the Macintosh and almost twice as fast as the IBM PC. The speed, together with built-in sprites (predefinable, animated graphic shapes), provide for a stunning level of animation. More importantly for the Macintosh comparison, disk access speed is like lightning. The snail-like speed of the Macintosh disk accessing is a problem for which the Apple machine has been criticized.
2. Multi-tasking—The Amiga can carry out several functions at once. Three custom chips work together with the central processing unit to permit direct memory access. This permits Amiga to run more than one program at a time, or to

allow more than one user to operate the system, or to print a document while the computer is being used for another purpose, or to play a duet with itself, or . . . who knows all the things users will want to do simultaneously?

3. Expandability—The Amiga does not have the "closed architecture" for which the Macintosh has been sometimes criticized. (Apple Computer, in fact, will introduce an open version of the Macintosh in the first half of 1986.) Many different things can happen to the system that the designers didn't manufacture into the model being sold in the stores. For example, for $500 a "Trump Card" will turn the Amiga into an IBM PC compatible machine.

4. Low cost—For $1,800 users get the computer, keyboard, 256K bytes of memory, a 3.5″ drive, a mouse, and a color monitor—in other words, everything they need, except a printer. This compares favorably to the price of a Macintosh and very favorably compares to the whopping price of a comparably equipped IBM PC.

In spite of its impressive credentials, three major problems will prevent the Amiga from penetrating the small-business environment that Commodore has selected for its target.

It is being marketed without the necessary software. It runs nothing comparable to Lotus 1-2-3, Symphony, or MicroSoft Word. An even more sinister fact is that no major software company has announced plans to release products for the machine in the near future.

The machine incorporates a non-standard disk operating system. It will be unable to compete successfully against the inertia established by the IBM PC and Apple.

Finally, the system will be very hard to develop software for. It incorporates a high level of never-to-be-explained complexity. A great advantage of the Macintosh's closed architecture is that the system is a software-developer's dream. Software engineers, however, will be chasing bugs through the internals of the Amiga in their worst nightmares.

As opposed to the small business/small office environment forming Commodore's main target for the machine, the Amiga has been touted by reviewers as the perfect *home* system because of its flexibility, graphics, sound, and low price. It will have a difficult time in this market as well, however, due to the problems of incompatibility and the difficulty of engineering new software mentioned above.

Commodore missed a good bet in not building into this machine compatibility with the VIC/64/128 line of machines. The Commodore machines run the most extensive library of home software in the world. The decision to ignore that great advantage will prove costly to the penetration of the home market.

Those Revolutionary Chips!

A microchip is a small, flat wafer of a crystalline substance. The substance is most often silicon, but may also be germanium or gallium arsenide. A single chip is one of many small pieces sliced or sawed from a larger, flashlight-size crystal ingot. The ingot is "grown" from a "seed" crystal smaller than the tip of your little finger. Molten crystalline material is poured around the seed crystal. As the material cools it re-creates the seed crystal's structure.

The face of the ingot is coated, or "doped," with up to ten layers of what are called impurities, even though they are very pure chemically. Each layer is electrically conductive. The layers are either positively (p) or negatively (n) conductive, depending upon the particular impurity used. Phosphorus, for example, produces an n (negative) conducting layer.

Lines are then etched chemically through the layers of impurities. The process is accomplished by use of "photomasks," which transfer the design of hundreds of intricate circuits onto the face of the ingot. As many as ten photomasks may be used to etch multiple layers of circuits onto the crystal's face. The lines, exposing one or another of the underlying layers of impurities, become conductors. Changing voltage through a p zone separating two n zones will cause the p zone to act as a switch. The switches are the "transistors" in the circuits. The relationship of the lines and zones together make a complete "integrated circuit" on each chip.

Doesn't sound like anything capable of fueling a revolution, does it? Tremendous power, however, lies in the size and complexity of each of the thousands of chips that come off of the original crystal. The chip, of the kind used in computers, is about a quarter-inch across and less than half a millimeter thick—about the thickness of five human hairs or a fingernail. Over 200 separate chips are carved from each half-millimeter-thick slice of the large crystal ingot. The entire ingot, depending upon its length, produces between 50,000 and 100,000 chips. Each chip contains its own complete copy of the integrated circuit. The chip is very small, but the circuit it contains is very complex. To the naked eye, the chip looks smooth, almost polished, but under magnification the face of the chip resembles a Chicago street map.

Millions of dollars were spent in the design of the circuitry; the original plan filled an entire wall of a large room and took years to develop. Once the circuit was designed and manufacturing begun, however, the actual costs of the chip became very low.

The story is told of the president of a microelectronics company who addressed the shareholders. Holding up a tiny microchip he declared, "This is the first chip we produced. It cost over $2,000,000." Then, reaching into a paper bag he held up a large handful of chips and, throwing them into the audience, declared, "And there is 17 dollars worth more."

Supremely complex chips came to be called Large-Scale Integrated Circuits (LSI's). As fantastic as they seemed, the complexity of LSI's continues to increase. Very Large-Scale Integrated Circuits (VLSI's) are now being produced that contain circuits thousands of times more complex than the original LSI's. Not only that, due to improvements in design and manufacturing technology, the new state-of-the-art chips are far cheaper in cost than the older, more simple ones.

Chip complexity will continue to increase, and costs to decline, for at least 15 years. Both increase in complexity and decline in price will be logarithmic. This will, of course, result in a not-too-distant super chip that will be millions of times more powerful than the best chips available today at a tiny fraction of the cost.

Several years ago someone pointed out that if the transportation industry had followed a development route analogous to computers, we could at that time buy a Rolls Royce for $2.50 that would get 10,000 miles per gallon. In the near-distant future the comparison will be to buying a 747 airplane for 25 cents that would circumnavigate the globe on a quart of water.

What's Happening With These Chips?

An integrated circuit is a combination of between a few dozen and a few hundred thousand tiny electronic switches, or transistors, etched onto a crystalline surface of (almost always) pure silicon on which deposits of impurities have been placed.

The impurities are the key to the operation of the circuit. The silicon is the "substrate," or surface, upon which the impurities are placed for etching. (For a description of how the chips are designed and made, see Those Revolutionary Chips!)

The nature of the transistors and their arrangement upon the chip determine whether the device being made is a microprocessor, a memory device, or some special-purpose chip. Sometimes, chips are combinations of several kinds of devices.

The qualities of an integrated circuit (IC) are determined by the kind of device it is designed to be and by the manufacturing process used to build it. For memory devices, important qualities to be considered are capacity, electrical power requirements, heat dissipation, and the ability to change the contents of the memory intentionally or accidentally. For more "active" components like microprocessors, look for such things as data bus width, word size, amount of memory that can be directly addressed, power requirements, and heat dissipation.

Many of these factors are determined largely by the process used to manufacture the chips. Some kinds of processes result in faster chips that take more power to operate, for example. In the past few years, an important process called "CMOS" (pronounced "Sea Moss") has been gaining in importance. CMOS stands for Complementary Metal-Oxide Semiconductor. It is a subset of the popular MOS technologies that have dominated the semiconductor business almost from its inception.

There are a few companies who manufacture devices called "bipolar" (pronounced "buy polar"), but on the whole these have not been very popular with system designers who decide what kinds of chips to build into their systems.

Two major design technologies in the recent past in the world of

MOS devices include CMOS and NMOS. NMOS and its predecessors dominated the MOS integrated circuit business for most of the history of semiconductors—a history that spans only about 15 years. In 1983, for example, only 14% of the MOS devices manufactured were CMOS chips. By 1986, though, well over half of the MOS devices will be CMOS type chips and by 1987 the CMOS devices will account for three-quarters of all the devices made. The primary advantage of CMOS over any other type of popular semiconductor design and manufacturing technology is low power consumption.

The amount of power consumed by a chip to operate its thousands of tiny switches is important to system designers for two reasons. First, it determines the amount of power required to operate the system. Second, it determines how much waste heat will be generated by the device, heat that must be removed somehow from the system. The higher the power required to run a chip, the hotter it will be when operating. High-power devices tend to gobble up relatively large amounts of electricity and run hot. The heat they generate can cause a number of problems, including the breakdown of the system in which they are used.

Still, for several years, system designers preferred NMOS and other similar technologies to CMOS devices even though the latter required far less power. The trade-off was power vs. performance. NMOS and similar circuits required greater power input and dissipated greater heat than their CMOS equivalents, but they could perform many times faster.

Engineers, faced with this difficult trade-off, often went with the performance and found ways of dealing with heat and power problems. Recently, though, advances in CMOS design and manufacturing techniques have brought CMOS to a point where its performance approaches that of NMOS and other higher power devices while maintaining low power requirements.

If the power difference were small, the shift to CMOS would probably not have taken place as rapidly as it has. But a CMOS device often requires only about 10% as much power as its NMOS counterparts—and generates only about 10% as much heat. Thus a typical microprocessor-based system using non-CMOS components may find itself facing a problem of dealing with heat more than 80 degrees hotter than the air temperature. This requires all kinds of expensive additional mechanisms to dissipate the heat safely.

On the other hand, the same circuit designed with CMOS will tend to operate only a few degrees above that of the surrounding air, requiring no special treatment.

Optical Disks

Optical disk systems have become familiar sights in department stores. Music and voice recordings are stored on these disks in a form that departs radically from the traditional LP records and tapes. Optical disks store and retrieve sound in a *digitized* form. In other words, the *waveform* that comprises a sound is analyzed and reduced to the kind of information computers can understand. When the disk is played, a computer processes the digitized information and converts it back to electronic impulses that are sent through a speaker to produce a sound that is very faithful to the original, recorded sound.

Huge amounts of information are required for high-quality voice and music storage. An obvious use of the technology for purposes other than storing sound would be to create a general-purpose computer storage medium. And, in fact, that is just what is being done.

Information is stored and retrieved on optical disks by use of laser technology. The power of the laser in many of its applications lies in its ability to bring its "coherent" light to a very narrow focus. (Coherence in light refers to the degree to which light resists its normal tendency to "spread out" from its source in all directions. Coherent light can be thought of as narrow-beamed and focused.) In the case of compact laser disks, the track on the disk is read by laser light reflecting from a number of small "pits" that mark the track. The pits are made by lasers and measure an incredibly tiny one micron across by one micron deep. Remembering that a micron is only one millionth part of a meter will help us understand that the marks are very small indeed. This provides for the mind-boggling densities that are possible with the technology. The little compact disk, for example, will hold 600 megabytes (600,000K bytes) of memory. That translates into 75 minutes of music, but into 300,000 pages of text. In other words, a single compact disk is large enough to hold an entire encyclopedia—with room to spare.

If you have money enough, you can get even more room. Large scale optical disk storage is now a reality. Before you dump your floppy disks into the trash, however, know for sure that you have plenty of money—for example, $80,000 to buy FileNet Corporation's OSAR optical disk drive.

One consolation—the $80,000 will purchase lots and lots of memory—in fact, so much memory that, according to FileNet estimates, the price per megabyte of storage on a Winchester hard disk is more than 80 times that of the system's optical disk storage.

OSAR works like a 1950's jukebox. Instead of a rack of 45 rpm records, however, OSAR holds a bank of up to 64 optical disk cartridges. One double-sided cartridge contains two "gigabytes" of memory. A robot arm retrieves the selected cartridge and inserts it into a disk drive. The duel "picker" arm will select a cartridge and return another to the rack in a single operation, cutting load time to a minimum.

The system will load a cartridge from the rack into the drive and begin operations by the computer in about eight seconds. Once loaded, disk access time is less than half a second.

The system is activated and operated by a controller that processes requests for the cartridges.

The optical-disk technology is still in its embryonic state. The current products mark only the beginning of an approaching storm wave of change in our methods of handling and manipulating information.

In early 1986, Microsoft Corporation hosted an industry conference on optical disks under their newly-fashioned title, CD-ROM (for Compact Disk Read Only Memory). The conference produced little short-term excitement, no consensus, and not a little confusion and disagreement.

This technology will become significant, however, in the late 1980's.

Laser Printing—Writing with (Coherent) Light

Imagine, if you will, a desk-top printer that produces a page every eight seconds. Imagine also that the pages have professionally typeset quality and the printing takes place in perfect silence.

This is not science fiction, but describes one of the laser printers, called LaserWriter, by Apple, Inc., already on the market.

The technology at the heart of semiconductor laser printing techniques is *the print engine*. It produces characters and graphics by directing a beam of laser light onto the surface of a rotating drum. The areas on the drum touched by the light take on electrical charges. In a copying-machine-like process, the drum rotates those places through a compartment filled with toner powder and the electrically charged areas on the drum attract powder. The drum then continues to rotate so that the drum's surface, with the powder on it, makes contact with the paper (or letter head or transparency or label) upon which the printing is to be done. As the drum is pressed against the paper, heat and pressure fuse the toner onto the paper, thus producing the image.

The revolutionary power in the laser-printing system resides in part in the speed at which the printer operates, and especially in the high quality printing results obtained by the technology. It achieves the quality because of the nature of laser light as "congruent"—the light waves all move in an orderly fashion in a single direction. As a result of its congruency, the light that activates the drum in the printer, and thus produce the letters or graphics, can be focused to produce very small dots.

The laser stream, in fact, can produce 300 dots per inch. That's not great, but it is very good. By comparison, a typical hi-res, dot matrix printer, like the Apple ImageWriter (the Macintosh printer) prints 80 dots per inch. The LaserWriter, therefore, represents a 375 percent increase in density. (The type you read in this book has about 2,000 dots per inch.)

The LaserWriter printers contain their own microprocessors, along with two megabytes of memory. 500K of the memory is ROM and is used for creating 13 different font styles. The other 1.5

megabytes of memory is used to convert the pages to be printed to the style and font dictated by the dot commands embedded in the text. The printer "bit maps" each character of the selected character set and stores the characters in a part of RAM, based on the outline for the characters taken from ROM. The entire page is assembled bit by bit in another part of RAM. A single page fills up a megabyte of memory. Assembling and printing the first page takes 30 seconds; subsequent pages follow at eight second intervals, though the time is increased for complex graphics.

Laser printer technology is producing an entirely new generation of printers. In the process of doing so, it is redefining the standards for top-quality computer printing capabilities.

Voice and Speech Systems—The Listening, Talking, Recording Machine

Within a few years, 80 percent of American workers will be engaged in information handling or office work. A bottleneck in the transmission of words and ideas occurs at the points of input and output. A major response to the bottleneck is the growing technology of *voice recognition systems.* Voice recognition will ultimately revolutionize the way computers are used and, therefore, will completely alter society's ways of conducting business and communications of all kinds.

While optical character recognition (OCR) systems allow computers direct access to printed words, voice recognition systems allow computers to receive spoken words. Voice recognition systems will someday lead directly to sophisticated voice as data systems that have a great deal of potential themselves.

Searching for the Perfect Wave

The basic element in sound is called the *waveform.* Use of voice for transmission of ideas and information centers around the technology of waveform analysis. Information about waveforms is put into a computer system and taken out again by processes of *encoding* and *decoding.*

Encoding and decoding have to do with the converting of information from its analog, waveform, state into a digitized form and back into the analog state. In its analog form, the information in the waveform can be heard; in its digital form, information that came from the waveform can be processed, stored, or transmitted by a computer.

A barrier to the swift implementation of voice recognition systems is the sheer amount of information contained in waveforms; the digitized representations of waveforms, therefore, occupy a great deal of memory. The complexity of soundwaves has imposed barriers upon digitizing efforts that are only now beginning to fall.

All practical applications of the technology of waveform analysis to the digital representation of sound, therefore, employ some form of compressing waveforms.

Let's briefly talk about waveform compression. The material below describes some of the ingenious methods engineers have devised in responding to this challenge.

"Here's What I Think She Said."

Linear predictive coding (LPC), as the name implies, makes a computer predict how the human voice should sound so that it can reproduce words and inflections on the basis of very little data obtained from a relatively infrequent samples of the original waveforms. LPC can require as little as 200 bytes per second.

In effect, the technique tells the computer, "Here is how the human voice sounds. Now that you know that, take this little bit of information about this particular communication and make it sound like a person saying words."

Obviously, LPC is not capable of the most faithful reproduction a person could ever imagine of an original sound.

Catching the Wave

Pulse-code modulation (PCM) techniques produce more faithful representations of the original sound than does LPC. PCM is an encoding standard used by telephone companies.

PCM takes samples of the amplitude of the waveform at regular intervals. The amplitude is represented as a digit, or binary number. Since the digit is recorded by a single byte, eight-bit microprocessors will assign one of 256 possible values to the waveform at any single point. (A binary number of eight places, one place for every bit, has 255 as its largest value, plus 1 for 0.)

PCM applications are used sometimes with four-bit representations, though eight-bit is standard.

The values possible in PCM are arranged in equal steps. For this reason, PCM is said to employ *linear encoding*.

Recording on a curve

Because of the way our ears work, high quality reproduction can be achieved if values are not arranged in equal steps. *Mu-law encoding* is an important *non-linear standard*. Mu-law uses more bytes per sample to weight representation of waveform samples more heavily towards lower amplitudes; lighter towards higher. Mu-law is the standard used for most digital telephone system in the U.S.

Because it uses more bytes, a big disadvantage of Mu-law is that it gluttonously consumes enormous amounts of memory—eightK bytes per second!

So What's the Difference?

Differential Pulse-Code Modulation (DPCM) applies a bright solution to Mu-law's profligate consumption of memory by recording only the difference of amplitude between samples of the waveform rather than recording the samples themselves. A brilliant extension of the solution is applied by an *adaptive differential pulse-code modulation* (ADPCM). ADPCM varies the scale of the differential value according to previous differentials. In the case of large differentials, the differentials will be assigned amplitude values recorded as multiples of the preceding values. ADPCM sharply reduces the amount of memory required to encode the waveform as digital information. As a result, perfectly good reproduction can be obtained from using only two-bits for representing amplitude values.

Don't Tell Me All That!

Delta modulation provides another way of representing waveforms for encoding and decoding. This technique is the Mr. Scrooge of memory allocation for voice conversion techniques.

Delta modulation represents each sample of the waveform with only one bit of information! Such a stingy allocation of memory is ingeniously accomplished by representing the amplitude of an individual sample as an extension of the previous sample and having a "slope" of plus or minus one. The limitations of delta modulation become apparent, of course, when modulation of the sound exceeds a slope greater than plus or minus one, which it constantly does in most applications.

Going with the Flow

Continuously-variable-slope delta modulation (CVSD) provides an excellent example of brainy people trying to have their cake and eat it, too. When waveform amplitude values returned by delta modulation remain constant (either $+1$ or -1) for several samples, CVSD simply doubles the value of change in the slope. You might guess that a drawback to CVSD is in requiring a high sampling frequency in order to obtain hi-fidelity results, and you would be right. You probably could *not* be able to guess, however, that in fact it might require 32,000 samples per second! This translates into 4,000 bytes per second.

Obviously, none of these techniques provide a final solution to the challenges of voice recognition. They do, however, demonstrate an increasingly sophisticated response to those challenges. The techniques illustrate how the technology of voice recognition is moving closer to the day when the input/output bottleneck in the transmission of words and ideas is absolutely broken and our machines can truly listen and speak.

5

Software Advances

During the mid to late 1970's, I taught seminars for people dealing with computer phobia. In my early discussions, I used to say to the participants, "A computer is a high-speed idiot. It only does *exactly* what we tell it, *very* quickly!"

This chapter will explore the "stuff" that makes a computer do exactly what we tell it. That stuff is called "software."

Everybody in the computer industry understands that their business is primarily software-driven.

"People buy solutions, not boxes."

"The greatest hardware in the world that doesn't run the program you want isn't worth bringing home at any price."

"Shop first for the software you think you want and then buy the best computer you can find that runs that software."

Advice and aphorisms like these are heard wherever people who aren't knowledgeable about microcomputers run into those who are and ask for help.

This wisdom wasn't always available. Most early computers were either difficult to program or ignored the subject of software completely—or both.

Apple Computer, Inc., was the first company to recognize the significance of software in the emergence and growth of the microcomputer industry. From the outset Apple encouraged programmers who did not work for Apple to use the machine, try new things with it, get it to perform feats even its inventors didn't envision, and, if possible, get rich in the process.

The software arena will be the scene of a great many important developments in the last half of the 1980's. The key idea will involve increasing *transparency*.

Hardware makers have been trying for years to make their products "user friendly." The phrase has been so overworked—and so seldom achieved—that we would be better off talking about the transparency of a system. What do we mean by transparency?

You turn on your television set without giving a second thought to the technology behind it, even though that technology was as startling and revolutionary in its own time as anything we're encountering in the computer revolution today. How does a picture, perfectly coordinated with sound, travel through the air—even through space—and reach your TV set at all? We don't think for one moment about it; we just turn on the switch and watch *Masterpiece Theatre* or fifth reruns of *Gilligan's Island*. The technology itself is transparent to us. The people who make televisions work hard to *make* it transparent.

On the other hand, television's equivalent of software, programming, is less transparent. We have to think about what show we want to watch. We learn to deal with the subtleties of on-the-hour program changes, commercial breaks, specific slots for news, and a host of other things demanding our attention. The programming, in short, is not transparent to us, at least not to the same degree the hardware is.

The same parallel holds for computers. Hardware manufacturers have typically worked hard to make it possible for us to turn on the machine and be able to begin doing something without having to know very much about the system and how it works. They do this with varying degrees of success.

Software, however, tends not to be very transparent to the user of the computer. It is the software we work with and think about as we manipulate data in a spreadsheet, write books with a word processor, or conduct exotic research over telephone lines with a whiz-bang telecommunications package.

"What was the command for moving down one line again?"

"How many characters can I put into the name field on this data file?"

"Am I supposed to use ETX/ACK protocol when I talk to this system?"

These kinds of questions tend to be in our minds—on one level of consciousness or another—when we use programs on our personal computers.

What happens to software has a more visible and meaningful impact on us as users of microcomputer systems than does the machinery itself. In that context, what the next five years hold in store for the software industry holds great interest for us.

Present Trends

There are currently dozens of mini-trends in the software industry as we move into the second half of the 1980's. Four software-related trends will be of particular interest and value. These include:

- a movement toward compatibility and transportability;
- media that will make software more widely accessible and less expensive;
- a blurring of the distinction between a programming language and an application program such that the distinction becomes unimportant; and
- a new idea, called "construction sets," which may make it possible for us to customize our computer environment to an amazing degree before 1990 arrives on the scene.

We will examine each of these trends in turn.

Making Things Talk to Each Other

Incompatibility. In some states, it's grounds for divorce. In business, it's a reason for changing jobs. In the computer industry, incompatibility is a major reason the boom in microcomputer sales didn't happen in 1984 as projected by many observers. In the last half of the 1980's, companies that do something about the problem will be in the forefront; those that ignore it or buck the trend will be losers.

A *little* incompatibility may be a good thing. It gives people a reason to choose Computer A over Computer B; and it gives the makers of those computers some guaranteed follow-on sales when their customers find that they must buy software, peripherals, and supplies from those manufacturers' dealers. But the industry has clearly overdosed on incompatibility.

The situation for the person who wants to make a decision to buy a personal computer for home use is particularly ridiculous. It is as if every channel broadcast on a television would require a special set that could only receive that channel and nobody else's. If that were the case, how many TV channels do you suppose we'd have today? Or suppose every brand of automobile required a different brand of gasoline or tires? How many brands of automobile would survive?

Yet the microcomputer moguls made exactly this kind of decision—obviously without concern for the needs of the consumers. Future winners in the microcomputer industry will respond to those needs; some already have. By the end of the decade, incompatibility with industry standards will equal failure.

Incompatibility manifests itself in a number of different ways. Operating systems vary from computer to computer, even those advertised as "100% compatible." Diskette formats vary from one system to another. And the interface to the outside world—where mice, modems, printers, and graphic devices live —vary from system to system, though there has been an earlier trend toward standardization there.

Programs written, say, in Pascal—a highly popular microcomputer language—for an IBM PC will not run on any other computer unless the other computer is designed to be compatible with the IBM PC. The operating system is the part of the computer that manages the use of the disks, printers, screen, memory, and other components. Operating systems cannot easily be transferred from one machine to another because they are "machine-dependent."

Companies that develop software for a living must choose the system, or a few systems, upon which they will concentrate their design efforts. Users who want the program will have to purchase a system that will run the program, never mind that they might have three computers at home already!

The industry has clearly dropped the ball on the home computer front, or rather, tried to juggle far too many balls.

In mid-1984, there were a number of contenders for the top

home computer company: Commodore, Atari, Texas Instruments, Coleco, Apple, Timex, and even IBM. None of these companies had an operating system that would run any of the others' software. There were, to be sure, some products available from other vendors that purported to make Apples run IBM software or a Commodore 64 manage Apple software, but on the whole these products tended not to be well received by a skeptical and overspent public who didn't understand why the manufacturers couldn't just get together and make life easier for the buyer.

Consumers wanting to buy a computer for home use were faced with a myriad of decisions, all of them being pitched in highly technical terms. Many of them concluded the wisest answer to be, "I'll wait until you people get this sorted out."

By mid-1985, only Commodore and Atari were in serious contention in the home market, though Apple was present in a much less forceful way. The others had gone by the wayside. Even the much-touted PC jr had gone the way of the TIMEX computer and other notable failures.

Atari and Commodore are fierce rivals. There is no chance the two will agree on a common standard in the near future. And Commodore's new machine, called Amiga, produced by an outside company, is incompatible with anyone else's software, even Commodore's. So the battle for the consumer has narrowed, but the consumer has not yet emerged victorious.

MSX is an attempt to standardize home computers. It is being promoted by Microsoft of Bellevue, Washington. Unfortunately, MSX is based on out-of-date graphics processors and technology. It is being introduced far too late to be of real value and will never attract substantial numbers of software suppliers. It is of much greater importance in Japan than in the United States.

The situation of small business computer operating system incompatibility began to show signs of being resolved when IBM entered the marketplace in 1983 and settled on MS-DOS and a variant called PC-DOS as its operating system. ("DOS," pronounced *doss*, is an acronym for "Disk Operating System.")

MS-DOS was designed by Microsoft (the same firm that designs and sells MSX, which is where the *MS* comes from), definitely a firm to watch in the last half of this decade.

IBM's imprimatur on MS-DOS sent computer manufacturers scurrying to make MS-DOS compatible machines. The key to success became, overnight, IBM Compatibility.

The problem is that IBM compatibility theoretically can't be achieved 100% without violating one or more of IBM's carefully protected patents or trade secrets. And Big Blue, as IBM is affectionately known in the industry, has been aggressive about pursuing look-alikes when such an infringement existed.

Nevertheless, the elusive goal of 100% IBM compatibility remains a target, which has been hit, so far as we know, only by Tandy and Compaq. (We were amused by Human Edge Software's attempt to deal with the issue. The labels of the disks of some of their products are marked "IBM PC and 98% Compatibles.")

The Argument over How Many Bits it Takes

IBM's decision to adopt MS-DOS as its new operating system set back its two main 16-bit rivals, UNIX and CP/M-86, a long way. The UNIX operating system is at least as easy to use as MS-DOS, and is clearly more efficient and transportable. Also, UNIX is the system of choice in Japan and has the considerable resources of IBM's chief business computer rival, AT&T, behind it. Apple, in its revolutionary Macintosh computer, has opted for non-standardization on its 32-bit microprocessor, and appears to be getting away with it.

In spite of all that, MS-DOS is winning the day in the standardization race. It is still argued by some die-hards that MS-DOS has not yet firmly established itself as the 16-bit standard, but this is a rather unrealistic position. The fans of UNIX and CP/M-86 are like loyal baseball supporters who are still at the park in the bottom of the ninth inning with the score 23-0 against their club, two out, nobody on base, and the pitcher batting with a two-strike count. The game's all but over.

Virtually all new programs—including important AI and expert systems packages—are being developed for the IBM PC world under MS-DOS. Many of those same programs are also being designed for other systems, UNIX and CP/M, chiefly, but almost no new software is being developed that isn't being created on MS-DOS or PC-DOS.

Apple gave tacit recognition to the *de facto* decision of big business to buy into MS-DOS when it introduced its Apple Office concept early in 1985. Even though Apple later retreated from this aggressive take-on-Big-Blue stance, the idea of IBM compatibility runs a strong second to technological innovation at the reorganized Apple Computer, Inc. Among other products, Apple plans to have available this year a means of connecting Macintosh computers and IBM PC's in a single network, permitting sharing of files and resources among all of the systems on the network.

Apple has, however, hedged its bet somewhat by producing for the UNIX system several implementations of the programming language known as C for Macintosh computers. These products are not being marketed yet and may never be since Apple co-founder Steve Jobs has left the company and a plethora of IBM watchers were left behind to run the company. But they are used internally in Apple in some key departments and groups, and there may be a portent of things to come in that observation. In early 1986, Apple bought a huge Cray supercomputer that it can use to simulate products and languages, and UNIX was among those being implemented. In the early summer of 1986, Apple conceded it needed IBM compatability and announced it would produce IBM-compatible Macintosh systems, as well as a UNIX-based system.

The distinction between 16-bit and 8-bit operating systems is significant. Briefly, the difference involves a question of how much data the microprocessor, the brains of the computer, can deal with at once. A 16-bit processor is more powerful. But an 8-bit microprocessor is still awfully fast by human thinking standards and the 8-bit processors will certainly still be around at the end of the decade.

The world of 8-bit microcomputers has one standard for the business world. CP/M, a product of Digital Research, has clearly established itself as the standard 8-bit operating system for the business community. Its only rival is Apple's own proprietary DOS.

Before departing from this subject, we should mention another aspect of compatibility that will almost certainly be increasingly evident in the years immediately ahead: the so-called "coprocessor" approach.

Plug-in boards, which permitted the Apple II computer to run some portion of the available IBM PC and CP/M software, were the first major entrants in this field. It is possible to buy co-processor plug-in boards for a number of computers that allegedly permit Apple users to run all or most IBM PC software.

The most recent addition to this market we know about is Seequa, a company in New England that manufactures a line of computers, including a portable dubbed the Chameleon. All of the Seequa systems can run both CP/M and MS-DOS software. Users have reported a very high degree of compatibility with MS-DOS and 100% compatibility with CP/M. The opposite solution is to buy MS-DOS machines with co-processor boards that will run CP/M software. One of these boards is appropriately called "Baby Blue."

Dayna Communications of Salt Lake City, Utah, introduced an interesting twist on the co-processor idea in mid-1985 with a product called MacCharlie that permits the Macintosh to run all IBM PC software. MacCharlie, which gets most of its name from IBM's extensive use of a Charlie Chaplin look-alike figure in its advertising campaigns, attaches to the outside of the Macintosh and the Mac's keyboard. It includes its own disk drives and memory and really only uses the keyboard and display of the Mac. Full IBM compatibility is not attained by this approach (programs that use graphics on the IBM won't run at all on MacCharlie), but spreadsheets, data bases and other more conventional programs work as expected. The market seems to have adopted an early wait-and-see attitude toward this expensive means of mating IBM and Mac.

One reason why attaining compatibility is so difficult in the microcomputer industry is related to the rate of change. The MSX standard is a good example. The *idea* of fashioning one microcomputer standard that all home computer makers would want to adopt was sound, but it took too long to develop. One engineer who worked on the design for the standard told us, "It was worse than trying to hit a moving target—our target was shimmering." By the time the team had finished its first draft, some of the technology was obsolete; today, most of it is.

The problem of standardization has plagued the consumer electronics industry from its inception. It shows no signs of going away, but between now and 1990, manufacturers of microcomputer systems who pay close attention to the problem and offer reasonable solutions will be more successful than those who don't.

A Media Glitch

The software and operating system incompatibility that prevails in the industry is made worse by the lack of a standardized format for diskettes, the main mass storage medium for microcomputers. Incompatibility of format is tantamount to the situation that would arise if every record company decided to manufacture records requiring us to buy a separate stereo turntable for each company's label.

Diskettes come in three popular sizes: 8-inch, 5-1/4-inch, and 3-1/2-inch. Each can be recorded in single or double density (according to how densely packed information is on the diskette), on one or both sides, and in all kinds of groups of information (called "tracks" and "sectors" and roughly equivalent to grooves and partial grooves on a record).

There is a single-density standard, developed by (surprise!) IBM. There is no standard for double-density 8-inch diskettes or for either of the other sizes. That means that if we have a program that will run on, say, an Apple II or a Commodore 64, we still can't simply sell it to owners of both machines: We have to create separate diskettes in the proper format for each machine.

As a result of this media incompatibility, software development companies don't make new programs available on all machines. Consumers must make choices among machines, choices that they probably shouldn't be required to make and are technically ill-equipped to make.

Software tends to be more expensive than it needs to be because of increased production, warehousing, shipping, and tracking costs, among other things, all caused by this incompatibility morass.

Inexpensive, Portable Media Envisioned

A company in San Mateo, California hopes to undo part of this incompatibility knot by making software available in printed form. The company, Data-Flex, Inc., plans immediately to market Cardette Reader Systems through computer manufacturers, electronic toy companies, and other outlets (see Les Parrish Has a Dream: Cardware). (It should be pointed out that the author is a founder of Data-Flex, Inc.)

Cardettes will be produced by conventional printing methods on plastic and, ultimately, paper. They will be smaller than a 3″ x 5″ index card and can thus be carried around easily. Cardettes will cost less than a dime to produce as opposed to several dollars per unit for disks. Finally, they are easy to use: The user merely slides the cardette into a slot in a reader and pushes a button. The reader automatically handles the assignment from that point forward.

Initially at least, cardettes are not being viewed as a replacement for diskettes. For one thing, they cannot have their information altered; that means users can't store accounting or word processing information on a cardette in the immediate future. For another thing, capacity will originally be limited to approximately 64K.

"We view these primarily as potential replacements for the far more expensive ROM cartridges used to store and transport computer programs," says Wallace X. Aron, marketing consultant in charge of early market development for Data-Flex.

Programs will be distributed easily and conveniently by many means, including being stitched into magazines, packaged in cereal boxes, and mailed in ordinary envelopes. The user can then read the cardette-contained software into his computer system and, if the software hasn't been protected against copying, store the program on a diskette for later use.

"A great majority of the microcomputer software on the market will fit in considerably less than 64K of memory, which is the capacity of the first cards we will release," cardette inventor Les Parrish points out. "In the case of smaller programs, we can do one thing diskettes cannot do: store the program for a number of different computers on a single cardette."

With that in mind, the cardette reader has been designed so that it can determine the kind of computer to which it is attached. A single program can then be printed on the surface of a cardette several times: once in Apple format, once for the Commodore, once for the Atari, once for a Radio Shack Color Computer, and so on. The user could then use the program on any of those four computers merely by having a cardette reader attached to the computer via the correct cable. To use a single reader with all four—or more—computers, he would replace only the cable.

Parrish envisions two future developments regarding cardettes.

First, he anticipates that with a totally transportable form of software available, someone will make what he calls the universal computer. "Just stick the cardette with the right software on it into the reader and, presto—your computer runs Apple software. Or Atari programs. Or whatever else you want."

There are some technical problems associated with that step, Parrish admits, but " . . . with co-processors available, a single computer could be designed to accommodate the entire user base of software out there." At that point, says Aron, "a lot of the barriers to widespread computer penetration as a consumer product disappear."

The second future development Parrish sees for cardettes is to give them the ability to have their contents altered, becoming, in effect, low-cost and highly transportable replacements for the floppy diskettes that virtually all home and small business computer systems use. Parrish is engaged in the basic research to make it possible to semi-permanently alter data on a disk. "I expect to introduce a read-write version of the cardette within two years or less," he says confidently.

The Trend to Low-Priced Software: Is It Real?

One of the biggest advantages of the cardettes—besides the ability to deal with the issue of compatibility—is low cost. They are inexpensive to produce, ship, warehouse, and account for. As a result, software publishers who use cardettes will be able to make price reductions without sacrificing profits.

By themselves, though, cardettes won't substantially lower the retail price charged for computer programs. Production costs are not the biggest component of computer software. In fact, computer software is a classic example of perceived-value pricing in the American marketplace. The price for a particular program generally bears little or no relationship to what it costs to manufacture, produce, or even develop the package.

The classic example of this is certainly WordStar, which is a full-featured professional word processing program published by MicroPro International of San Rafael, California. WordStar has by far the largest installed base of microcomputer word processors on the market; its share has been estimated as high as 85%. The product has been on the market without any substantial change—and therefore without substantial new research and development investment—for several years. The cost of producing a copy of WordStar, including the bulky manuals with which it is shipped, is less than $25. Yet it sells at retail for more than $300—and is recommended as high as $500 with all of its options.

MicroPro released its new product, WordStar 2000, in early 1985. The market response was less than enthusiastic, in part due to the price tag, which was still in the several-hundred-dollar range for a product several reviewers found less than exciting.

There are a few such products at the very high end of the price spectrum. Most people who buy these products tend to use only a small part of the features available to them. Some users are beginning to recognize that paying for the name and for the additional power isn't necessarily all that intelligent. There is a shift, slight at the moment, but one that will grow in momentum as the 1980's wind to a conclusion, toward less expensive software that does the job it is designed to do without pretending to be all things to all users.

We'll look at two primary examples of this trend; there are dozens of companies and individuals who are doing battle with the high-priced software world and emerging with some scars and some victories. The first idea is one called "freeware," typified by Jim Button, founder of ButtonWare, Inc. The second is a slightly (but only slightly) more conventional approach being taken by Paperback Software, a firm founded by portable personal computer pioneer Adam Osborne.

Freeware: It's Not Really Free

The term "freeware" has come to be applied to a host of programs being offered by dozens of small companies around the country—in most cases one- or two-person operations. The idea is that people who buy the program make copies of the disk on which it comes and give it to friends, who are obligated to send some money, always less than $50, to the publisher if they decide to keep and use the program. The idea is of relatively recent vintage, but it has a great many devotees among computer enthusiasts who see it as a way of getting programs that perform well at low prices.

Button, whose firm, ButtonWare, Inc., is located in Bellevue, Washington (coincidentally, the home of software behemoth Microsoft), sells four programs for the IBM PC. The two best-known are PC-File, which sells for $49, and PC-Calc, priced at $48. The first program is a small data base manager and the second, an electronic spreadsheet.

Both programs have been well received by IBM PC users involved in user groups on CompuServe, the electronic information service, where word of their availability spread quickly among several thousand ardent fans of the PC. Two other recently added programs include PC-Graph for $47 and PC-Dial for $29.

Since he doesn't have to pay for advertising, doesn't manufacture or distribute diskettes, doesn't publish documentation or offer instant support (his recorded message advises users with problems to write to him and document the problems thoroughly because " . . . we've found that phone support can be very frustrating on both ends of the line"), he can pocket most of the nearly $50 per program he receives. On the other hand, he probably gets paid for far less than half of the copies of the programs that are made and "distributed."

Companies like ButtonWare, Inc. will not flourish in the last half of this decade, although there will probably be many more of them in that period. There are two reasons for this. For one thing, Americans still get suspicious of products that are priced *too* low. Second, the established software companies are beginning to realize that price-conscious consumers are increasingly less likely to buy overpriced programs. Software for Apple's popular Macintosh, for example, is almost always in the under-$100 range. Companies that make a living out of selling low-priced software will find their markets being taken away.

Some freeware products—notably PC-Talk, a telecommunications package from Headlands Press, Inc., of Tiburon, California—have been highly successful. That will inevitably spawn imitators. Button says, not without some justification, "You're paying for the name when you pay high prices for software." On the other hand, industry analyst Bill Coggshall says the low price tags make consumers wary.

Coggshall, president of a Mountain View, California, research firm known as Software Access International, says. "Low-priced can mean cheap, which can mean there's something wrong with the product."

Inexpensive, Not Cheap

Adam Osborne, who single-handedly transformed the personal computer industry by introducing portable computers and software "bundling," has turned his aim on the software industry in his latest venture. The outspoken Osborne presided over one of the most spectacular rises—and falls—in the history of American industry, Osborne Computer. Osborne Computer built the first low-priced microcomputer on the market that included software in its price. It was also the first portable micro to be mass manufactured.

Osborne has moved more cautiously into his new area. He founded the firm in early 1984, but the company's first products were introduced in late 1984 and early 1985. Chief among them are two word processors and a spreadsheet program, all priced under $70.

The obstacle Osborne must overcome to make Paperback Software International successful is different from the one he dealt with in his earlier company. The Osborne I was all alone in a new niche. With low-priced software, Osborne has the negative image of what he rightfully characterizes as "a lot of garbage" programs that have been placed on the market at lower prices. This has led to a situation where consumers have no confidence in low-priced computer programs. In other words, people have tried to sell low-priced software, but with no polish or professionalism.

The trend to low-priced software, often with reduced capability, will almost certainly continue as the microcomputer catches on more and more in the home and school where price is an issue. WordStar, with a hefty price tag, can do a great many things that the vast majority of its users never touch or need. Scaled-down word processors that incorporate the needed features most people would like to use in their routine correspondence, and even in professional writing, need not incorporate every conceivable feature. In fact, the more features a particular program has, the harder it may be to learn to use.

Some established software companies—including Creative Software and Software Publishing Corporation—are already pricing products in the $100 and under range. Philippe Kahn of Borland International has become something of a hero in the computer industry in the past two years, offering extremely low-cost, fully-functional software. Beginning with the wildly successful Turbo Pascal (estimates of sales for the $70 programming language range into the hundreds of thousands), Borland has built a reputation for meeting market demand with product typically priced under $100 that offers real functionality. SideKick, the memory-resident program on the IBM PC and Macintosh computers, handles appointment scheduling, telephone list management, phone dialing, and note-taking with a well-designed word processor. The program was *InfoWorld* magazine's 1984 Product of the Year when it was available only on the IBM PC.

Borland and its colorful, if controversial, president will force the software industry to settle for reasonable profits while still supplying effective customer support. By 1990, the era of big-ticket software will have passed us by and we will be able to buy programs far more sophisticated than we can even envision yet for considerably less than $100.

Expect to see more and more low-priced software on the market, at first from freeware firms and pioneers like Osborne, but ultimately from most major suppliers of software to what will once again become a booming market after mid-1986.

Construction Set Software

Besides lowering prices, one other way for a software company to increase its customer base is by making programs better suited to individual users' needs. Thanks to the "construction set" programs, that capability is no longer limited to big business clients willing to pay thousands of dollars for customized software.

The idea behind construction set software is the same as the old Tinker Toys many of today's middle engineering managers grew up with. Give users a box of tools and let them construct their own environment for creating a word processing program, a data base management program, or an educational program.

Construction set programs let users define how things will happen, in what order, and in response to their kind of commands or inputs. It is possible to write programs that provide this level of user control. Several companies we talked to while researching this book are readying such products for market later in the 1980's, some as soon as early 1986, though none cared to be identified by name because of the secrecy involved in their projects.

Some of these products are even more ambitious than simply permitting users to define their work environment. These advanced ideas are built around artificial intelligence methods for determining how users prefer their environments to look simply by observing the users' behavior and then shaping the environment accordingly. Toward the end of the decade, the self-adjusting word processing package will become available to home computer users.

The construction set idea for microcomputers started, logically enough, where a great many of the best ideas in the micro world originated: in the game environment. Electronic Arts, a home computer software development company that flourished in 1984 with innovative packaging, marketing, and products, introduced a pinball construction set package and later a music construction package. Instead of selling the finished pinball machines on a disk, which was the early product direction, EA decided to sell the means for *creating* the pinball machines. Give users a bunch of elements to work with and let them design their own pinball machine that they can then save on disk and play as often as they like.

A similar approach was taken with the music package. Users moved symbols around on the screen, positioning notes, staffs, sharps, time signatures, and other components of a musical score, and then listened to the composition being played.

Another variation on the construction set software theme came from a different region of the game world. People often designed new characters for games like the widely popular Dungeons and Dragons.

When that game and other role playing games got shifted to the computer, some variations slipped in. One variation enabled users to define characters using predetermined building blocks. From that early, cultic beginning, Robot Wars developed. In that program, each user defines a robot in terms of character traits and combat strategy. Then these user-created machines would be placed into combat situations against other robots. The competition was fierce and real.

Recently, a child's version of the customized robot idea has been introduced. Robot Odyssey, from The Learning Company, enables the younger set to build and use robots and to learn from the experience what makes robots successful or not.

A Cyclic Reversal?

In some ways, this trend toward construction set software brings a software design cycle to a close. It is a cycle about which nothing has been previously written, but it is a clear cycle nonetheless. Briefly, it involves a swing from fully customized software through off-the-shelf programs to what can be classed as a "template" or do-it-yourself software building program. These frameworks became known as templates because, like the template used in making products out of sheet metal, they were laid over the underlying program and turned the program into a useful form for solving a particular type or class of problems.

The difference between the starting and ending points for the current cycle is the issue of who does the customization. A few years ago, all customization work was, of necessity, done by programmers. Now with tools being made widely available, the user is doing his own customization.

To expand on this idea, let's examine the field of financial analysis software. In the early days of computers, all computer programs of any kind were done on an individually tailored basis. A company that needed a financial forecasting tool for a minicomputer simply hired a programmer or a staff of programmers to design and create one. There was no other way to *obtain* software.

Then, in the mid to late 1970's, software vendors selling programs for minicomputers started appearing in huge numbers. These companies had found a great deal of commonality between the various financial planning programs companies were using and decided to capitalize on that essential *kernel* of the software by making it available far less expensively to companies who were willing to let someone else do the program design. This meant, of course, that the financial analysis program you could buy was not always precisely the one you would have designed for your own company's use. But it was close enough and the system of feeding it information and analyzing the results could be adapted to the idiosyncracies and limitations of the program.

Then, in 1980, a small Sunnyvale, California, company named Personal Software (later VisiCorp) introduced VisiCalc, the first electronic spreadsheet for microcomputers. Its developers predicted it would be the first program that would help sell computers: They were right. As a "blank page" kind of program, VisiCalc did not have to be programmed to understand anything about the numbers put into it or the formulas it was called upon to carry out. Anything a financial planner or accountant might have used a ledger sheet and pencil for, VisiCalc could carry out more easily and efficiently.

It isn't clear five years later who made more money from VisiCalc, Personal Software, Software Arts (the developer of the program that Personal Software marketed), Apple Computer (the only machine on which VisiCalc was originally available), or an army of template writers. This last group consisted of all kinds of people, from independent one-person consulting shops to large, established companies that designed the frameworks and set-ups for people to type into VisiCalc formats for certain tasks.

The template era spawned dozens of what came to be known as "VisiClones"—new, more elaborate, more powerful electronic spreadsheets. The very word "spreadsheet" went from an accounting term many business managers didn't know to a household word, practically overnight.

In terms of the software product cycle, the template took a giant step in the direction of customization. In many cases, the electronic spreadsheet let users do their own customization. For a reasonable price, they could buy a spreadsheet they could then customize to do any number of a broad range of tasks inside the company, each task designed in a way that was very close to the way the company wanted the task done. Compromising with limitations was not a thing of the past, but was clearly on its way out. Furthermore, it was quite easy for companies lacking the resources and interest to learn VisiCalc or one of its imitators to employ consultants to write templates. Even rather complex templates were fairly easy to create.

For a time, between 1980 and 1983, it was almost impossible to have lunch in the Santa Clara Valley without having or hearing a conversation about a new template.

Electronic spreadsheets are, however, limited in one sense: They only work with numbers. In fact, they only work with numbers in columns and rows. They are not word processing packages. Nor are they "idea processors" that help their users organize thoughts and concepts.

At this point, construction set approaches to software development and design have the greatest potential to change the way we think about, buy, and use software. Such methods of design will permit users essentially to create their own work environments, or to buy one of what will be a veritable sea of templates.

Such construction set systems will be quite graphic. They will make extensive use of *icons*. Icons are little symbols of various activities and instructions which, for example, lay at the heart of Apple's Macintosh user interface.

Austin Henderson of Xerox's prestigious Palo Alto Research Center (PARC) predicted that the use of icons will become widespread in the construction set business in the near future. He confidently maintains, "You'll have icons representing, for example, various types and formats of documents, the various steps in the document editing and printing process, typeface selection, and anything else the user might want to control."

The user's job will be to assemble the icons into meaningful groups so they can create a different work environment for each of several different kinds of documents or program situations without having to stop and reset system parameters before beginning to work.

It is difficult to forecast exactly how such construction set programs will operate, or what they will permit us to control. It is not, however, difficult to predict that such programs will play a significant role in the software world in the next few years.

When is a Language Not a Language?

When construction set software becomes the accepted way for microcomputers to do things, it will signal the virtual end of widespread use of formal programming languages. Already the distinction between people who can program and those who can't has blurred beyond recovery. The trend will continue into the rest of the 1980's and beyond.

This doesn't imply that there will be no computer programmers in the future. There clearly will be, but their jobs will be different from the jobs of most programmers today. Given a standardized computer environment, access to powerful symbolic tools, and the lack of necessity for understanding the computer's intimate details, tomorrow's programmer can become more of a system designer who invents and implements efficient and comfortable solutions for people using computers. This will merely be the logical extension of what's been going on in programming for the last five years.

As we indicated, the arrival of VisiCalc on the microcomputer scene in 1980 resulted in thousands of people finding themselves in the business of writing programs. Only instead of learning esoteric programming languages with archaic commands and weird symbols, these New Age programmers manipulated numbers and formulas, the familiar stuff of business life. Familiarity with the subject matter—financial planning and forecasting, modeling, accounting methods—was essential. An understanding of the computer and ideas like loops, control logic, conditional processing, and file structure was unimportant, even cumbersome.

Template designers can certainly be *called* programmers: They give the computer sets of instructions to follow to reach desired conclusions. But most template designers would be lost in the world of BASIC, COBOL, LISP and APL. (See Languages: High, Low, and In Between.) They focus on the *task*, which is expressed in terms of manipulating data, and not on the *technology*, which is thought of in terms of manipulating the machine.

Another step in the direction of blurring the distinction between programmers and users took place when Ashton-Tate, Inc., introduced dBase II, a microcomputer-based data base manager with its own built-in language. One can easily use dBase II without knowing how to program it. But to do something exotic or more powerful than routine data management tasks, the power of the dBase II language was accessible. Thousands of programs written in this straightforward language appeared on the market, catapulting dBase II onto the best-seller list of microcomputer business software. Users became programmers for their own specific needs and some of these users turned into entrepreneurs, selling the solutions they'd discovered to their own problems to other people with similar needs.

The first successful, fully integrated microcomputer software package was the enormously well-received 1-2-3 from Lotus Development Corporation. It burst onto the scene with an imbedded programming capability that was relatively more difficult than dBase II to use, but required minimal knowledge on the part of the user and spawned thousands of 1-2-3 templates.

Lotus followed 1-2-3 with Symphony, a related integrated package that unashamedly incorporates something called "Symphony Command Language." SCL is not as easy to use as some of its imbedded predecessor languages, but it is more powerful, bringing much of the clout of more traditional programming to Symphony users who may never have thought of themselves as computer programmers.

In fact, such imbedded languages have made more people into programmers than all of the universities and colleges in the country combined; though the new programmers would deny in loud tones their status as programmers if you asked them. Remember, setting up a spreadsheet model is a form of programming. So is defining a data base structure, outlining a report requirement, setting up the parameters for displaying a pie chart, printing a graph, or any of dozens of other activities in which one engages while using 1-2-3, Symphony, Framework (Ashton-Tate's integrated product), or any of the other similar products on the market.

Symphony carries the idea one step farther with "Learn Mode." When IBM PC owners use Symphony to undertake a set of tasks that they may want to repeat frequently, they can instruct the computer to "learn" by watching and recording the steps taken. The steps are saved in the spreadsheet the users are working on at the time exactly as if they had programmed the steps in SCL. The next time they want to use the same sequence of steps, they simply type the name given the list of commands when Symphony's Learn Mode was invoked and Symphony handles them automatically.

This "keyboard capture" method of programming is extremely powerful and easy for the typical Symphony user to figure out. Because of this, more and more users will begin to do their own programming for complex, repetitive tasks.

Keyboard Enhancers: Of Mind Readers and Mediators

In 1985, a whole new genre of software called "keyboard enhancers" or "keyboard utilities" began to emerge. By year's end, dozens of packages bearing names like Prokey, Smartkey, and Superkey, were available to the IBM PC-using public. The purpose of these programs is simple and powerful: allow the user to define specific key combinations on the keyboard to carry out specific functions. Their success derives from the fact that they greatly simplify otherwise complex tasks. Operations that are performed repetitively can be given one or two keystroke names and then performed on demand without the user having to carry out the individual keystrokes, which can range into the thousands of keystrokes for each so-called keyboard "macro."

These programs obviously do Lotus' keyboard-capture method of macro programming one step better. For one thing, they are application-independent. A user may have a single file of these commands, some of which are used in his word processing and some in his spreadsheet, some in games and some in programming. Or he may have large, separate files for each of these functions, calling up the one he wants to use at a given moment. In any event, the user has the *luxury* of doing any or all of these things while Lotus' programming approach only works inside its integrated programs.

Surely more and more such programs, with increasing capability, capacity for keystrokes, and flexibility, will continue to emerge in the next two or three years. But the real future may lie in the direction taken by a transplanted and transformed cognitive psychologist named David Taylor (see David Taylor Wants Computers to Help Minds).

Taylor, once a well-established professor of cognitive science at the University of Rochester, specialized in what are called "high-speed mental events," (mental steps and processes that require a few milliseconds to execute). Taylor was engaged in attempting to track and analyze these, but is now an entrepreneur in California's Silicon Valley. He started a company called Predictive Systems and introduced a product called The Mediator. A mediator, he points out, is a go-between. His mediator goes between a user and his computer.

"Using The Mediator," Taylor explains, "you simply load it into your computer's memory exactly as if it were a keyboard enhancer. It sits there and waits to be summoned into use. When you call it up, you tell it you want it to learn what you are about to demonstrate. Everything you type from that point on—letters, numbers, symbols, commands and, most powerfully, the names of other, similarly defined tasks—gets stored in a procedure that can be given a very English-like name." The Mediator accepts English sentences as input; all commands start with a capital letter (which the program automatically handles if you forget) and end with a period. In between, a number of words and phrases defined as different types can appear. Keystroke sequences are called "skills," while collections of sequences and skills are called "actions." In addition to skills and actions, The Mediator's sentences can contain:

- variables (words containing information)
- formats (words describing information)
- conditions (decision words)
- relations (comparison words)
- topics (subjects The Mediator can explain)
- screens (different kinds of screen layouts and formats)
- key filters (patterns that lock out certain keystrokes)
- experts (specialized versions of the product for specific purposes)

In addition, The Mediator incorporates a feature called "predictive recognition" that comes quite close to AI natural language processing. If you type a keystroke that corresponds to only one skill in The Mediator's vocabulary, for example, it will finish the typing for you automatically. Similarly, if you are not teaching the program a new skill but trying to use an existing one, it won't let you make a typographical error. It "knows" what is in its vocabulary and won't permit you to type any sequence it can't relate to.

The Mediator clearly further blurs the lines of distinction between utilities and programming languages, but it does so at a level of understanding of human input that is exceeded by anything we've seen on the market. (In fact, The Mediator may be on the market under a different name by now. As we went to press, Taylor was seeking a corporate partner or joint venture partner to assist him in marketing the product, having decided he is not cut out to set up and run an ongoing company.)

Where is The Mediator headed next? Taylor reveals that his next project, although still only an idea in outline form, will be the creation of a similar product that is capable of accepting freeform input from the user, drawing associative and combinational relationships and acting as an " . . . extension of the human user's memory, allowing the user to keep his personal memory for more current and important ideas and events."

Another product that is uncannily like The Mediator in some ways and yet totally unlike it in others is Mind Reader, a word processing program for the IBM PC introduced in mid-1985 by Businessoft, Inc., of Annapolis, Maryland. Like The Mediator, Mind Reader contains a built-in feature that attempts to anticipate what the user is trying to type. But Mind Reader's purpose is not to have the computer learn commands and keystrokes but words and phrases in a word processing context. Mind Reader inventor Kallman Toth received one of the first U.S. patents issued to a software designer for his algorithm that handles the anticipation of the word or phrase the user is attempting to type.

Mind Reader is billed as a word processor for "busy professionals who may or may not be good typists." For people who type less than 45 or 50 words per minute, the program is able to stay ahead of the typist and offer choices of words. As the user types a letter, Mind Reader examines its vocabulary to see if it knows a word that starts with that letter. If it has any (and it often does, of course), it creates a pop-up window at or near the point where the typing is taking place. The window contains all of the possible words Mind Reader has stored that fit the current letter pattern. The user can select any of the words by typing the number next to the word or phrase in the window or by pressing the semicolon key if his choice is the highlighted, most logically expected word or phrase. The user can not only save large numbers of keystrokes, but can be assured that words are spelled right. Plurals, -ing endings and past tense forms of words can be created with single function key presses.

But Mind Reader's real cleverness lies in its learning skills. As you use the program over time, it learns which words you use most often in given letter combinations. It adjusts its display of word options so that the one you choose most often is the highlighted, logically expected word or phrase. You can add words or phrases to its vocabulary as well, and these become part of the pop-up window scheme of typing assistance.

Mind Reader essentially takes the front-end concepts of a portion of The Mediator and builds into them some program functionality. Taylor chose to let other people supply the functional programming—word processors, spreadsheets, data base managers, etc.—while he furnished the intelligent front end that was the same regardless of the underlying program being run. Both products could as easily have appeared in this book in Chapter 1, Extending Our Minds, but since both are general-purpose software products with broad application, we chose to present them here. Both offer a tiny glimpse at what intelligent software may someday be like.

One of the most powerful productivity packages with imbedded languages is called, modestly enough, Knowledge and Mind Amplification System—KAMAS for short. It is published by KAMASOFT of Aloha, Oregon, and is the brainchild of Adam Trent.

On the simplest and most elegant level, KAMAS is an outline generator and idea processor. It helps to organize thoughts and ideas into a structured framework, much like Ashton-Tate's Framework package.

One level below the outline processor is a powerful language that could be used to build hundreds of user applications. Unlike languages in dBase II, Symphony, and other packages, KAMAS' built-in language is oriented toward text applications. In fact, it is similar to the FORTH language, with the addition of what KAMASOFT calls the KAM™, Knowledge Access Method. But the language is part of the environment within which users work and interact with the system. It is accessible; if a user would like to add a function, it is possible to do so. Users can, therefore, admittedly with some difficulty, expand and enhance KAMAS to suit their own taste.

Trent, commenting on his particular vision of the future, said, "We think that knowledge processing and imaginative ways of applying the computer to text manipulation will become an increasingly important software ingredient in personal computing systems. We're seeing an awakening awareness and growing demand for this kind of software. It's a shift from information and data processing to knowledge processing. At KAMASOFT, we are banking our future on this shift."

KAMASOFT Systems is unique in an interesting way. Trent, who personally designed and programmed KAMAS, wrote it for the 8-bit CP/M operating system, an operating system many observers have shoveled into an early grave. Trent said, in a recent interview, "Instead of abandoning CP/M, we saw the neglected CP/M market as a golden opportunity. An enormous base of users is being bypassed by the software industry they helped make successful."

KAMAS is not only not the *only* outline and idea processor on the market, it is clearly not even the best-known. The easy leader in this field is Living Videotext's ThinkTank, a product available for both the IBM PC and Macintosh systems. MaxThink, a later competitor with arguably more capability and speed, but available only on the IBM system, emerged toward the end of 1985 as a serious competitor. More such products are destined to appear and have their impact on a market hungry for tools that make peoples' minds more productive and useful in the next few years.

Next: Expert Templates?

Artificial intelligence and expert systems hold the key to the future of the microcomputer industry (for more, see Expanding Our Minds). In AI, too, we will see the trends we've been discussing very much in evidence: compatibility, low cost, construction sets, and the blurring of lines between using a program and programming a computer. In fact, if anything, the trends in this area will be accentuated.

Jeff Perrone, president of Jeffrey Perrone and Associates, Inc., of San Francisco, believes, " . . . there will be a huge market in the next five to ten years for the expert systems equivalent of templates." What is termed "value-added software" development will take place.

Expert system development tools like Expert-Ease, Insight and Exsys—all available for less than $1,000—will spawn another sub-industry of people. These people will design and sell knowledge bases in specific subject areas that users will employ to get advice and direction about decisions in those areas.

Some of these packages, notably Expert-Ease, have taken some direction on their user interface from their spreadsheet and integrated package cousins. These packages tend to be relatively easy to put data into and to use, once their different approach to problem analysis is grasped.

Expectations

Expert systems tools and their template-related products are certainly not the only way AI will be felt in the microcomputer industry during the last half of the 1980's. Building on a mid-eighties genre called "logic games," entertainment software using AI principles, and even created by artificially intelligent systems, will emerge in the last half of the decade.

The logic game market is typified by Robot Odyssey I from The Learning Company. The program requires user/players to assemble a robot by using sub-components that produce a microchip containing elements necessary for the robot to carry out certain tasks. As players send robots into the "world" in which they must function, they learn by trial and error and logic what works and what doesn't. Over time they perfect an understanding of the robots' needs and of the environment within which they work. It is no coincidence that the program carries the designation "I"; follow-ons are a logical outgrowth of the initial product entry.

A Macintosh game called Chipwits has some of the same charm, a vastly different approach to robot design, and a highly graphic implementation. It, too, is a logic game. (For a full discussion see page 30.)

These games and others that resemble them have a number of things in common, chief among them is the fact that players must use intelligence and logic to train their micro alter-egos to attain a pre-defined goal. A conceptually short, though complex, step leads from there to a game in which artificial intelligence adds a new dimension. Before 1990 dawns, games and entertainment products with an AI base will appear on the market.

One product already well past the conceptual stage is a scaled-down version of a larger computer game called Truckin' (see Just Truckin' Along). The game pits players' abilities to define strategies and formulate plans for carrying out those strategies. It is one of the most popular programs at Xerox PARC, where it is used to demonstrate, explain, and spark discussion about artificial intelligence. Mike Weiner, a former Xerox manager, formed a spin-off company to market such products, and plans to introduce a microcomputer version of Truckin' sometime in the next year or so.

It is not difficult to envision games in which the program, being artificially intelligent, learns from its mistakes. The more it plays its human opponents, the better its play becomes.

In fact, exactly such a program that plays draw poker was developed by Dr. Donald Waterman as he undertook his doctorate work. Now a leading AI researcher at the Rand Corporation in Santa Monica, California, Dr. Waterman's program may serve as the prototype of such pastimes in the next five years—and beyond.

A substantial difference exists between this approach to computer program design and the more traditional difficulty adjustment approach. In those designs, the program knows in advance how to play a more challenging game. It merely adjusts its level of play to coincide with that of its human opponent, subject to the human's override, of course. Difficulty adjustment has been used in a number of chess programs that have emerged in the past few years.

An artificially intelligent program, on the other hand, begins its game-playing with nothing but a few basic principles and rules. It then builds a knowledge base from its interaction and experience with one or more human opponents.

From this beginning, we can envision computer programs sufficiently well designed as learning systems that users will swap copies of their knowledge bases with one another in an attempt to outsmart even these smart computer programs!

An alternative objective will be to build a super-smart program with an extensive knowledge base because of a broad range of experience with a variety of human competitors.

It is neither expecting too much of AI nor belittling its contribution to predict that the advanced science will make its first highly visible mark on the world of microcomputers in the area of games, pastimes, and entertainment. Note the qualifier, "highly visible." To be sure, earlier programs may well be full-blown, professionally usable expert systems. But the general public may get its first real taste of AI in the way many new concepts have come to their attention: through the world of entertainment.

Programming With Pictures

All this talk about construction sets, logic games in which players build robots, and programs that learn from their users would be far less tenable if it were not for a final trend we will see in the rest of the 1980's. All these advances depend, to some degree, upon the ability of a large number of people to write computer programs to carry out very sophisticated tasks.

There is an interesting parallel here with the world of microchip design (see Chapter 4, Hardware Advances). A very small number of people in the world know how to design integrated circuits. By contrast, many more people understand how to design *systems*. The way to produce sophisticated electronic gear, therefore, is to enable system designers to become chip designers. This is exactly what several companies are doing with new approaches referred to generically as silicon compilers (which happens to be the name of the leading company in that industry).

In the world of software systems design, to draw the comparison, there are, relatively speaking, very few programmers compared to the number of people trained to look at a situation, spot a problem, and design a solution to that problem. The trick, then, is to make it possible for these problem-solvers, who are knowledgeable in specific areas of human endeavor, to design computer programs to solve the problems.

A variety of approaches has been suggested, from automatic program generators to high level compilers and interpreters that offer a very forgiving environment within which to implement solutions. Automatic program generators almost never do what their name implies. They facilitate program design and produce usable program code for a very limited range of applications. They have, to be sure, served some useful purposes, but are, as of yet, incapable of carrying us into the era of the design of intelligent programs.

The next generation of such gap-bridging products is foreshadowed by a soon-to-be-released product from a little-known Palo Alto company, VPL Research. The firm, headed by young Jaron Z. Lanier, is working on a product called Mandala (see Graphic Language Interpreters on the Horizon). For security reasons, Lanier was unable to give a complete description of the product, but its potential is great.

Implicit in the design of Mandala and other yet-to-be-unveiled graphic language interpreters is the idea that a great many people can visualize and describe graphically what they want to happen but are unable to do so in words using the strict grammatical and associated syntactical rules required by traditional computer languages. Many people, therefore, are simply unable to learn to program a computer with any facility.

If we can use internationally meaningful symbols instead of English-like command words to program computers, graphics-based programming languages will overcome traditional human language barriers. This will result in many people programming and developing expert system templates, devising new computer environments in the context of construction set approaches, and generally making computers in their own environments more humane in response to their own needs.

Opportunities, Strategies, and Decisions

Much of what we have said in earlier sections applies to the subject of software as well. In fact, it is the software driving the industry that *leads* to those other conclusions and recommendations. But for some very software-specific thoughts about the microcomputer revolution and its effect on you, try these on for size.

Careers If you are reading this book with a *career* orientation, one message should come through loud and clear: Programming careers are not where it's at in the micro industry in the next few years.

If you're really interested in programming, prepare yourself for a career by becoming knowledgeable in an application area (like art, music, design, or engineering) *or* focus on connections between hardware and software and plan to join the ranks of system programmers who will continue to be in strong demand for the foreseeable future.

If you are examining career opportunities outside programming, don't let yourself get hung up in the computer literacy craze by thinking you have to learn to be a programmer. As we have shown, programming languages are not going to be major driving forces in the near future. At the same time, think of ways the computer can and probably will affect your chosen vocation or profession. For example, if you are considering a career in the law, it would be smart to learn something about telecommunications, on-line computer aided legal research, and other developments that will have great impact on the profession in the next few years.

No profession will be untouched by the microcomputer. Bet on it.

Investment If you are considering an *investment* strategy in high-technology companies, the message to get from this chapter is that software companies will move from the spectacular, no-holds-barred growth of the early 1980's to a steady growth with some shake out in the late 1980's. Beyond that generalization, though, look for companies that seem to understand the broad implications of computers, not just the technological innards.

Be particularly wary of companies that focus most or all of their energies on providing tools and development aids for programmers.

If you find a company with real understanding of AI and its

template-like potential, that may be an investment opportunity to examine more closely.

Management   Management implications of software are far-reaching and evolutionary. For openers, in projecting personnel needs during the next few years, look to the issue of whether your non-computer personnel can and should learn to develop templates and otherwise design their own applications, thus reducing the number of programmers needed on your staff. In addition, at the system level, begin emphasizing compatibility and transparency as key issues to be dealt with, but not necessarily by the ordinary expedient of buying less-than-the-best equipment for the sole sake of such compatibility. In other words, force developers to bring you solid equipment that can be made compatible with existing hardware and transparent to your company's users.

If you're really interested in far-reaching implications, give serious consideration to conducting training seminars for your key personnel in knowledge engineering, the use of AI techniques in program design and development, and other such avenues of future growth in micros.

Graphic Language Interpreters on the Horizon

The marriage will certainly be logical. Icons, created by Xerox and popularized by Apple, will become the symbols by which programs are developed, replacing words and esoteric-looking commands like "CADR."

The first such graphic language made a public debut late in 1984 on the front cover of the prestigious *Scientific American*. The language is called Mandala by its creators, VPL Research of Palo Alto, California. Jaron Lanier is the president of VPL Research and the idea man behind Mandala. (Mandala, for those uninitiated in Hindu culture, is the word for the Hindu symbol for the universe.)

Moving Commands

Programming in Mandala involves two steps: placing icons representing various kinds of program action in an appropriate arrangement on the screen and activating the controlling icon so it moves from icon to icon, carrying out our instructions.

Scientific American reproduced part of the program on its cover. The controlling icon is a kangaroo that hops from the three treble clef signs that activate a program to play a three-part musical composition to another symbol that enables the user to look at the music in conventional notation, and finally to a slightly melted ice cube, which "freezes" the icon and allows the whole previous sequence to be redefined as one new symbol.

Mandala and other graphic languages may hold the key to the future ability of computer users with no programming experience being able to customize the environments within which they work with their computers. Combining the ideas behind graphic computer languages with the concept of construction set software (see page 271), it is possible to envision a word processor that is rearranged specifically by each person who buys or uses it for his or her own particular needs and quirks.

An early attempt at such an environment was Filevision, a program produced for the Apple Macintosh computer by Telos Software. Filevision permitted users to create data bases using graphic symbols they had created and were therefore meaningful to them. Filevision stopped short of permitting user redefinition of the environment, but it presaged the emergence of products like Mandala and others that are sure to come along in the last half of this decade.

David Taylor Wants Computers to Help Minds

A lifelong fascination with understanding the mind has led David Taylor on a path to the development of an intriguing new microcomputer product called The Mediator. Along the way, he has become an acknowledged expert in the little-known, but critically important field of cognitive science, of which he is certainly qualified to bear the title "founder."

"I got into cognitive psychology because I thought it was broad enough a discipline to embrace the overarching questions in which I was interested," Taylor says. "It turned out I was wrong. The questions I am dealing with are not addressed by psychology at all and only a relative few are addressed even by philosophy. Mostly, though, they're ignored."

Behavior as an Evolutionary Topic

One of those important issues Taylor is referring to centers on the issue of whether behavior patterns are learned, inherited, or part of the broader process of evolution. "Does behavior evolve?" he wanted to know. "If so, how does it?"

To derive answers to this question, he turned to the computer as a tool. "I had always loved computers," he recalls, "and they seemed incredibly well-suited to this investigation." As a member of the faculty at the University of Rochester (New York), Taylor had access to the facilities he needed.

"I developed a simulation. I began with an island populated with inhabitants who were capable of making two kinds of decisions: motor (move up or move down) and sensory (detect danger, detect food). Then I gave the island food, predators, and surrounded it with a hostile water environment."

By introducing mutations periodically—within what he says turned out to be "incredibly narrow and precise limits"—he developed a system that improved its behavior over time. "At first, the inhabitants, left to their own devices, would do things like run into the water and drown, trample their food and starve, or try to eat a predator and be killed. This went on for generations and generations of inhabitants. Then one morning I noticed that the inhabitants had developed a sense of what to do next."

This development arose from Taylor's introduction of layers of what he calls, for lack of a better term, "associative cells" between the two major kinds of decisions. By altering the patterns of these cells over time, he could influence behavior; the patterns of cells were made the object of behavioral changes and mutations modified them further.

"I was intrigued and captivated. I felt I was on the verge of answering an eternally important question," Taylor says, still animated with the excitement of his find. "But when I submitted a paper on the subject to a conference on cognitive science being held on my campus, my colleagues rejected it. They thought I was just fooling around. They couldn't figure out what I was doing or if it was even science. I was hurt."

Soon after that experience, Taylor turned to writing a book, *Mind: The Human Difference*, published by Simon & Shuster in 1982. The book is about mind, consciousness, and intelligence. In the course of writing it, a coherent idea of what an intelligently designed machine would look like began to emerge. "Then I got excited," Taylor recalls. "I kept saying, 'I can build this. I can build this.' So when the book was published, I walked away from tenure and moved to California to try to build the thing I had envisioned in my book."

The First Step

Taylor, true to his scientific roots, first broke the concept down into progressively smaller parts until he could focus on a potential product that was feasible, practical, and useful. That is where the natural-language, front-end product called The Mediator originated. "The total project looked like a five to seven year undertaking. I needed to market something as a way of funding the rest of the project. The front-end interface that maps English into computerese and mediates between the user and the program seemed to be a strong beginning point."

Although The Mediator did not meet with great market success, Taylor gained visibility in the software community. He is confident the product will emerge in some form, probably with some other company in charge of its marketing. "What I have discovered," he says candidly, "is that I am not the chief executive type. I'm happiest when I'm in the lab, shirtsleeves rolled up, working on the beast." When we last talked, Taylor was busy trying to put together an acquisition or joint venture of his company, Predictive Systems, to enable the product to be successful as he moves on to other projects.

The Future

"For the first time," Taylor says wistfully, "cognitive scientists are going to be worth something, and they're going to be worth a lot. I want to stay involved at the leading edge of that movement."

He has already mapped out a design for his next product: a free-association, unstructured collector of facts and experience that can act as an extension to a human memory. "It's something we'd use every day and which would, over time, learn how we think, organize, process, and use information," he says, somewhat vaguely. The product idea is not yet crystallized but he says he'll know it when he finishes it.

In the even longer term, Taylor has sketched a way of designing parallel computer systems effectively for knowledge representation and management. "Parallel systems are the key to the future if we're going to build really smart machines. We need hundreds, thousands, or tens of thousands of computers working on a problem simultaneously. How they relate to each other, exchange information and share tasks is critical. I think I have a way of doing that."

At the bottom line, he says, "Within our lifetimes, we will see disturbingly capable mental machines and systems and we're going to have to make tremendous adjustments to their arrival if we are to assimilate and use them."

Les Parrish Has a Dream: Cardware

How about software for six cents a copy, on a virtually indestructible card you can carry in your pocket until you're ready to load it into your computer?

His ultimate contributions to society may well come in the arena of space travel, but for now Les Parrish has a dream that's a little closer to the surface of planet Earth. The dream: make personal computer programs less expensive to produce so that they can be distributed at low cost, perhaps even free.

The vehicle by which he expects to make that happen is the Cardette Reader System, a patented device Data-Flex, Inc., of Sunnyvale, California, plans to introduce into the marketplace.

The system includes a reader that accepts "cardettes"—palm-sized, thin, plastic cards printed with patterns of dots. The reader translates the patterns of dots into computer programs that the host computer, video game player, or other device carries out exactly as if the instructions had been stored on an expensive cartridge, diskette, or tape cassette.

Computer programs in large quantities may be produced by this method for less than ten cents per copy, as compared with two to seven dollars per copy for other program production methods.

Unsuccessful Forerunners

The idea of printing software so that it could be distributed inexpensively or free is not new and did not originate with Parrish. Bar code readers are perhaps the best-known attempt at a commercial product of this type, though magnetic and optical-disk approaches have also been either suggested or tried by a number of companies, all without much success.

Industry observers have concluded that previous efforts to use such an approach to software manufacturing had one of two problems: low density or high cost. In 1984, for example, a bar code reader called Oscar I appeared on the market. But bar codes are inherently not very dense; a 4K program took several sheets of paper and required several minutes to load into the host computer. It was easy to make mistakes because the user had to pass a wand across the surface of the paper with the bar codes printed on it; the angle of the wand, the speed and regularity of movement, and a number of other factors would frequently contribute to unusable loads, which then had to be repeated.

Magnetic media that pass through a slot where data is encoded magnetically on a credit card-like surface have also been attempted. The load process is fast and simple, but the reader is expensive and outside the range most people wish to spend for such an additional peripheral device for their home computers. Magnetically encoded software is also subject to being undesirably altered or even destroyed by stray magnetic fields and a host of other fairly common problems.

A Low-Cost, Fast, Easy Method

What is required for paper-based software to succeed is a method that is fast, easy to implement, and cheap. And that is where the Cardette Reader System fits. Tentative plans call for the reader device to be available at retail, probably bundled with several programs, for as little as $50. The time required to load a 4K program is approximately five seconds and the time does not go up proportionally to the size of the program, thus a 64K program loads in 10–15 seconds.

Creating Software for Cardettes

To produce software on cardettes, publishers of the software simply pay Data-Flex a license fee under one of several arrangements. They use a program Parrish authored to convert the machine-stored representation of the software into patterns of rectangular shaped dots that are printed on an Imagewriter printer hooked up to an Apple Macintosh computer. The process works equally well whether it's reading binary machine code or ASCII representations of BASIC commands.

The resulting printed paper product is taken to a print shop where it is converted into a printing plate, which is then affixed to a printing press. Plastic sheets are then fed into the printing press and software rolls off the other end.

Inside the reader, a patented combination of ultraviolet light-emitting diodes (LEDs), thin fiber optics, and an array of light-sensitive sensors are hooked together to perform the special decoding that is the heart of Parrish's invention. "Previous attempts at such reading designs have all run into the problem of density vs. cost," Parrish says. "By designing and implementing a special address decoding scheme, I've found a good way around that combination of problems."

Available for Most Computers

One of the first places Data-Flex will test the cardettes is in the educational business.

Parrish and Data-Flex intend to put together deals in which software, printed on inexpensive cardettes, is distributed in cereal boxes, through magazines, and other unconventional (for software) ways.

Many other applications are possible. For example, people could receive huge amounts of data in the mail from, say, their stockbrokers, for very little money.

Units are being planned, Parrish says, for the IBM PC, Commodore, Atari, Radio Shack, and Apple computer families. In addition, he thinks there may be a large market for the low-cost, lightweight, low-power readers in the exploding portable computer market. "How'd you like to be able to carry your whole software library around on a pack of cards you can slip into your pocket or purse?" Parrish asks hypothetically.

In the next year, Parrish expects to complete work on a high-density cardette that will accommodate as much as a megabyte of program storage on one cardette smaller than a 3" x 5" index card. His next project: using newly developed chemical techniques to provide write capability to cardettes, making feasible a low-cost, high-density, and very portable replacement for diskettes.

Just Truckin' Along

The world of microcomputer software in the next five years will see the introduction of the first recreational and entertainment products based on the concepts behind artificial intelligence.

At least that's what Mike Weiner, founder and president of Microlytics, Inc., and a long-time Xerox Corporation planner, believes. And he should know; he plans to introduce the first such product himself.

The product Weiner hopes to bring to market on a micro is called Truckin'. It has been used inside Xerox's Palo Alto Research Center (PARC) in northern California for the past couple of years to demonstrate the potential of AI programs for solving real-world problems. The program in its original form runs on a Xerox 1108 minicomputer. Weiner plans to release the program under a different name.

Learning by the Rules

At its simplest level, Truckin' offers multiple players the opportunity to define relatively complex strategies for directing a truck through a sequence of transactions involving travel, buying and selling various commodities, and avoiding robbery by two thugs named Bonnie and Clyde. In true AI style, the players' roles "end" when they've all defined their strategies. From that point on, the program takes over, running the players' trucks through a sequence of events, making decisions based on the rule set defined by the player, and keeping track of how players are doing in terms of gaining money and staying out of trouble.

The screen for Truckin' most nearly resembles a traditional playing game's board layout, with squares representing various events and conditions. The truck, which can be of any type defined by the player from a list of options, moves along the highway path between the rows of squares, stopping at intervals for various kinds of transactions.

Defining Rules

In the process of defining rules, players not only have the largest role in determining the likelihood of success, they also learn how rules are defined, how they affect other rules and decisions, and how to think about rule-based systems. This learning process is the most important part of the product in its Xerox life; in its commercial application, Weiner thinks some of that value may have to give way to more simple player definition processes and increased player involvement during play.

An example of a simple rule the player might define in the Truckin' program might be to determine when to begin to look for a gas station. The player might write a rule that looks like this: If fuel less than 1/4 then stop_for_gas. This last item—stop-for-gas—is a built-in function of the Truckin' program that carries out certain sequences of events to achieve the desired result. By controlling the circumstances under which the truck will refuel, the player can either create or avoid problems for himself during the play of the game.

Players sometimes will create rules that don't work for them. They can modify strategy based on what they learn. For example, if they find that by waiting until the gas tank is at 1/4 or below before looking for a gas station they run out and get bumped off the road a lot. They can then change the rule and look for a gas station when the tank gets below half-full.

More complex set of rules, with more subtle and longer-term results, will be built around the question of which commodities to buy and which to sell at which points. Users must take into account questions like how much money they have earned, how much they have in cash, the price of the commodities, and a dozen other such factors. Failure to judge correctly here won't result in the player being stranded and defeated dramatically (as would running out of gas when Bonnie and Clyde happened to be in the neighborhood!), but would ultimately result in the player losing the game.

There are dozens, perhaps hundreds, of such functions upon which the Truckin' players can call to define a rule. Once a rule sequence is defined, it can be named and so become a rule. Thus, over time, very complex strategies can be condensed into terse statements.

Others to Follow?

If we combine the idea of AI-based games like Truckin' with the concept of construction set programs as described earlier, we could envision some highly intricate games where strategies almost become alternate views of reality or experience and where parameters change as the system and the user grow and interact together.

Given the fact that most major software developments have taken place first in the arenas of games and recreational programs, the last half of the eighties will see a number of AI-produced or AI-based game programs. To the extent that these micro-based programs are easy to use, adaptable to different users' interests, and even customizable, they could become a raging success.

Languages: High, Low, and In Between

People involved in the computer software industry often speak of "talking to the computer" as if one could actually do that: speak audibly and have the computer both hear and react. That is, alas, not yet the case. (The essay, Systems and Interfaces, gives you some hints about when, if ever, it might be). But in one limited sense, programming is very much like talking—both use languages.

We may call programming languages "languages" because they bear resemblance to human languages. Or we may use the word "language" in this context as a convenient way of referring to the symbols we string together in dealing with a computer. Leaving the meaning of the name aside, what exactly is a computer language? How many kinds are there? Why are there so many? And where's language going anyway?

First There Were Bits

The first thing we need to understand about computer languages is that they all, except one, are artificial as far as the computer is concerned. The computer really understands only two "words": 1 and 0. Anything in a computer is stored inside the computer itself as a collection of 1's and 0's; whether it's an address, a priceless novel manuscript, a computer program, or a video game.

The first computers were programmed directly in these 1's and 0's. This was referred to as "binary" programming or, more popularly, machine language programming, because programs were written in the machine's "native" tongue.

Pretty soon, though, people got tired of typing strings of 1's and 0's into a computer. In fact, they couldn't even be *typed* most of the time but had to be put into the computer by tediously setting and resetting whole rows and banks of mechanical switches. The process was not only tedious, it was also terribly error-prone and nearly impossible to debug if a problem crept in. So someone wrote what was called an "assembler."

Low Level Language #2

Assembly language bore little resemblance to either machine language programming in 1's and 0's or to speaking English (or any other human language for that matter!). It did, however, have the advantages of fewer programming key or pen strokes and a mnemonic quality that made it relatively easier to remember how to cause certain things to happen in the computer. There was still a one-for-one correspondence between a single step for the machine and a single instruction in the assembly language.

Assemblers, like their predecessor, machine language, were still "low level languages." Lower level implies being down on the machine's level of processing.

High Level Languages

In the mid-1950's, high level (i.e., English-like) computer programming languages emerged. The first, FORTRAN (which stands for FORmula TRANslator), was an IBM effort. The second, COBOL (COmmon Business-Oriented Language) was produced by the U.S. government.

Both languages made it possible to write, debug, and implement computer programs faster than their low level predecessors. In addition, another benefit was produced: Programs written in HLLs, as high level languages came to be known to insiders, could be "ported," or moved, from one kind of computer to another far more easily than those written in machine or assembly language. An accounting system written in, for example, assembly language for an IBM computer could not be simply moved over to, say, a Univac system. It would have to be completely rewritten since the Univac's assembly language was totally different from the IBM language. In fact, low level languages must be difficult to transport because they are designed to work with specific processors inside specific computers in specific environments.

Compilers and Interpreters

The key idea behind the development of HLLs is interpretation. Someone writes a computer program in the machine's language. The program translates HLL commands into sequences of machine language instructions the computer can understand and carry out. There are two classes of such middle-programs: interpreters and compilers.

Interpreters examine the HLL as it is typed in by programmers. The HLL interrupts the process if they type something the program doesn't understand.

Compilers, on the other hand, ignore the process of program entry and examine the entire collection of instructions written in the HLL in one (or more) compiler "passes." (A pass happens each time the compiler goes through the entire section of program instructions looking for specific things.) It prints out at one time all the mistakes it finds. The programmer fixes those problems, runs the compiler program again, and gets a new list of bugs. The process continues until the program runs free of errors.

Both interpreters and compilers have their advantages and their disadvantages. Compilers change the entire program into machine code only once, so they run faster. Interpreters change the program one line at a time, each time the line is executed, and may thus need to change the same line into machine code many times.

In the microcomputer world of the 1980's, almost all programs are interpreted, although compilers for languages like Logo and LISP that have formerly been interpreted are becoming available on personal computers.

Classifying Languages

There have been other schemes for classifying languages into generations, orientation (procedure oriented vs. problem oriented), and other categories. None of the schemes seem to be all that helpful in trying to simply understand how to program a microcomputer. We'll leave all of that theorizing to the linguists, computer and human. Here we want to deal only with one other language idea: LISP.

LISP is generally recognized as being the one language that has transcended all generations, orientations, and designations as it has evolved from the time of its invention in the early 1960's.

In one sense, LISP is very much like any other HLL: It is not at the machine level and therefore requires interpretation or compilation to be useful to the system. In another sense, though, it seems closer to the assembly language level because many of its commands are not English-like. To be sure, some instructions are very understandable (commands like FIRST, LAST, REVERSE, PLUS). Others, though, defy description and originate in the Dark Ages of computer history. An example is the cryptic CADR, whose name comes from the way certain instructions and hierarchies were handled by an early mainframe computer system!

Because LISP is continually evolving and spawning new dialects—dialects with names like PLANNER, STRIPS, and CONNIVER, —it defies categorization. Once we figure out what neat little niche in a neat little hierarchy of languages is best suited to contain LISP, the language, chameleon-like, changes and becomes a new and undefinable genre.

As a result of these observations, we shall resist the temptation to classify LISP at all except to say that it is and remains the language of choice among most serious AI researchers and developers.

Index

Introducing

THE TECHNOPOLIS STRATEGY: JAPAN, HIGH TECHNOLOGY, AND THE CONTROL OF THE TWENTY-FIRST CENTURY

by Sheridan Tatsuno

It is the year 2000.

Japan's vision of a network of 19 high-tech cities is a reality. As a result of long-term planning for the twenty-first century, Japan is ready to lead the world with its innovative ideas and cutting-edge technology. Is the U.S ready to meet the Japanese challenge?

Sheridan Tatsuno, an industry analyst specializing in the Japanese economy and strategic industrial development, discusses the specific tactics Japan is pursuing to insure the success of the project, and what these government-backed high-tech cities, or "technopolises" will mean to the West.

In this eye-opening book, he addresses major questions surrounding the Technopolis Strategy:

- *Will Japan Take The Technological Lead?*
- *Is the Technopolis Concept Feasible?*
- *What Are The Problems And Pitfalls Of The Technopolis Program?*
- *What Can The U.S. Do To Remain Internationally Competitive In Science And Technology?*

It is the year 1987.

Is the U.S. prepared for the challenge?

PRENTICE HALL PRESS, A Division of Simon & Schuster, Inc., Dept. #3, 200 Old Tappan Road, Old Tappan, NJ 07675

Please send me _____ copy(ies) of *The Technopolis Strategy: Japan, High Technology, and the Control of the 21st Century* @ $19.95(0-89303-885-7, 66-03885).

Enclosed is my ☐ check   ☐ money order. Or, please charge my ☐ MasterCard   ☐ VISA. I've included $1.50 postage and handling for the first book and $1.00 each additional. For quantity discounts contact: Market Contracts, Prentice Hall Press, 1 Gulf + Western Plaza, New York, NY 10023.

Name _____

Address _____

City _____ State _____ Zip _____

Account # _____Exp. date _____

Please add appropriate sales tax, regardless of payment method.

Prices subject to change without notice.   Dept. 3 GR-TECH-CI (3)